D1245339

THY
PEOPLE
SHALL BE
MY
PEOPLE

THY PEOPLE SHALL BE MY PEOPLE

BY RUTH JUNE PERL

FOREWORD BY
CHARLES LEE FEINBERG

Dedicated
To the One
who made me Ruth
and to
Mike—my Boaz

FOREWORD

MORE THAN A DOZEN YEARS AGO it was my privilege to
have as students two dear friends, Mrs. June (Ruth) Carter
and Mr. Myron (Mike) Perl. She studied New Testament
Greek with me, and excelled to the degree that I was happy
to use her services in grading class papers. He, desirous of
ministering to his lost Jewish brethren, received individual instruction from me in Hebrew. From their early contacts at
school and in Christian service I realized a bond of love in
Christ was born in their hearts. Therefore, I was not surprised
to find that, each finding the will of the Lord for herself and
himself, both arrived in the Holy Land about the same time.
But you must read the thrilling account for the details and
the joyous outcome.

Here is an account of God's gracious dealings with two
committed servants of His with hearts aflame with unquenchable love for Israel, His beloved people. The Book of Ruth
is made to live again! The style is clear and polished, and will
carry you on almost effortlessly. I warn you that you will
not be able to read it dispassionately.

It is a privilege to write this word of introduction to
the book, which should have a wide reading. May God use
it mightily to quicken zeal and passion for the lost sheep of
the house of Israel, for Israel shall yet hear and live!

CHARLES LEE FEINBERG, *Dean*
Talbot Theological Seminary
La Mirada, California

PREFACE

IN THESE DAYS, so obviously the last days of the Church Age, a new sound has arisen—the shout of "God is dead." Recently it has been taken up and re-echoed throughout the land. To us who have experienced the new birth from above and enjoy daily fellowship with a resurrected, living Saviour, it seems indeed imperative to declare to the floundering multitude around us that God is very much alive. We have found Him so!

For a number of years it has been my heart's burden, coupled recently with a sense of urgency, to share with others the story of my life and His precious, tremendous, inescapable workings. Because many have remarked that my story is like reading a book, or upon hearing it have encouraged me to write a book, I dare to do so.

Man proclaims and it cannot be denied that history repeats itself. Therefore, it should not seem unrealistic to find the plot of my life written centuries ago—and recorded in the Bible, the Book of the Author of history himself.

What seemed to be the end of life to me was of a surety death—but to the past life of self-living, self-seeking, self-satisfaction. In reality, although I could not know it at the time, it was but the threshold to a new, beautiful life, centered in Jesus Christ. With the new life came a new name and I found myself reliving the story of Ruth, amazingly following in her footsteps.

Though the circumstances could hardly be identical some thirty-three centuries later, yet the plot is essentially the same. Only a truly living, very real God could have master-minded and directed the intricate duplication detail by detail. It is

9

not God who is dead, but the hearts and souls of those who have not found eternal life in Him, God the Son.

I am forever grateful to my husband, Mike, for his unending patience and source of encouragement throughout the writing, and to Mrs. Diane Stocking who lovingly typed and prepared the manuscript.

In writing I have tried to help make the Bible the living Book it is, to show forth a living faith, to reveal a miracle-working God, and last, but not least, to present the Jewish people as the wonderful and needy people they are. It is my sincere prayer that the true experiences set forth on the following pages will be a source of inspiration and challenge to my readers who already know Him. And may those who have not as yet met the living Saviour personally, and who honestly seek to know the truth, find herein the One who is himself truth, the Lord Jesus Christ.

CONTENTS

Part I DECISION AND DIRECTION

CHAPTER 1 of RUTH of the HOLY BIBLE

THE STORM

THE SUN-ROOM WINDOW FRAMED a dark and fierce winter storm. The branches of the trees bent at every whim of the domineering wind, dramatically helpless against the backdrop of a blackened sky. Suddenly in the midst of nature's agony a ray of sunshine, of warmth, a sign of peace and hope, broke through. It seemed as though nature itself were portraying the great drama of the conflict of the human soul—of our souls as we waited fearfully, hopefully, desperately.

The storm had raged within for eight days now, eight torturous days while doctors and nurses worked desperately to preserve a life, a home, a future—my future! Now was the time of life or death. All was in God's hands. Man had done his best, but could not conquer the powerful invisible enemy stamping out the life of the one who meant life to me.

Without Doug the world seemed empty, lonely, unbearable. The void left in my heart since the death of my mother had been filled by this one who seemed about to be snatched away from me. The terror of being left alone without him had suddenly, moments before, subsided as a strange peace flooded my soul, bringing a feeling of light and hope, even as when the sun had suddenly broken through the storm clouds. The tempest was still raging, but I was strangely aware of a loving hand overshadowing and sheltering, bringing an inner calm. Did this mean God would fulfill His promise as we were hoping? The next minutes or hours would tell. We waited in the stillness.

Tragedy and terror had struck so suddenly. Doug was so full of life, and at the age of twenty-two had the hope of a successful future before him. Our lives were all bound up in each other—two idealistic, romantic young people with our heads in the clouds. Unhappy home situations for both of us had caused us to desire above all else a happy close-knit relationship. Our love was young, exciting, beautiful to us, and we felt sorry for others around us whom we were sure did not have what we had! We were going places and would make a mark for ourselves—not spectacular, but comfortable, secure, respectable. Doug was studying to become an architect and doing very well. We had just built our own little three-room home, a little "doll house," having designed it ourselves. Working as a carpenter while learning designing was a wonderful experience and what could hinder our future? Our aim was to enjoy life to the fullest and our goals, when realized, would fill the yet empty spot in our hearts, we were sure. But now suddenly our hopes and dreams—my whole life—was about to be snatched away and there was nothing I could do!

It had started the night before Thanksgiving. Doug was working late out in the tool shop of my uncle's business when suddenly he cut his thumb quite badly on a power-saw. We rushed him to the hospital where our doctor attempted to save the thumb. Given the required tetanus shot we felt no concern in that direction.

A strange foreboding came over me. For three weeks I wondered why I should be so fearful over the possible loss of a thumb—which surely was not that important. Then suddenly Doug had begun to feel strange. Before two days had passed we realized he was very ill and rushed him to the doctor's office. Unable to walk inside alone, he was carried in and immediately examined by the doctor. His words still echoed in my ears: "You worry me, Doug. I'm afraid of tetanus, lockjaw. We had better get you to the hospital right away."

I looked at Doug hardly able to move. He tried to brave a smile. "Surely it will be only for a few days," I tried to reassure him, hoping this would somehow bring assurance to my own fearful heart. Soon the ambulance whisked him away, and I quickly followed in our car.

Cold, icy fear of the unknown was taking control of me. As I walked up the stairs to the hospital entrance, my heart was pounding more heavily than my feet on the stair. The doctor met me at the entrance to the ward where Doug had been put to bed. "I am going to give him a tetanus shot, and from the reaction we will be able to determine if this is our problem or not. You wait here while we do so."

Having learned to pray as a child, it was natural to turn my heart to prayer. Childlike, my heart pleaded with the Lord I had early loved but strayed from in teen-age years, "O Lord, please heal Doug. I couldn't live without him. Please, please make him well."

Suddenly I knew I must pray for his life. Great waves of fear flooded my soul, leaving it all but numb. Somehow I was aware that another doctor and a nurse had hurried past me to where Doug was. A tank of oxygen was rushed by.

Previous pleading turned to desperation. "O Lord, please save his life. Don't let him die. O God, if ever I needed You, I need You now. I beg of You, spare Doug."

Bargaining born out of desperation became a straw to which to cling. "Lord, I know we haven't been living for You— only to please ourselves. If You will please save Doug's life, then we will serve You the rest of our lives." Then with the presumptuous boldness that honesty plus carnality can bring forth, I dared to add, "And if You don't spare Doug's life, I will never again believe that there is a God, because You will be defeating Your own purposes since I've promised that we will serve You if You do save him."

A gracious and merciful God (an understanding Saviour who himself had suffered heartbreak and separation), looking down upon a trembling form and hearing a desperate heart try to bargain with Him for a life, must have lovingly smiled and tenderly thought, "Wayward child of mine, My ways are not your ways; My ways are far higher than your ways. You cannot bargain with Me. But I will lovingly lead you, carefully mold you into My paths, and you will see My way is best."

In the other room a gasp for breath revived some hope for the young life which had nearly slipped into that foreboding darkness of the unknown. "He is not yet ready for eternity," must have been the mind of God. This boy must exchange his condemnation because of unpardoned sin for the righteousness acceptable to a holy God. Seven days the faithful convicting Spirit must yearn over and woo this soul.

After what seemed an eternity, fearful and trembling I

17

tried to read the doctor's face as he approached me. "It is tetanus." These words were vague to me—not then knowing the severity of this disease. Proceeding, as if reading my questioning face, "If he lives three days, then there will be some chance of recovery; if eight days, a fifty-fifty chance. He had an attack a few minutes ago that almost took him. He had stopped breathing, but we were able to bring him back this time. We'll keep him in oxygen and administer the serum for tetanus and hope we can get the bug before it gets him. The only thing left to do is pray. It is in God's hands."

Now I understood my overwhelming compulsion to pray for his life a few short minutes before. What I did not, could not, understand then was that God was moving into our lives to begin to fulfill His purposes planned from before the foundation of the earth. Some will listen to the Lord only when He touches that which is most dear to them, the treasures or the idols of their hearts.

CHAPTER II

WAITING

THE NEXT SEVEN DAYS were days of prayer, fear, torment. As I sat by his bedside, hardly daring to leave, hour upon hour the pleadings rose unceasingly to the One in whose hand lay the balances. Memories of having loved Jesus as a child, of sweet and real fellowship with Him (even though the attractions of the world in early adolescence had caused me to stray), encouraged my efforts in prayer. Surely God wanted us to serve Him; surely He would raise Doug up so we could!

The realization came that in all fairness I should tell Doug of my promise since the bargain included him. Doug had not grown up in a Christian home, had never professed to be a Christian. But he had willingly gone to church with me whenever the Spirit of conviction drove me there for appeasement of conscience. Surely he would be willing, I mused. Just a little while before when the pain seemed unbearable, I had told him to call to the Lord and He would help him. And then his lips had moved silently and he seemed to relax and be comforted a little. Yes, he even seemed pleased when I told him I was praying for him and also that our Aunt Leona had asked her church to pray for him! However, I didn't tell him that her pastor wanted to come to see him, for fear he would then think he was going to die. The thought itself might be too much for him.

So, when opportunity afforded itself, I said softly, "Doug, I've promised God that we will serve Him the rest of our lives if He heals you. And we will, won't we?" Painstakingly, he managed an affirmative nod. My heart was greatly relieved, for knowing Doug's essential honesty, I knew he would never agree unless he meant it. Little did I understand then the process of the Holy Spirit in bringing his soul to a place of yieldedness to the Lord.

He had passed the third day. Now if he could live eight days, his chances of recovery would be half and half. But by the seventh day the doctors feared that dreaded pneumonia was developing. Somehow I knew a crisis was coming. We must lay hold of God in a special way. When members of the family came to the hospital that evening to learn how Doug was doing, I asked them to please meet with me later that evening in his brother's home to pray.

And so it was that Doug's brother, sister-in-law, mother, father, my brother and my Christian Aunt Leona gathered with me to plead with the Lord for the one we loved. As we implored in prayer peace seemed to come upon us, and we felt assured that the Lord had answered, "All will be well with Doug." This must mean he would live. We could think in no other terms! That night the presence of God and the quiet assurance that flooded our hearts made me know confidently there was a God. No matter what happened, I could not doubt Him again after such experience!

The next morning dawned gray and stormy, and before the household stirred, I was dressed and on my way to be with Doug again. What would the day bring forth?

Upon reaching the hospital I found Doug was anxiously awaiting my coming. He wanted to tell me something. He had had a dream of a black marble casket with white handles on it. And he had felt he was floating in the air. He was frightened.

How thankful I was I could tell him of our prayer meeting of the night before, and our assurance that God was going to heal him. And now I dared to tell him of Aunt Leona's pastor who would gladly come and talk to him if he wished. He might be able to say something to quiet the fears within. He agreed immediately to Pastor Dugger's coming. Obtaining permission from the doctor for the pastor to come in the afternoon, I quickly called Aunt Leona, asking her to contact him. It was arranged that he should come after lunch.

Just before lunch the crisis came. Doug couldn't breathe! Immediately I was sent from the room. In rushed doctors and other nurses! I fell to my knees in the corridor pleading with all the strength of being within me, "O God, You promised last night to save him. It is now or never! You promised! You promised! It must be now, Lord! Please!"

Through tear-filled eyes I looked up to see Aunt Leona coming down the hall. A few minutes before, as she was driving near the hospital, a strong compulsion to stop in had come upon her. Quickly changing her previous plans, she obeyed what was the leading of the Lord and arrived to find me there in the hall praying desperately.

Locating a telephone, she quickly called her pastor, "Don't wait. Come now!" Hanging up the receiver she turned to see Doug's mother and father coming through the entrance. Also obeying a strong urge, they too had come. The Lord had brought us together to wait while He worked out His plan for us all.

The nurses tried to make us comfortable in the sun-room adjacent to Doug's room. Through the large picture windows we could feel the warmth of the sun as it broke through the storm clouds, and could watch the seemingly angry gusts of wind swirl the strong branches of the trees around as though they were mere straws. Foreboding clouds hid the rich blue of the sky, except for now and then when they would permit the sun to gently peep through as though trying to melt the icy fear in our hearts.

Suddenly the doors swung open and in walked a large, kindly looking gentleman. After introductions, Pastor Dugger suggested prayer. I prayed openly, unashamedly, "Lord, You promised to heal Doug last night! It is now or never. We are expecting You to heal him."

Pastor Dugger, having known the Lord intimately for many years, knew God's ways are not always our ways. Quietly, deliberately, he opened his Bible and began reading to us, "Delight thyself also in the Lord; and he shall give thee the desires of thine heart" (Ps. 37:4).

"Why, my heart's desire is that Doug shall live!" I exclaimed.

Tenderly he answered, "If we are delighting ourselves in the Lord, we will want His will."

What was he trying to tell me? "Do you mean," I could

21

hardly utter the words, "I must want God's will more than Doug's life?"

"Yes."

In the stillness that followed, the Spirit of God was searching out the inner hearts of us all. Finally, breaking the silence, I questioned, "How could I ever do that? I don't want to live if Doug doesn't."

There was understanding in his fatherly face. His reply was gentle but definite. "Look at the next verse." Then reading, " 'Commit thy way unto the Lord; trust also in him; and he shall bring it to pass.' He will enable you."

And somewhere in the inner recesses of my being a spiritual transaction was being made, as the unspoken prayer, "All right, Lord, Your will be done," brought peace and rest to a weary, frightened soul. A sense of overshadowing love now relieved the pain of waiting.

Pastor Dugger's voice was comforting. "A verse comes to me, but I feel it is for him in there rather than for us here. In fact, parts of two verses: 'The everlasting arms are underneath. . . and God's love shall be thy cover' " (modern speech versions of Deut. 33:27, 12). As God had promised, everything would be all right. "As for God, his way is perfect" (Ps. 18:30).

CHAPTER III

TURNING FROM IDOLS

MY MIND REVIEWED the two years we had been together as husband and wife. Vividly I recalled the many times the Lord had convicted me of my selfish life—living only for "us," going to church spasmodically, and then only out of a sense of duty. Painfully came the remembrances of almost nightly prayer, "Lord, please bring me back into fellowship with yourself," and the fears of the day that He would do it!

Doug had never professed to believe in Christ, although he was sympathetic with my weak profession. I had allowed him to become an idol in my life. Somehow, not knowing the power of the Spirit to change a life which has yielded itself to the Lord, I could not see Doug living a Christian life. It had not been too long ago when under great conviction I had told Doug I must get things settled with the Lord. He had responded, "I don't know if I can live a Christian life or not, but I'll go as far as I can."

If only I had yielded to the Lord then as His Spirit strove with me! How different things could have been. But fear had filled my being. "If I turn to the Lord I'll lose Doug. He means more than life to me; I can't live without him." My rejection quenched the working of the Holy Spirit for a time. So as the torrent of conflict within my soul—the battle between spirit and flesh—subsided, things settled back to normal.

God is a jealous God, in the righteous sense, not allowing us to attach our hearts to idols no matter how normal or even good the idol might be. Since I had given Him my heart as a child, I belonged to Him and He could not let me sin against Him indefinitely. "For whom the Lord loveth he chasteneth, and scourgeth every son whom he receiveth" (Heb. 12:6). After sweetly, faithfully, lovingly trying to draw me back without success, He had no other choice than to touch my heart in its tenderest spot. He had put His hand on my idol, not to snatch it cruelly from me, but to carry it gently to His own bosom, knowing my heart would follow its treasure.

And so it was that the long wait was finally broken by my being summoned out into the hall. My strength seemed to ebb away as I faced the doctors and nurses waiting for me outside his room. I knew what they were going to tell me, but somehow hoped my terrible foreboding was wrong.

"He's gone."

There was a cruel finality in their words. A great sense of helplessness flooded me. There was only One to turn to now. In my heart a prayer was uttered, "All right, Lord: I said Your will be done. You have taken him and left me here for a purpose. Please let me finish my work quickly and follow him home."

Back in the sun-room a lone figure quietly dropped to her knees. "The Lord hath given, and the Lord hath taken away. Blessed be the name of the Lord." Another soul was born into the kingdom of God. A mother's heart had followed her son into the bosom of the Saviour. Life was born out of death. Already the higher purposes of God were being revealed.

As for me the first step had been taken in the direction of a new, God-planned life. I was soon to learn of another young widow whose life my own would strangely parallel. Long years before, Ruth, the Moabitess, widowed young, after relinquishing her idols, even as I, had found the sweet refuge and balm there is in the God of Israel.

CHAPTER IV

ASSURANCE FOREVER

IT WAS NOT UNTIL several days later that a thread of doubt and fear was sown into my thoughts, penetrating my heart. The person who uttered the thought had not meant to bring new pain. No, I would not allow myself to voice, much less dwell on any possibility that Doug was not in heaven with the Lord. Had not God given us assurance the night before his death that all would be well with him? And since it hadn't been meant physically, it had to be spiritually.

And then there was the funeral, which I was sure I could never attend! It was a stronger power than my will that took me there, a power present in that service that spoke peace and beauty, dispelling the hopeless grief of separation and the darkness of death. It was as though the curtain of heaven had been pulled aside and the Lord had allowed me a spiritual glimpse into the joys my beloved was experiencing.

> "I come to the garden alone,
>   while the dew is still on the roses,
> And the voice I hear falling on my ear
>   the Son of God discloses;
> And He walks with me and He talks with me,
>   and He tells me I am His own;
> And the joy we share as we tarry there
>   none other has ever known."

The strains of this precious hymn were still soothing my weary mind. Even as the words were being sung, closing my eyes, it seemed as though I could see Doug walking hand in hand with the Saviour. This had given such comfort I dared go on to the cemetery, even though previously I had been sure I could not stand to see them put his body into the ground. My mother's death when I was twelve years old had seemed so final; my life and heart had been left so empty. I was fearful that seeing him interred would make our separation seem final too. This I could not bear.

However, now I found the One who comforts the brokenhearted, the God of all comfort, had gone before. As the procession entered the cemetery gates, with my spiritual ears I could hear beautiful angelic choirs singing praises to His holy name, and I knew in my soul there was my Doug in the midst of them. Imagination, no matter how vivid, cannot fill the soul with joy in the midst of sorrow, nor give an endless hope in the face of a hopeless end. Surely this way the Lord revealed to our hearts all was well with his soul.

And that blessed Presence that had walked with Doug in the garden was walking with me daily. He knew the tiny fear of doubt the enemy had sown. Sweetly, tenderly He began to work to remove the doubt forever before it could grow into a stumbling stone bringing torment and spiritual destruction.

Christmas Sunday, five days after Doug's death, found me in church, Pastor Dugger's church. My still freshly borne sorrow laid me heavily upon his heart during his afternoon meditation and prayer time. Although it was not my intention to return to services in the evening, late in the afternoon I felt the need to go for strength and comfort. After the evening services, Pastor Dugger called me aside to tell me that while he was praying for me in the afternoon, the Holy Spirit had come to him and clearly spoken, "Give June this verse." As he read I Corinthians 3:23, my mind searched beyond the obvious words for the Holy Spirit's message to me. "And ye are Christ's; and Christ is God's." My questioning expression prodded an explanation.

"This little word *ye* in the Greek (original language of the New Testament) is plural. Ye are Christ's."

Catching a glimpse of hope I asked, "Whom do you mean by ye?"

"Him up there and you down here," with quiet assurance he continued. "You and Doug both belong to Christ now and Christ is God's."

My heart soared with praise. Even though Pastor Dugger did not know my unvoiced doubts, the Lord did!

Later Pastor Dugger told me he had seen Doug for just a moment before he had come to us in the sun-room. Though he could not deal with him, Doug had managed four little words, his last, to Pastor Dugger. "It's all right now." This was his own testimony that his heart which had been so fearful only a few hours before had found peace, and he could leave this world saying in a sense, "It is well with my soul."

This would have been sufficient to quiet my fears forever, but our Lord delights to do the exceeding abundantly. Two weeks later, a letter I had learned of only hours before was unexpectedly placed in my hand. It had been written eight years earlier to my mother in the hospital. Perhaps because she died before the letter reached her it was kept by the sender for eight years. As I opened it now there was assurance that the Lord had a message in it for me. Trembling with excitement I scanned the contents. Included was a verse of Scripture. "The eternal God is thy refuge, and underneath are the everlasting arms" (Deut. 33:27). It was one of the same verses the Lord had given through Pastor Dugger for Doug in the hospital. The Lord had given the same verse for both my mother and Doug on their deathbeds eight years apart! Could I ever again doubt God or His wonderful love and compassion for me?

These were paradoxical days: days of overflowing tears, and abounding joy—loneliness for a voice, an ache for the touch of a hand, and yet the sweet comfort of a loving Presence that continued with me day and night. Now I truly belonged to Him. His purpose in leaving me here alone must be fulfilled soon, so I, too, could join that happy throng around His heavenly throne.

CHAPTER V

RUTH DECIDING

THE GLITTER OF THE WORLD and the pleasures of self-satisfaction held no meaning for me now. My previous goal of enjoying life to the utmost was empty, meaningless. Without Doug there was no world for me. The life of this world had died to me when he died. My heart had gone with him to his new residence on high, leaving me with only one purpose in life: to find the will of God and complete it.

My daily prayer had become, "I'll do or be anything, go anywhere You want me to, Lord Jesus; just please don't leave me sitting." I felt sure I could bear anything of pain, sorrow, or even martyrdom, for it would have been easier to die than to live on alone. My great fear was that of being left to the emptiness of normal, everyday living, which without Doug could only bring me pain. My heart cried out, "Please don't put me on a shelf. Let me burn out for Thee." My only solace was to completely lose myself in Him and in His work for me. The inner realization that I was left behind to do a job which no one else could do was so strong I felt nothing could touch me, that I was hedged about until that work should be completed. How could I discover what that work would be?

Because of the great strength and sweet comfort the Lord had given me, my heart went out to lonely, suffering ones who do not know the Comforter. These were the ones I longed to help, the brokenhearted, the unloved. And since I now had no binding earthly ties (I would never remarry, I was sure, for if God had wanted me married, He would surely have spared Doug!), and having the blessings of good health and youth (being just twenty years of age), I felt I should fill the gap where most others could not go. China? Perhaps. At least the needy foreign mission field tugged hardest at my heart. Feeling I had the message for those suffering as Doug had, my next thoughts turned toward nurses' training.

As I waited on the Lord in prayer, and sought Christian counselling from Pastor Dugger, the Lord began to lead me step by step. The need of learning the Word was presented to me; the desire to learn the Word was stimulated by the Holy Spirit within; and then finally the closing and opening of doors made the path clear.

Meanwhile, in God's own providence, evangelistic meetings had been scheduled during January at Pastor Dugger's church. The Spirit of God was striving with different members of the family. Our rejoicing was joined by the angels in heaven as one by one many of them sought refuge and cleansing at the foot of the cross. One particular night when the invitation was given, a great burden for my unsaved brother in the audience came over me. As I felt the crushing weight of the burden for his lost soul, agonizing pleadings rose incessantly from my innermost being. Suddenly I was aroused from prayer by the pastor's voice, "Stand up and see your brother coming!" It was all I could do not to run to meet him. The victory was glorious, the joy overflowing.

By the end of the meetings thirteen persons, having seen the vanity of this life—its swift and sudden end—having been brought to the very threshold of eternity by Doug's crossing over, had bowed before the One who has paid it all. We realized in Him the Good Shepherd, who having taken up a lamb in His arms, carried it forth in order to draw the mother and others of the flock to follow. If we ever wanted to ask, "Why? Why did he have to die so young?" thirteen salvaged souls would forever stand as a monument to the answer.

It was during those meetings the Holy Spirit spoke clearly to my heart, "Biola Bible College in Los Angeles." And the urgency of desire burned within, giving full assurance, "This is My will." However, it was only two weeks before the beginning of the spring semester. Could I possibly be accepted at such a late date? To our omnipotent God there is no obstacle. He is the One who delights in moving mountains, in making paths through the sea, in leveling walls before us. And had

He not spoken clearly? I quickly made application. Knowing there would not be time to prepare after receiving my acceptance, I proceeded to put my affairs in order, pack my suitcases, and then to wait with the joy of anticipation. So strong was the assurance that the Lord wanted me at Biola right then that I knew I had to go, accepted or not! Anticipation gave way to fulfillment when on the day of opening registration my acceptance arrived.

And so it was that seven weeks after Doug's death, like a frightened little sparrow pushed out of its nest by the mother bird, God lifted me out from the comfort of family love and flung me into the strange new world of preparation. As Ruth the Moabitess had chosen to follow the way that separated her from her secure world of family and any hope of remarriage, into a life lived solely, devotedly for the God of Israel, even so the Lord had drawn me away from the love of the world and shelter of my loved ones into a life given over entirely to Him. My days at Biola were days of leading and learning that proved eventually to bring me also to the land flowing with milk and honey.

CHAPTER VI

THE JOURNEY

THE PATHWAY HE WOULD TAKE us is not always smooth and beautiful, full of sunshine and easy to tread. Perhaps if it were, we would become so enraptured by our surroundings, by the blessings along the way, we would soon forget our need of the One who is our guide. Our desire would be drawn out after the blessings rather than the Blesser. Even so, the first days and weeks at Biola were mixed ones. There were mountaintop experiences, catching glimpses of the beauties of the living Word through the written Word. There were feasts as the Bread of Life was broken for us. There were showers of blessings in sharing with others the precious experiences and lessons along the way.

Then, too, came the valleys when the crushing loneliness hid momentarily the beauties of His face, and the famines and parched deserts when my love-starved heart cried out for the touch of the hand, the embrace of the arms that could not be regained. At such times the only solace was the deserted roof of the women's dorm, fourteen floors above the din of a busy metropolitan street, the closest I could get to heaven. There I could go alone to weep and pray and hope that soon, very soon, my work would be finished and I, too, could go Home. Or, better still, that even this night the trumpet call would sound and He would come in the air to claim His own, all the redeemed! Blessed hope! Lifting face and heart heavenward, pleading for courage to go on, I would drink in the needed strength, the refreshing hope that the precious Comforter always so freely gives. How sweet His fellowship became to me as we walked this path of sorrow together.

The time came when there awoke within me the realization of the depth of His mercy in saving Doug's soul when we had hardly given thought to that need. How very narrow is the margin between life and death, between heaven and hell. How grateful I was that the Lord had spared him those few days, and tenderly brooded over him until his soul was born anew into His marvelous salvation. I shuddered to think of the outcome had the Lord allowed his life to end that first day in the hospital! Oh, the multitudes around us standing on the very edge of that awful precipice, ready to plunge headlong into the chasm of outer darkness! Little do they realize that Jesus hung on a cross between heaven and hell choosing death that they might gain life! His triumph over the grave three days later swung open the glorious gates of heaven and took the ultimate sting, the finality, out of death. Such need, such love that answered this need, compelled me to go on—to go out to tell the wondrous story.

My thoughts turned again to the Bible and the story of Ruth. It must have been a difficult, weary journey for the little Moabitess as she trudged alongside Naomi across the mountains and through the valleys and deserts toward a land she never before had seen. She perhaps mused in her heart upon the workings of Naomi's God which had brought her this way; His leadings through the years, unrecognized then, but clearly evident now.

I, too, looking into the unknown future, found comfort in reviewing His workings of the past. The Lord had put His hand upon me as a small child and claimed me for the mission field. When simply told the Son of God had died on the cross for my sins because He loved me so, my child heart responded, though I had not had as yet my fifth birthday. For several years thereafter my life's ambition had been to be a missionary. And although the cares of the world had gradually choked out the vision, yet in love, God had laid His hand upon me to claim that which was rightfully His. So, through no carefully laid plans of mine, here I was preparing in Bible college for His place of service for me.

The first summer vacation found me happily home again with my loved ones. How sweet our fellowship was as I shared the rich treasures of the Word gleaned at school. Doug's mother had truly become a Naomi to me as the Lord knit our two bereaved hearts together in a spiritual bond of love.

The little church where the Lord had worked so marvelously some months before became a well of refreshing, a special place of spiritual delights. Like King David, "I was glad when they said unto me, Let us go into the house of the Lord." At times it would have been the fullfilling of my heart's desire if I could have pitched a tent in the church patio and spent every moment enjoying the sweet atmosphere of Christian love and fellowship that satisfied a hungering heart. It was that very summer, however, that the Lord taught me through experience that the reality of His person and presence, rather than His blessings, are the ultimate for satisfying the human heart. So often it is through experience that our understanding becomes enlightened in previously learned spiritual truths.

It was necessary for me to work during that summer in order to save enough money for re-entrance at Biola in the fall. At times I would meet with a childhood friend for lunch in the park. One day as we sat on the grass enjoying the cool shade of the trees, she began unburdening her heart. As school girls together, we had shared the intimate thoughts and desires of our hearts, and so, even though she had not shared my spiritual experience of rebirth, it was not unusual for her to reveal her heart to me. She bared a hungry soul—seeking love, understanding, fulfillment; but a soul intent upon finding satisfaction in the fleshly realm of this life. How my heart ached for her. What could I tell her more of the beautiful satisfying love of the Saviour than what I had told before? How could I disclose to this one the fullness He would exchange for her emptiness?

While lifting my heart in silent prayer, I became conscious of a Presence behind me. So strong was my awareness that I turned to look, and there a few yards away, under a tree, my soul visualized an unseen Presence. A sweet fragrance, a loving warmth reached me from that Presence as He seemed to say, "All I am and have is for her too." A sense of awe, then joy, sweetly filled me—a quiet, deep abiding joy that the world cannot know and cannot take away.

The Presence remained with us and after departing to go back to work, I was aware that He went with me. He was so real that the eye of my imagination could visualize the long flowing white robe and the sandled feet. There was strength and power in that form, and above all, the glowing warmth of love. Wherever I went my unseen companion remained with me, my spiritual sensitivity to His presence becoming so strong I could all but see where He was in the room. There was at times the reality of the nodding of His head in affirmation to or negation of my questioning directed to Him in the silence of my heart when decisions had to be made. He had become to me a living companion and abundant provider of all my needs. Was this what He meant in the written Word, which I was memorizing daily, when He said He would be a Husband to the widow? I thought so!

It must have been this same Presence who walked with Ruth and Naomi as they made their way to Bethlehem. The knowledge that she had given up forever, it seemed, the hope of a home and family of her own, to go to a strange land and a strange people who might not accept a little foreigner like herself must have given her grave misgivings. The way was rough, traveling over the barren hills of Moab, the provisions for these two widows meager. Could it have been anything other than the love and strength of that Presence walking with them that enabled them—enabled Ruth particularly—to set her face unwaveringly toward Bethlehem? Little could she or I know the beautiful valley of fulfillment that lay before us at the end of the long, hard journey. But with this Presence by our side the fears and forebodings were hushed, and the pain of widowhood soothed.

I felt sure that Ruth must have longed many times for a shortcut. Perhaps as she lay on the hard earth at night with only a rock for a pillow and closed her weary eyes in sleep, she would think how wonderful it would have been to be able to open them the next moment in Bethlehem. Little did she realize that each step, each moment of this slow and difficult journey, was giving her time to learn of Him and preparing her for the work of faith and labor of love awaiting her in that strange land which was to become her home.

Back at school in the fall I found there were no shortcuts for me either in the training and preparation necessary for the work He had left me to do. How my heart longed to put away the books and find a place where I could be satisfied by being poured out in behalf of needy lives and souls. And though the restless flesh sought many times and ways for shortcuts, His faithful Spirit held me fast. Each step was needful for rooting and grounding and ultimate preparation to becoming an effective vessel later. All the lessons were not learned in the classrooms from the textbooks. Each exercise of soul wrought by the divine Teacher caused the roots to sink deeper.

The Bible became a living book, Old Testament personalities, especially Ruth, real people whose experiences with the Lord inspired and challenged. In compliance with future purposes the Author of the Book was creating in me a deep love not only for the Book but also for the people of the Book.

Missionary conferences kept before us the overwhelming need of a lost and dying world. Always the question uppermost in my mind, "Where, Lord, is my field of service?" sent my heart searching in prayer with each new missionary challenge. When departure time came for my second summer home from school, I knew the Lord had not yet spoken, "This is it."

CHAPTER VII

DIRECTION

COULD IT TRULY BE August 29 already? The summer had gone all too quickly and only another week remained before returning to Biola for the fall semester. It had been a wonderful summer, making my regret to see it end all the stronger. There had been precious times of service in daily vacation Bible school, and counselling junior girls at camp. How marvelously the Lord had moved in young hearts, bringing some to salvation and others to dedication. Many doors had been opened for testimony, and I had again tasted the bubbling up and running-over joys of serving the Lover of my soul. It would not be easy to return to the loneliness away from loved ones and the restricted dormitory life. Later I would learn that even this was necessary missionary preparation. And, of course, there would be great compensations in feasting upon the Word under godly and scholarly men, as well as new doors of service which surely would open.

So, with mixed feelings I prepared to attend my last midweek service of the summer at my beloved church. Who did Pastor Dugger say was going to speak tonight? The name Elias Zimmerman did not sound especially interesting to me, nor did I know what his message was to be about. Somewhat disappointed, as I so enjoyed our pastor's usual Bible lesson, I set out for the church, not knowing this was to prove one of those steps ordered by the Lord—in fact, one that would give my life an entirely new direction.

After a stimulating song service, the speaker, a small elderly man with a face of sunshine, began his message. He introduced himself as a Hebrew Christian, and began to tell of a people, his people, and more important our Lord's own people—the Jewish people who have not known the One who came to them centuries ago. Why, it had not occurred to me until right then that they were a mission field just as truly as any people on a foreign shore!

Mr. Zimmerman's words painted a heartrending picture for us of a suffering, abused, neglected people. Here were those who had not only missed their longed-for and long-awaited Messiah, but also had come to suffer terrible inhumanities in His very name! The persecutions begun by blinded religious zealots such as Saul, who later became the great Apostle Paul, were taken up and continued down through the centuries— often by religionists! Here lifted before us was a bruised and heartbroken, hopeless, suffering people who needed the ointment of love and the salve of understanding, the healing touch of the "Balm of Gilead."

Strong responses of love and compassion began to fan the coals of my heart. The Holy Spirit was moving to answer a prayer of more than one and a half years! My heart was prepared and ready when he challenged us, "What will we do when we stand before God if we have done little or nothing to win His own chosen people to Himself?"

My heart cried out, "Lord, I will go. Send me; send me!" A sensation of joy and peace came over me, but was immediately cushioned by a cautious hesitancy. Was this truly the Lord's call to me? His choice of a field of service for me? My immediate prayer, "Lord Jesus, please don't let me be led astray by an emotional experience if this has not been Thy call; but on the other hand, if it is, please move me in that direction and show me clearly," was to be answered quickly and with abundance. August 29, 1951, was to become one of the most indelible dates in my memory.

CHAPTER VIII

SIGNPOSTS

It has been said, "The Lord cannot steer a parked car." Fully persuaded of this, I took advantage of a notice posted on the bulletin board in the lobby at Biola shortly after my arrival back at school. The Los Angeles Hebrew Mission needed volunteer visitation workers. What better test could I make to prove my call to Jewish missionary work than by becoming involved in it? The required telephone call to the mission resulted in an invitation to attend their next fellowship meeting called the "Watchmen upon the Walls Club."

Meanwhile, for practical Christian service training, I received an assignment to the Hollywood Street Team, which held services each Saturday night. Later, much to my utter amazement and joy, I found it to be a Jewish street team led by a Hebrew Christian, David Sanders.

My curriculum this particular fall included New Testament Greek. For many months I had been anxiously anticipating this study, having previously received a taste of the richness and depth of meaning found in the original language. The class turned out to be so large it had to be divided, and it fell to my lot to be removed to help form the new class. Surprisingly, but providentially, I am sure, our new teacher proved to be none other than Dr. Charles Feinberg, Hebrew Christian professor! Suddenly everywhere I turned I was involved with or confronted by the Jewish race! Were these incidents His signposts of assurance for me? To the Christian there is no coincidence—only divine incidents!

Shortly after school had begun, Doug's mother and father came to the Los Angeles area to visit friends. At their request

I received permission to spend an afternoon and evening off campus with them. In order not to fall behind in Greek, which demanded daily study time, it seemed wise to take my assignment along with me. During the afternoon as I was attempting to complete it, I noticed a puzzled expression on our host's face. He questioned, "Why are you studying Greek, of all things? Why not Spanish, French, or some other popular language?"

To which I replied, "I want to be able to read the New Testament in its original language."

He then surprised me with, "Isn't the Old enough?"

"Oh, no!" I explained, "The Old only prophesies of Christ's coming while the New records His actual advent."

Whereupon, I was taken aback to hear, "I didn't know He had come."

Before I could open my mouth again his wife called him to the kitchen. Could it be? Excitedly I turned to mother, "Is he a Jew?"

Her affirmation thrilled me, for this was my first witness— though unknowingly at the time—to one of the chosen seed of Israel! How rapidly and clearly the signposts were being revealed along the way!

One of the most outstanding incidents at the time was the Watchmen upon the Walls Club meeting later in the month, and just a few weeks after what was fast proving to be a definite call to Israel. I arrived at the meeting with as much curiosity as anticipation. This was all so very new to me. The atmosphere was warm and friendly. Glancing about the room my eyes fell upon Hebrew lettering on the walls. I later learned these were portions of Old Testament Scriptures revealing God's appointing of watchmen upon the walls of Jerusalem who were to warn of approaching danger. How appropriate, I thought, to use for a Jewish mission; for truly we who know the Messiah, should act as watchmen upon the walls, heralding the message of impending eternal doom to all—and most assuredly to God's own chosen race!

The meeting not only was enlightening educationally, but also increased my burden and my love for the Jew. Several gave their testimonies as to why they as Jews believed in Jesus as the long-awaited Messiah and only Saviour of the world. The most impressive part of the meeting was the unique testimony of a young man who less than a year before had become a believer in Jesus, the Christ. He had been reared as an orthodox Jew (adhering to the strict laws of Moses in the Old Testament) but had not found it satisfying to his soul. Life had become so difficult, so empty and meaningless for him, that he made plans to commit suicide. A Christian friend who had dealt with him through the years, just at that crucial time pointed him once again to Jesus Christ as the answer. And right on the very verge of casting himself into eternal torment he was saved—snatched from the very edge of the abyss. Life was no longer unbearable to him; he emitted a glow of joy, voicing deep appreciation and love to the Messiah who had changed his life completely.

Though I saw this young man only from a distance—across a very crowded room—and had given no particular heed to his name, his testimony so penetrated my heart and thrilled my soul that I went back to Biola deeply moved and bubbling over with renewed enthusiasm. The next day my chief topic of conversation was the tremendous story of a young Jewish lad who was gloriously saved on the brink of suicide.

I had truly lost my heart to the Jewish people. As I learned more about them my heart was drawn out more and more with a desire to help them. Here was a people who had suffered undoubtedly more than any other people in history. The race leading to the Messiah, and to the ultimate fulfillment of God's plan for this world of a righteous kingdom on earth, has always been a target of Satan. He has sought to destroy them down through the centuries: through Pharaoh at the time of Moses' birth (if all the male Hebrew babies were destroyed, the line would be exterminated eventually); through Haman at the time of Queen Esther's intercession; through King Herod at the time of Christ's birth; and often through professing Christians since His birth.

Could it have been other than Satan who conceived the thought in the hearts of the Crusaders to plunder and kill the Jews on their pilgrimage all the way across Europe to the Holy Land? The historians of that day wrote that the Crusaders rode through town after town holding forth a cross in one hand and a sword in the other demanding the Jews to bow down and worship Christ or be killed. To the Jew, who knows nothing of the Trinity, to do so would be to break the first commandment that says, "Thou shalt have no other gods before me" (Ex. 20:3). They heroically chose, rather than to deny their faith, to pay with their blood. So many were slaughtered, Jewish blood literally ran like rivers in the streets. And the unenlightened Crusaders emerged feeling they had done God a favor. Surely herein lies the secret of their gross failures, for has not God promised to curse them who curse Israel? (Gen. 12:3).

For centuries the Jew has been made an outcast of cities and even countries which had been their family home for generations because of their "terrible crime" of having been born a Jew. Persecution has broken out time and again, the Jew conveniently being made the scapegoat of anything and everything. And so often in the name of Christ!

In our own time one-third of the known Jewish population was mercilessly destroyed by Hitler and his cohorts, the grotesque atrocities against six million Jews still coming to light! Truly this was a people with whom and for whom I could suffer. My own experiences of sorrow gave us a common bond and enabled me to understand them, compelling me to love them! Even as Ruth had entreated Naomi, my heart cried out to my precious Redeemer 'who himself came to us a Jew, "Thy people shall be my people."

By the end of another school year, as a result of the many opportunities to participate in Jewish evangelism under the Los Angeles Hebrew Mission, the assurance of my calling had come with abundance. And as I served them, the very people of The Book, I felt awed and richly blessed at this special and high calling to God's own chosen people.

CHAPTER IX

COMPULSION

My last year at Bible college was to prove not only very eventful, but also very decisive regarding the future. One of the highlights of my curriculum was an evening Jewish Missions course, directed by a dear Christian man with a great love for the Jews.

During the first class session in order to establish the ultimate aim of the group as well as a more intimate class relationship, our instructor requested each student to stand in turn and with his personal introduction to present his purpose for having enrolled in the class, Many of the students voiced an interest in helping Jewish people learn about their Jewish Messiah and Saviour. One young man, standing to his feet, replied that he himself was a son of Abraham, called of God as a missionary to his own people, and was looking forward to service in Israel.

It was a rich blessing indeed to have in our class an actual Jew who knew and loved the Lord Jesus. During recess I made it a point to inform him of the wonderful Watchman upon the Walls Club meetings which I had found so profitable and enjoyable. Much to my surprise, I found he had been attending them also. Strange we had never met there! As we fellowshipped a little more, the astounding realization dawned upon me that this was the young man whose testimony had so thrilled me a year ago at my introductory meeting of the club. This was he who was on the verge of suicide when he yielded to Christ and was saved! Mike Perl was a very warm person who drew people to himself. His zeal reminded one of the Apostle Paul—bolstered by his 5' 5½" stature and typical Jewish appearance.

The Lord's ultimate purpose in bringing Mike to Biola was yet to be revealed. He had been attending another Bible college when he felt the need of acquiring a more complete knowledge of biblical Hebrew. There was one major problem to be faced. He was attending school under the G.I. Bill, and the government had shortly before made a ruling against transfers from one college to another. He might have been defeated without trying except for two things: his personal knowledge of a miracle-working God and his previous army experience which had taught him that usually exceptions can be made to any rule.

After extensive prayer, Mike picked up the phone and dialed the local Veterans Administration. The voice on the other end of the line displayed a slight chuckle in answer to Mike's pointed question, "Can or cannot a student transfer schools under the G.I. Bill?"

"If you have a good reason, you might be able to do so."

"Well, I cannot get Hebrew at my present school and I feel I need it for my future work."

The answer was encouraging, "Sounds like a good reason to me, but of course I am nobody; I don't have the authority. There is a form you will have to fill out."

Mike's army experience prompted a note of apprehension, "Is it a long form?"

This time the chuckle was less concealed, "No, not this time. It is a short one!" He must have felt he was talking to Sgt. Perl by now!

"Do you have one?"

"Yes! Now wait a minute, I had better check to be sure." After a few moments, "No, I don't. But I know where I can get one. And I'll tell you what I'll do. I'll put it in an envelope with your name on it and leave it at the desk. You won't have to wait for it when you come."

The response was gratifying, "Great! I'll be down for it in a half hour!"

When the submitted application was returned in seven days, Mike was sure it was bad news! It seemed to him that whenever the army put anything through in a hurry, it was "no!" Much to his surprise and resultant elation, it read, "APPROVED." The Lord had overruled again!

A bond of friendship grew between us as we fellowshipped together concerning our common interest and love, Israel.

Mike Perl became a cherished friend, someone to counsel with as I sought the Lord's next step for me as college days drew to a close.

The Lord had also given me a bosom friend and companion during my years at Biola. I had met Diane at Pastor Dugger's church, and her compassionate heart had been drawn out to me from the beginning. She had been led to Biola my second semester there (even through my encouragement!) and her presence proved a great help many times.

Diane had been gifted with an understanding heart and a good listening ear. These were much exercised during the two and one-half years we were together at school. Faithful like Job's friends (though with much better understanding) she was the one who sat with me through the soul struggles while I tried to understand and determine God's direction for my life. It was to her first I confided the great desire burning within my soul to go to the land of Israel. Many an evening we spent hours strolling the streets or sitting in the dormitory trying to analyze, through discussion and prayer, what was assuredly desire kindled by the Holy Spirit within or what should be considered desire motivated by self. So many encouraged work among the great number of Jews here in America, feeling sensationalism was the attraction to Israel. Some of the compulsion and struggle was recorded in letters to Diane after she left school in the middle of my Senior year:

> I've lost my heart to the Jews. I can't explain so great a love as I feel for them. I wish I were a Jew so very much. . . . I long to be one of them, to fight for them and with them, to laugh and cry with them. . . . I love their spirit. Their heartaches are mine, their persecutions, their loves and joys are mine. . . .
>
> Last night I felt so definitely that my place is in Israel. . . . I could just see myself with dungarees on, sleeves rolled up to the elbows working side by side with the Jewish people in their land. I feel that is where I belong. . . . They need someone to be one with them, to encourage their broken hearts, someone to love them. . . .
>
> This morning He gave me clearly, "I being in the way, the Lord led me to the house of my master's brethren" (Gen. 24:27). What house is this but the house of the Jews?

And again:

> I know God is doing something in my life—I feel
> He is working out beyond my little sphere where I can-
> not see—but I'm sure soon He will open the future to
> me. I know I shall be thrilled to see that not only has
> He been preparing me, but also that which He has for
> me. "He will perfect that which concerneth me" (Ps.
> 138:8). All I know is that it is in my heart to go to
> Israel.

> Last night after Jewish prayer band we saw the
> Jewish Declaration of Independence. How it thrilled
> my soul and warmed my heart. I love their land, too,
> and am so glad they have it back. How I would love to
> help rebuild it. I feel within me the spirit that I think
> they must feel about Israel. I've never seen it, but I
> love it—pictures of the land thrill me—and I want to
> get my hands in their soil. My very being cries out
> to go and yet I cannot plan until God definitely opens
> the door and shows me how to get there.

A highlight came early in April.

> Diane, I just felt I had to tell someone. . . . When
> you feel something wonderful in your heart you just
> want to share it. Just think, the people I am going to
> already have a knowledge of the true God, and as I
> study their heritage, culture, and language I will in
> reality be studying the Word of God.

> These are God's people—the people of God's book,
> and how much nearer Him I feel because of it. It is a
> privilege to be called of God, but I feel an extra priv-
> ilege to be called to the Jew, and I can never be happy
> or satisfied until I have given my all for Him among my
> people, Israel. After all, Diane, we aren't living for
> this world—it is only preparatory for life with Him.
> And truly I count not my life as dear to me, but I am
> willing ". . . not to be bound only, but to die at Jerusalem
> for the name of the Lord Jesus" (Acts 21:13).

There must have been a similar yearning in Ruth's heart
when she said to Naomi, "Intreat me not to leave thee, or to
return from following after thee; for whither thou goest I
will go: and where thou lodgest I will lodge: thy people shall
be my people, and thy God my God" (Ruth 1:16).

CHAPTER X

STEPPING-STONES

As MY HEART THUS YEARNED after what was to me a strange land and people, the Spirit of God seemingly wooing my heart to them, obstacles began to arise. When one is walking in the will of the Lord, obstacles are made to become stepping-stones to the ultimate fulfillment of that will.

One of the first obstacles to appear was the information that the land of Israel was not then open to missionaries as such. The Jewish people there have no objections to Christians in their land, but are very opposed to what they consider proselytizing, or Jewish evangelizing. They would not understand that my desire was not to try to change them into Gentiles, an impossibility, but rather to help them become completed Jews; for the one who stops at Malachi, the last book in the Old Testament, has stopped short of all God's plan for the Jew. How greatly I longed to share with them the unsurpassing love and joy and peace I had found in their very own Messiah.

It was at this time through Diane that the Lord put into my possession, unexpectedly, a wardrobe trunk. It was as though the Lord was saying, "This is my will for you. Get ready to go!" But how could I possibly get into the country? Should I seek to find a mission board when missionaries are not as a rule being accepted? This first obstacle gave rise to a stepping-stone when I heard of the Hebrew university at Jerusalem. Could this be the answer? I would enter the land as a student and continue my schooling at the university! I could in this way become one of the people of the land. What better way to contact the people and to gain friendships which would enable me to speak to them of the One who taught the wisdom of Jehovah from that very land?

Saturated with much prayer, a lone letter requesting the necessary application papers for entrance into the Hebrew university went winging its way to Jerusalem, Israel. Soon, by return mail, came the next obstacle! Along with the application paper came a letter of information—all lectures (at that time) were given in the Hebrew language, the revived modern Hebrew, now the national language of Israel. This seemed to set my schedule back possibly two or more years, until I could learn Hebrew sufficiently to attend lectures at the university.

After the first wave of disappointment, submission to the seeming will of God brought peace, though the deep longing to go remained. This longing was only increased when the Jewish boy, Mike Perl, came to me and asked if he could have my application to the Hebrew university since I couldn't use it. He felt the Lord was leading him within the next few months to enter Israel as a student even as I had planned! Not with little anguish of heart did I part with it. Only those who know the experience of surrendering willingly a heart's desire to the Lord can understand the paradox of sweet pain or joy in sorrow. Soon the soothing ointment of His precious peace mollified the disappointment.

Shortly after this a door opened that turned this obstacle into a stepping-stone. Mike was this time the instrument of God. He had learned through the Jewish Agency of a government language school (the Ulpan) in Israel, which taught modern Hebrew by the direct conversational method. Again this was indeed the answer. To learn Hebrew in the land itself would be the quickest method possible, as you would have daily opportunity to put your classroom learning to practice. At the same time I would be receiving orientation to my new land and people!

The Ulpan would begin in July. There was no time to lose. Easter vacation was upon us. While at home I would locate my birth certificate which would be essential to applying for my passport. However, to my dismay, the certificate could not be located, necessitating a delay while obtaining a duplicate from the courthouse. It was May 4, just one month before graduation from Bible college, when I was finally able to submit my application for the passport. As I placed the compulsory form before me on the counter, I inquired as to the length of time before I could expect to receive my passport. The answer was disheartening, "Usually from two to six weeks. This being coronation year, many people are going to Europe for Queen Elizabeth's coronation in England, and so it is generally taking the longer time!"

My heart sank. Another obstacle. "But surely, if the Lord is in this," I reasoned, "then it will become a stepping-stone."

And it did so definitely seem the leading of the Lord even to the preparation of the hearts of my loved ones. Had not Mother written recently, "You sound as though you wanted to leave for Israel right after school. Do you think it might be that soon? Don't see how you could; but if the Lord really wants you there, I'm sure He will open the way. I'm about reconciled to the fact that you won't be around much. It really has been grand to have you all this time. I feel I've been richly blessed!" It had been wonderful having a mother again in Doug's mother and I would greatly miss our sweet times together.

Then word came that the school I wanted to attend would not open until the fall. However, there was a school in a Kibbutz (a collective farm) opening in July which I could attend. We would work all morning and study all afternoon. This was not an obstacle to me, but rather an added blessing in gaining experience and knowledge of Israel and her people. And even as I had desired, I could really roll up my sleeves and work with them! Application was made.

Knowing I must proceed quickly now, by faith I made reservations on an airliner to arrive in Lydda, Israel, June 29. Great was the joy of anticipation with each new step leading me closer to the chosen land, which even the many required shots and vaccinations (steps again taken in faith) could not dim. Each obstacle, turned stepping-stone, only increased the joy and certainty that soon my eyes would behold "Jerusalem, a quiet habitation" (Isa. 33:20), even my future home!

And so it must have been with Ruth of long ago. As each distant hill appeared an obstacle, but conquered became a stepping-stone toward Bethlehem, her joy and certainty of final arrival must have increased. And an unseen hand guided her as surely as that unseen hand was guiding me now.

Such a vital step for me certainly required definite assurance that this was the Lord's plan for my life and not just my own engineering because of human zeal. The Lord had His servant to help me at this time. The experience was shared with Diane:

". . . Mr. K. from the Watchman upon the Walls Club and I were the only ones driving out to the Jewish Beach meeting Sunday as Mrs. K. has the flu. On the way back God definitely spoke to me through him. He asked me what I was going to do when I got out of school. I told him I wasn't sure. He said he feels we can definitely know what God's plan is for us but that only comes through waiting on the Lord in prayer and fasting. He didn't know God led me to fast twice last week!

"Anyway, he said first we must wait before the Lord—sometimes on our faces (literally) before Him and let Him search out our hearts and show us what must go. Then when our hearts are clean before Him and nothing is between Him and us, He can speak to our hearts and tell us His will for us. He said that as we wait in prayer it isn't always talking but often just waiting—and it is amazing what He brings to our minds that we never thought of before. Then after we know God's place for us, we should in the same way seek out how He would have us carry out His will for us.

"For example, Moses knew he was to be a deliverer, but he didn't know how God wanted him to carry it out, so he took things in his own hands and killed the Egyptian, and then God had to train him in the desert for forty years.

"Now, Diane, I've known since last summer that fasting was of God, but not until Sunday afternoon did I really understand the reason for it, and I would not have then except for last Tuesday and for Saturday morning when I fasted. Mr. K. said when you fast you become weak and when you are weak you will yield, submit, and cast yourself upon Him when you ordinarily would not.

"I know that is the purpose now, for those two days I was so weak physically I felt I could not hold myself up, and I prayed for real strength. And Diane, when I felt so weak, I could do nothing but cry out to God and cast myself at His mercy whether to go to Israel or to stay here. His strength is made perfect in weakness; His spiritual strength—our physical weakness. I felt sweetly resigned to Him."

In this attitude, there was much heart searching on my knees before the Lord and in the Scriptures as I analyzed and weighed all details. Then, because of the shortness of time, I felt prompted to pray shortly after my return from the passport office, "Lord Jesus, if it is Your will for me to go to Israel and now, please bring my passport in the shortest possible time. If it is of Thee, please make the application go through on the top of every stack of applications all the way to Washington, D.C., and back again."

If the passport arrived in two weeks this would give me approximately two weeks to obtain my visa necessary for entry into Israel. After two days of earnest intercession, the assurance came, "In two weeks." Looking up from prayer to my wall calendar I observed that exactly two weeks from then would be May 20. With joyful assurance I praised the Lord and had no liberty to plead again. Rather my daily prayer became, "Thank You, Lord, that my passport will be here by the 20th."

I arose the morning of the 20th with mixed feelings. My first thought was to remind the Lord that this was the promised day and thank Him for my wonderful expectation. Then came a little twinge of fear. What if the passport doesn't come today? What if this has all been only hopeful thinking on my part—and the Lord had not really spoken?

Pushing the doubt aside with another prayer of praise and thanksgiving, I headed for class. After the first mail delivery, with hopeful anticipation I checked my mailbox. No passport. Well, it was early yet! An hour later upon making another check the mailbox was still just as empty. Surely next time! However, by noon the greatly desired envelope had not made its appearance.

A slight disappointment now caused me to face the fact it may indeed have been my strong desire that prompted me to misinterpret what I had felt sure were the words of the Holy Spirit. But I could not, would not, give way to doubtings yet. There was one last scheduled mail delivery in the afternoon. The Lord still could answer my prayer the way it seemed He had promised.

Returning to my room to freshen up before lunch, I found a note pinned to my door. I quickly scanned the contents. My heart fairly leaped within me. "There is a registered letter for you in the office." Of course! Nearly bursting with excitement I sailed down nine flights of stairs—unable to patiently wait for an elevator—hardly touching a step! Breathless, I presented my note to the girl at the desk, and upon receiving my letter wanted to shout upon beholding in the upper left hand corner "Washington, D.C." The Lord had certainly spoken, and His assurance was clear and convincing. There was no mistaking His will for me now—to go to Israel at this time—and He was overcoming every obstacle! The next weeks were to prove that He and He alone was making an open door for me to Israel.

Passport in hand, with inner fear and trembling, I went forth. The Jewish people in general are very kind and warm. However, knowing my missionary intentions gave me an apprehensive feeling as I approached them for a visa permit into their land. It was especially so, knowing that a missionary nurse, also a student at Biola, had a few weeks previously been refused a visa—after exhausting every avenue—because it was believed she had missionary intentions. Even so, thoroughly paving the way with the prayer, "Lord, please give me full favor and great grace in their eyes," I dared go forth to the Jewish Agency.

There I informed them of my application to the language ulpan, with further studies at the Hebrew university as my prospective goal. I was interviewed by a very kind gentleman who seemed to take a personal interest in me, even to the invitation to see some films that afternoon which they were viewing of Israel. All in all, a profitable four and one-half hours was spent working for my visa that day. There were more interviews on succeeding days. There seemed a definite reluctance on their part, but they had not said no yet! More earnest supplicating prayers for favor and grace ascended heavenward.

June 2, graduation day, marking my departure from Los Angeles, necessarily became my deadline to obtain the essential visa from the Los Angeles Israeli consulate, thus making a July 1 debut in Israel possible. June 1 arrived with still no visa in hand. The shipping company also arrived to pick up my wardrobe trunk, packed and ready for shipping to Israel.

By faith, my face was determinedly set toward Israel—and my trunk now, too!

The kind gentleman who had befriended me at the Jewish Agency, realizing the urgency of time (perhaps mixed with my importunity!) took upon himself to call the Israeli Consulate and plead in my behalf. His last words to me were, "I am going to ask the consulate to give you a visa. But one word of warning: never mention the word missionary to any Israeli officials!" The word had not passed my lips, but he had guessed my heart's intent! How great was the favor and grace that had been granted!

I quickly assured him of compliance to what I had already realized should never be done, and went out rejoicing that I was to pick up my visa the next morning at the consulate. But the next morning, to my chagrin, they tried to put me off once again, asking me to return the following morning. Nevertheless, perseverance and prayer overruled, and on June 2, my deadline, with the precious visa stamped in my passport, there was only praise and wonder at the marvelous miracle working of God. Invisible doors had opened one by one before me and June 29 was just around the corner!

Part II GLEANING IN THE FIELD
CHAPTER II of RUTH of the HOLY BIBLE

CHAPTER XI

TO THE FIELD

GOOD-BYES ARE NEVER EASY when departing from those you love. Now on the first lap of my journey to Israel, soaring high above the Western United States, winging our way through the blue toward New York, there was much time to reminisce. The days since graduation had passed so quickly, with so much to do, so many to see! And then, finally, the good-byes at the airport. Even the joy of anticipation could not ward off the tears that unashamedly flooded up and overflowed.

Was it hard for the Ruth of long ago to say good-bye to her loved ones, too? She surely realized she might never see them again. I could now better appreciate her sacrifice! How great her love for Israel's God and for Naomi! Only a deep sense of love and devotion could have compelled her to cry out: "Intreat me not to leave thee . . . thy people shall be my people, and thy God, my God" (Ruth 1:16). Her words again echoed in my heart. Yes, they too would be my people, as their God was my God. Love was drawing me ever onward, even as it had her, constantly increasing my desire to become one of them, one with God's Chosen People in their promised land.

With one day of rest and sight-seeing in New York, I was again winging my way toward my final destination. Breakfast in New York, afternoon dinner over the Atlantic, and at 10 p.m. (Pacific Standard Time) by my state-side-set watch, a sunrise breakfast in Shanon, Ireland! Next stop—Amsterdam, Holland. Until now there were English-speaking passengers helping me feel somewhat less detached from my native land. By the time we landed at Frankfurt, Germany, however, the

55

strange sounds falling upon my ears, as well as strange words greeting my eyes, brought home the realization that I was indeed alone, very far from home, and in the midst of a foreign people and land.

The great boldness with which I had departed the States began to fade into great wariness! The initial thrill of seeing faraway places I had read about previously began to diminish with a growing sense of anxiety and loneliness. My only comfort came from the faithful One who had called me forth. Inwardly in desperation I clung to His Word, "I will never leave thee nor forsake thee" (Heb. 13:5).

The next hours to Istanbul, Turkey, and then on to Lydda, Israel, were spent in ceaseless praying, intermingled with restless sleeping. There was continuously the mixed sense of His protecting presence and of my weak and defenseless self— so far from home and loved ones—so alone! Somehow, some way, I knew He would see me through the first hours and days in a strange land with a strange people of a strange tongue. He was aware of my need and would surely guide me in a plain path as He had done hitherto!

I was suddenly alerted to the present by a stir of excitement. Above the drone of the engines came the word "Israel!" Far below bright lights glistened through the darkness. The plane, like a huge bird, banked and turned and floating downward, soon was lighted upon the ground—the hallowed ground of the Promised Land! With mixed emotions I breathed deeply of the hot and humid air of a summer night in Israel.

Within minutes, perhaps like the little Moabitess, with a sense of awe and trembling, my feet first touched Israeli soil. The darkness of the night around us could not dim the inner glow of knowing I was home at last—the home for which my heart had hungered so long! Was it any wonder the Yemenite Jews of the recent exodus from feudal and barbarous living conditions, out of sheer joy and thanksgiving had knelt down and kissed this soil? These who had never seen an automobile were borne on the wings of eagles (Operation Magic Carpet Airlift) even as their prophet Isaiah had foretold. So sure were they that this was fulfillment of prophecy, the first question many asked was, "Where is He?" They fully expected the Messiah to meet them there at the airport.

As I followed the crowd up to the customs building, we overtook a group in front of us who had arrived on another airliner just prior to ours. As we approached the group it seemed suddenly to open up and there in the midst was a familiar form! Looking the epitome of astonishment, with hand on forehead and mouth dropped open, stood Mike Perl. Needless to say, my heart overflowed with the joy of relief. The Lord had wonderfully provided. Here was a true friend in the midst of a strange people. Loneliness and fear vanished as two hearts and minds together were swept up into the excitement of seeing Israel for the first time.

As yet I had no idea as to how the Lord had worked to provide this needed companionship for my first days in the land. Later Mike related how he almost missed arriving when he did. Having stopped off at Athens, Greece, for a few days of sight-seeing, he sought for a reservation on the flight arriving in Israel, June 29. On his stopover in Rome he had been told there was no flight from Athens arriving in Israel on that date. Having previously understood differently and having been persuaded in his heart that the Lord had shown him he would arrive in Israel on June 29, he persisted in checking it out. Whereupon he was told that there was such a flight after all, but it was already filled. Still convinced the Lord had spoken clearly, he persisted in seeking for a seat on that plane, and in answer to much prayer was finally told he could have one.

When departure time from Athens came, the flight was delayed. The delay was of enough duration that the passengers were told they could not hope to arrive (apart from a miracle) before midnight, changing their landing day from the 29th to the 30th of June. Mike took it to the Lord in prayer: "Lord, I don't understand. You impressed me I would arrive in Israel June 29. If this is Your will, please move this airplane along miraculously, and bring us in before the 30th." Later, upon inquiry, the stewardess informed him that they had a strong tail wind and were making excellent time. More prayer! And the miracle was wrought! Mike Perl stood upon Israeli soil before midnight, June 29.

And as he later reported to me, his mind had turned to thoughts of me because of the way the Lord had used me to help him get to Israel. But his thought had been, "Poor June;

she'll never make it here." His knowing my tremendous longing to go to Israel had wrought a sense of pity for me. Then his strong doubts against my desire materializing had produced the astounding shock at my appearance. Now what a blessed time of fellowship we had as we shared the ways of the Lord with each of us since last we had seen each other far across the seas in Los Angeles.

When Ruth went out into the fields to glean she faced a new culture, new customs, a new land. She undoubtedly felt fearful and wary. But with a determination born out of love and necessity she went forth boldly. And how sweetly the Lord directed her steps to a part of the field belonging to Boaz. It was from this Jewish bachelor the little widow received direction, comfort, protection, friendship.

Ever mindful of His children's needs, the Lord had not left this modern foreigner without direction, comfort, protection, and friendship, too, upon my arrival in my new land and home. As surely as Ruth's steps had been directed to this meeting of Boaz, even as surely He directed my meeting with Mike. As they fellowshipped, Ruth's own love and devotion for the God of Israel she found equaled in that son of Israel. I, too, rejoicingly found in this modern-day son of Israel a deep devotion, a rich love, a complete consecration for his God, the Messiah of Israel. It had not always been so!

CHAPTER XII

THE TESTIMONY

MIKE HAD BEEN BORN into an orthodox Jewish family. His father was an unusual orthodox Jew in that he drank heavily and gambled. This brought havoc to the family atmosphere, as often money needed for necessities had been 'drunk up' or gambled away. The many quarrels and fights that ensued made him an unhappy, hard-to-manage child.

At the age of six he was deposited with a childless aunt and uncle, who then sent him to Hebrew school. This gave his little heart new hope. Already he had come to feel that family life was a failure. Here in religious training he felt he would surely find joy and peace and something to live for. By the age of thirteen, preparing to become a rabbi, he had become a little Pharisee, striving hard to keep the 613 commandments in the Law of Moses as well as the endless traditions of Judaism.

Shortly after his Bar Mitzvah (confirmation of a Jewish boy at the age of thirteen) his uncle with whom he was living died. This was a great tragedy to this boy who had found solace in his uncle's home. He went to his rabbi seeking comfort and the answer to the mystery of death. "Rabbi, where did my uncle go?"

The vague answer came, "Your uncle was a good man and we hope he is now in Gan Eden" (the garden of Eden—the orthodox Jewish idea of heaven).

This did not satisfy the inner cry. "Rabbi, can't we know if he is there?"

"No. We cannot know such things. Keep on being a good

boy—study hard—and we hope that some day you will be a big rabbi."

This uncertainty, however, began to shake his faith in Judaism. Did Judaism have the answers to life after all? It did answer where we come from, but could not definitely reveal why we are here or where we are going.

In his search to learn what life is all about, and seeking satisfaction in pleasure, he succumbed to the evils of the society around him. Unfortunately, he was living in a very wicked city in northern Wisconsin, where there were more than seventy-five saloons in a town of only three thousand population. The back doors were open to the teen-agers; and before his fourteenth birthday, Mike knew what it was to be dead drunk, and before his fifteenth birthday to have a gun pulled on him, by a man more than thrice his age, in a poker game.

A year and a half after his uncle's death, Mike's father died. There was a different rabbi at the synagogue at this time, and Mike dared to think he might know more than the previous one. And so he questioned him as to where his father had gone. Explosively, this man retorted: "Don't stick your nose into God's business!"

Now completely disillusioned with Judaism, and even losing faith in the God of Judaism, Mike next decided the answer must lie in education. Out of high school, he entered the University of Wisconsin, where, influenced by his professors, he accepted the doctrine of atheism. This not only provided him with no answer to the "why" of life, but also gave him in place of the sadness of Judaism the badness of atheism. With no God or judgment to face in the future, the word sin was struck from his vocabulary. This only deepened his inner conflict and misery, feeding the obsession of suicide which had begun to plague him from childhood days.

Realizing education was not giving him the answer he needed, he withdrew from the university to seek the answer in money. At the age of twenty-three he was buyer-manager of the men's wear department of Baron's, the second largest department store of Madison, Wisconsin. The future looked only bright as the childless president, drawn in a fatherly way to Mike, began to groom him for the future presidency of the store. By the time he had earned enough money to purchase most of the material things he desired, he found money could not buy peace of mind, nor give him the answer to or purpose in life. Distressed, he walked out on this promising future, and his steps providentially led him to Rockford, Illinois, where he went to work in a ladies' shoe store.

The first day on the job a fellow salesman came up to him saying, "I hear you are Jewish." Since about the only time Mike's race was brought up was when someone wanted to make trouble, these words meant a fight! Not one to start trouble or to run away from it, Mike clenched his fists. Seeing this reaction, Claude Sprague quickly spoke up, "Wait a minute, fellow—don't get excited. I love the Jewish people!"

This was new and strange to Mike and he felt sure there must be something wrong here! Later he received his answer when Claude informed him that he loved the Jews because his Saviour, Jesus Christ, was a Jew. Did he know that Christ was his Messiah? Mike answered, "Some say so, and some say no. As for me there are two things I don't discuss: religion and politics."

Claude, however, persisted in speaking to Mike of Christ, telling him how He had straightened out his own life for him. Opening their hearts to Jesus had brought peace and harmony into the Sprague's home and marriage. Christ would straighten out Mike's life for him, too, if he would let Him.

When the opportunity presented itself, in order to get away from Claude and Christ and the crisis in his life, Mike transferred in the company to Aurora, Illinois. He was there but a few days when in the door walked Claude. He was transferred, too!

Here he continued to speak to Mike of Christ at every opportunity. So when another opportunity came to transfer to Joliet, Illinois, Mike again seized it. Within a few days again in walked Claude! Mike was relieved to learn that Claude was to be there only part time, however, and so could work on him only part time. He did not know then that Claude had gone to his knees and asked the Lord to use him to lead Mike to Christ. However, refusing to receive Christ, Mike continued to be miserable, depressed, and disgruntled with life.

World War II broke out. Here was his golden opportunity! Mike would join the Army, ask for combat, die an honorable death for his country, and thus be out of all of his troubles—

he hoped! But at the end of two and one-half years he was still in the United States frozen in a technical position. In order to get into combat he volunteered for the Infantry Paratroops. He qualified and went overseas late in the war. Crossing the Atlantic his ship was rammed by another in their own convoy! Sixty-eight men drowned round about him and he was spared. He wondered why, as he didn't want to live. He wanted only to die. Several weeks later his outfit arrived in France to find they had missed their scheduled jump over the Rhine in which many of his buddies had been killed. The next thing the war was over and he hadn't a scratch on him.

While overseas he had picked up letters from the Sprague family further pleading with him to turn to Christ, and offering their open home and hearts to him upon his return to the States. He could not ignore nor refuse this kind of love. And so back in the States Claude continued to speak to him of Christ.

Once again to escape this, Mike fled into Chicago where he went to work as a salesman. After a short time his body broke out in boils. He went through a fine clinic trying to determine the cause. After a thorough examination the doctor spoke to him frankly. "Young man, we find nothing organically wrong. You are in better health than many a fellow ten years younger than you. What you need is peace of mind."

A faint hope sprang up, "Doctor, I think you are right. Where do I find it?"—only to be dashed to the ground; "If I had the answer to that question, all of my troubles would be over!"

Perhaps a change of job, environment, a change of pace might help. Also to get far away from the preaching of Christ, Mike headed for California in 1947. By this time he had exchanged the badness of atheism for the madness of agnosticism. He would neither admit nor deny there was a God. This brought only conflict. "Maybe there is no God so I might as well kill myself and get out of my misery; but on the other hand, maybe there is and I would be facing His judgment. Maybe there is a heaven and I'll miss it—or a hell and I'll go to it!"

The conflict of trying to be neutral was maddening.

About six months went by after he had settled in Los

Angeles when one day Mike picked up a letter postmarked Colton, California (about sixty miles east), and read, "Yes, Mike, we are in California, too. We like it fine and intend to stay. We will be coming over to see you first chance we get." Signed Claude, Clara and the children.

Claude had felt if he didn't follow Mike up and lead him to Christ no one else would. So, on the promise of a job in California he had quit the good job he had, put his wife, six children, a nephew, and a dog in a nine-year-old jalopy and headed for California, arriving with $42 in all of their pockets put together! Again and often Claude and his family pleaded with Mike to turn to Christ.

Finally February 7, 1951, rolled around. Because of extreme depression and weary of the battle of life, Mike decided this was the end of the road. That day, unexpectedly, Claude came in to see him. Since they had been out of touch for several months, Claude had felt burdened for Mike. When asked how he was, Mike answered, "You know that hole in the ground? Well, I've got both feet in it this time."

Claude pleaded, "Don't do it, Mike. You'll only send yourself to an eternal hell."

Mike would not be restrained. "I don't believe any more that there is a God, or a heaven or hell, so this is it."

Finally Claude put out his hand, "Mike, will you promise me one thing? If you are still alive at the end of this day, will you get down on your knees and ask the God in whom you claimed to believe at one time to show you the truth about Jesus being your Messiah, your Saviour, and the answer to your problems? If you will, I am willing to abide by the results. Here's my hand and I'll say good-bye." Wanting to get rid of Claude and not expecting to be alive to keep such a promise, Mike slipped his hand in his in agreement.

For four hours that night in the privacy of his apartment Mike tried to end his life. In answer to fervent prayer God was staying his hand—unknown to him then.

Weary from the struggle, he realized he couldn't do it that night. Remembering his promise, he felt he had to keep it as a man or he should be dead! His family had taught him always to keep his word.

Skeptically, he dropped to his knees, although as a child he had been taught as a Jew he should never kneel. Such was for the Gentiles. Looking up, Mike said, "God, if You are a God and if You are up there (I don't know where You are) and if Christ is my Messiah and if He can straighten out my life for me, let Him do it. I'm whipped, beaten, defeated, and helpless, and if You are a God and You are up there, You know what I intend to do about it, so You do something about it now—that's all there is to it!"

Getting up from his knees, disgusted with himself for praying into thin air and expecting an answer, he threw himself on his bed crying out, "Let me die; just let me die." Fatigue overcame him and the next thing he knew it was morning, and nothing had changed! Somehow, hoping this day might be the turning point in his life, he went through the mechanics of going to work.

By noon the next day he had quit his job, and went home determined to accomplish what he had not been able to do two nights before. Shortly after arriving home the telephone rang. Hesitating at first, he finally decided to answer it. San Bernardino was calling, Clara Sprague was on the line. Claude had lined up a good job for him in San Bernardino. Would he come over right away for an interview? Realizing it would be a shame to kill himself on what could be the eve of his ship's coming in, he promised to go. After all, he could always kill himself later if it was another false lead. He arrived on Friday afternoon but was asked to return Monday for a definite answer. The Spragues insisted he stay with them even though there were four adults and seven children already sharing their two-bedroom home!

Early Saturday morning Claude took him to the local Christian Business Men's breakfast meeting. There he met fine, wholesome, peaceful-looking men. They manifested something Mike wanted! During the course of the meeting when introductions were made, Claude remarked, "This is my friend about whom some of you have heard. I don't want to say anything that might embarrass him. He has had enough trouble in life. Mike, would you like to say something?"

Responding, he replied, "Men, it is true that I am at the end of my road. I used to believe in prayer at one time, but I do not anymore; but since you men do, please pray for me."

The chairman stood up and said, "I believe this calls for prayer right here and right now. Bill S., will you pray, please?"

Bill stood up, a tall midle-aged man, with a shining face. He addressed Mike, "Young man, you sit where I sat forty-two years ago. I was at the end of my road when someone told me about Jesus. Christ came into my life and since then these have been the best years of my life." Then he prayed, "Lord, light a fire underneath this boy's heart and don't let him be satisfied with food or drink or anything until he comes to You."

That night Mike was awakened from a sound sleep feeling unduly warm. Pushing back his blankets, even the cold February air could not cool him. He thought he must be ill but he could detect no fever! Suddenly he recalled, "That man had prayed, 'Lord, light a fire underneath this boy's heart. . .'!" He put his hand on his chest. That was from where the heat seemed to be coming. Upon checking he found the rest of his body was cool! Looking up in the darkness he said, "If something is happening, just let it happen." Then the conflict for a soul began in earnest.

"This seems to be what I'm looking for."

"But what will your orthodox family say if you, a Jew who once wanted to become a rabbi, turn to Christ? Can you face your Jewish friends and tell them you believe in Jesus Christ?"

"But wouldn't they be happy if this straightened out my life for me?"

"Your mother who traveled five hundred miles just to be in the synagogue for the Jewish holidays would never forgive you. The thing for you to do is to get up and end your life right now."

Yet there seemed to be something, Someone, saying to him, "This is what you are looking for—this will give you peace and answers to all your questions." And so the battle ensued until once again fatigue overtook him.

Upon awakening in the morning Mike could not escape attending church with the Spragues. He did not understand the minister's message but did understand the appeal to accept Christ at the close. He refused, "Not me!"

That evening one of the Sprague daughters invited him to the young people's meeting. He declined, stating that he was too old. When asked his age, he answered, "I'll be thirty-five."

"When?" she asked.

He replied, "In May."

Victoriously she persuaded, "Thirty-five is the deadline and this is February—C'mon." His heart was touched by the young people and their wholesomeness—by their pleading prayers for him. He felt if he had met young people like these years ago how different his life could have been.

After the meeting was over he wanted to be alone and so withdrew into the field behind the church. There he stood looking up. This time the words came spontaneously from a melted heart, "If this is real, and if it's true—if it's lasting and for a Jew, let me have it, no matter what it costs or what it doesn't cost." At that moment this bruised and bleeding Jewish soul was born into the redeemed family of God.

As the Spirit of Christ entered into him, out went the misery, the desire to drink and gamble, the obsession of suicide. In came love, hope, peace, faith, and the desire to live to tell others of this glorious gladness which he had already begun to taste in his own Jewish Messiah. Now he could hardly wait to re-enter the house of God and tell everyone that he had at last found the answer to death and life, the key to peace of mind, and purpose in living. At long last he had exchanged a hopeless end for an endless hope.

CHAPTER XIII

FIRST DAYS

MY HEART WAS FAIRLY BURSTING with excitement and delight. Opening my eyes I glanced at my watch—5:20 a.m. Closing them again, my mind relived the events of just a few short hours ago. Was it all true? The strange sounds from the street already falling on my ears, the balmy air, and ocean smells removed all doubt. How wonderful of our faithful Lord to have led Mike and me together at the airport! How lost I would have felt in this strange land all alone. I recalled Mike's having to negotiate with the taxi driver in Yiddish. So few seemed to speak English, contrary to what I had expected! We had finally arrived and acquired rooms at the Central Hotel on the Tel-Aviv waterfront.

A slight shudder passed through me as I remembered my quick shower just before retiring. If I had not felt so grimy and sticky from nearly twenty-four hours of traveling, I certainly would not have invaded the privacy of the several large black beetles chirping away in the corner of the shower room! Watching them out of the corner of my eye, I had quickly washed away the last traces of the long, weary journey and hastily but thankfully slipped into the inviting bed. Safely home, at last!

Now restless with anticipation I set about to ready myself for Mike's knock on the door announcing breakfast time and the beginning of our first day in the land. It came about 8:30. We found the dining room on the second floor overlooking the calm Mediterranean Sea. Breathtakingly beautiful it was, glistening in the early morning sunshine—and such elegant shades of blue! Breakfast, not as elegant, began to initiate me into the strange customs of my new homeland. Set on a plate before me was a piece of strange white cheese (I later learned it to be a goat milk cheese), a couple of small pickled herring, a roll with jelly, and three garlic olives. This with a cup of tea I found to be a typical hotel tourist breakfast. Occasionally an egg was added!

Out on the streets I found the tiny shops just as strange to me. Unfamiliar words in Hebrew, German, French, Spanish, and other languages caught our attention in the windows. We were amused to suddenly come upon a sign that read (in Hebrew): "Hebrew spoken here"; (in German): "German spoken here"; (in French): "French spoken here"; and (in English): "English spoken here"; and at the bottom, "American understood"!

The streets were bustling with traffic and noise! Autos impatiently honking horns, buses chugging past, bicycles dodging in and out, and braying donkeys slowly pulling carts or wagons—all together made a confusing but picturesque scene.

Tel Aviv, a city of nearly 400,000 in 1953, had only forty-five years before emerged out of the sand dunes as a suburb offspring to Jaffa. Now she had outgrown the mother-city and had become the commercial and industrial, as well as cultural, center of this infant state.

No less confusing than the street scene was the sound of voices all around with no distinguishable words. Since Israel's population had flooded in from over seventy different countries, almost any language could be heard somewhere on any one day. However, it wasn't always possible to find someone at the right moment who spoke yours! Relying on Mike and his Yiddish, what would have been frustrating if not nearly impossible was accomplished with little strain.

Israel has been rightly called not a melting pot but a pressure-cooker. In the early days of statehood, with the great influx of exiles, when there was insufficient food or water, lack or failure of needed electricity, and the thousand and one irritating problems always cropping up, the wonderful Jewish sense of humor came to the fore. A stock comment was often heard, "For two thousand years we Jews have been hoping and fighting and praying to return to our homeland—and it had to happen to me!"

As we boarded a city bus I glanced down at the strange

coins in my hand. Five prutot for the bus fare. It must be this coin with the 5 on it! Already apparent was the necessity of learning the value of Israeli leirot or pounds! This became one of our first goals.

Unaccustomed as I was to the very humid heat, I began to feel dehydrated. We could find no drinking fountains which are so readily located in the stores or on the sidewalks in our American cities. Plentiful water, so taken for granted by us, was as yet a luxury Israel did not possess. Soda-pop had to meet the need!

Everywhere one could hear a vendor calling "Artic!"— "Artic!" and it did not take long to learn that this was an ice-cream bar—understandably very popular in Israel, which is blessed with a radiant climate of unbroken sunshine a full one-half of the year. Also popular in season was the vendor pushing a wagon with a large barrel of hot, steaming corn-on-the-cob! In the place of the American hamburger or taco stand was the Israeli falafel stand. This was actually an Arab pocket-like tortilla filled with something that looked like a deep-fat-fried meatball (but was actually made of mashed chickpeas) along with shredded lettuce, tomatoes, or other ——? and seasoned very hot! One could never feel quite sure just what was in it!

We found the people friendly and willingly helpful. Many appeared to be in want and need. Although the struggling government did not let anyone starve, everywhere we saw beggars, deprived mothers with babes, old helpless people, exiles who had arrived here carrying all of their possessions on their backs or in one hand. Our hearts cried out to be able to help them, longing for the time when we could speak to them in their own language and tell them of the One who could not only supply their material needs, but also mend their broken hearts. Walking down the streets, looking into faces, I knew these were the brokenhearted ones my heart was longing to comfort. These were not to me just a mission field but rather, like Ruth, I felt these were indeed my people. There was a deep, abiding peace and a grateful feeling of belonging.

The Sabbath began Friday evening at sundown. The streets became quiet, stores and shops were closed, and public transportation came to a complete halt. These were the only outward signs of Sabbath-keeping according to God's ancient demands. Saturday morning found more people on the beach than in the synagogues. The law of Moses was flagrantly violated. At the close of the Sabbath, after the first three stars made their appearance in the Saturday evening sky, the streets and beaches quickly came alive again and were crowded with a gay throng, in sad contrast to the earlier half-filled synagogues. And so ended our first Sabbath in the land.

CHAPTER XIV

JERUSALEM AND ONWARD

TODAY, SUNDAY, WOULD BE A SPECIAL DAY. With transportation operating again, we decided it was time to move out and see a little of the land before checking in at the Kibbutz (communal farm) the next Sunday to begin our language training. Our first stop would be Jerusalem.

We boarded the out-moded bus at the station and hung on for dear life as we bounced and bumped along the well-worn road leading southeast. We looked out across dry, denuded fields standing in surprising contrast alongside yellow grainfields or lush green cultivation. Everywhere could be seen the ancient and the modern existing side by side—a factory proudly defiant rising upon the neglected wasteland—oxen slowly, laboriously pulling a wooden plough. After a time we began a winding ascent into sparsely covered hills. Now and then along a road lined with dusty green eucalyptus trees we would pass by the rusty, twisted wreckage of armored vehicles left where they had fallen. We learned that these were war mementoes to those who five short years before in the War of Liberation had sacrificed their all to gain a homeland, a haven for their exiled brethren who had recently survived the Hitler holocaust.

At last surmounting the rocky, barren hills of Judaea, coming around the shoulder of a hill, we found ourselves rumbling into a narrow populated street. Could this be Jerusalem? My eyes scanned the quaint little shops lining the street.

Here and there we passed men, young and old, dressed in the dark or drab colored long coat of the eastern orthodox

Jew, bearded, and with the long side curls (Peot) dangling from beneath a broad-brimmed hat or a beany type yarmelḳa. The little boys were as picturesque in their short pants, knee-high stockings, and similar curled locks swinging from beneath a skull cap.

A spirit of awe descended upon me as I felt assured this was indeed "Jerusalem, the eternal," the very heart of the Jewish nation through all her generations. I remembered that the Lord had spoken to me through Isaiah, "Thine eyes shall see Jerusalem, a quiet habitation" (Isa. 33:20). Her scars bore testimony of other days and past years of tribulations when many strove to and sometimes succeeded in conquering her. It was no wonder David had exhorted, "Pray for the peace of Jerusalem; they shall prosper that love thee" (Ps. 122:6).

Silently we lighted from the bus, stepping out into the dry, brisk air. We both wanted to focus our attention fully upon the reality of this blessed experience.

As in all of Israel this too was a city of contrasts. Broad avenues gave way to narrow twisting and hilly streets. Neat modern shops stood in marked contrast with small cluttered ones. The streets were filled with people wearing the modern western-world dress, as well as those with the often unkempt eastern flowing robe. Intermingling with the civilians were rugged, well-groomed Israeli soldiers—men and women. Compulsory military training for both sexes is necessary because of Israel's precarious position—surrounded on three sides by enemies sworn to push her into the Mediterranian.

Modern Jerusalem had sprung up outside the western wall of the Old City, separated from it by a narrow corridor called "no-man's land." Our heart's yearnings to cross over and see beyond those austere walls were quickly deterred by the evidences of Arab sentries standing guard. To our outside world those high walls hid from sight and sound the busy Arab world within.

We found our way to the American Church Mission of the Christian and Missionary Alliance and introduced ourselves to the workers there, who in turn introduced us to others of like precious faith. Friendships were made that were later to prove profitable and rich in blessing.

Our second day in Jerusalem was spent mostly in visiting the places cherished not only because of the past, but also because of their future. Climbing up Mt. Zion to the south of the Old City wall, we rested under the cool shade of old olive trees. Welcome breezes seemed to be softly chanting our thoughts: "Beautiful for situation... is mount Zion..., the city of the great King" (Ps. 48:2). Our hearts echoed: "The law shall go forth of Zion, and the word of the Lord from Jerusalem" (Micah 4:2). What glories await this land and people when, in fulfillment of His Word, Messiah will reign in majesty and power from this very hill!

We strolled into an old synagogue and beheld pious Jews prayerfully chanting or weeping before the ancient tomb of King David. This was a substitute for the inaccessible wailing wall while the Old City remained in Arab territory. Our hearts were broken in the chamber of horrors beneath the synagogue which displayed awesome mementoes of the suffering Jews in our century.

Here among other things we saw parchment vests, made from the Old Testament Scrolls for purposes of smuggling, stained with the lifeblood of fleeing Jews who sought to preserve their Torah from enemy soldiers. Candles were burning in memory of the millions who had died by the murderous hands of the Nazis. Only a calloused person could emerge from there dry-eyed.

Later as we visited the headquarters of the Hebrew university (the new buildings were at that time still in blueprint stage), unaccountably, I somehow felt I would never attend it. Perhaps the university had been only a means to another end in God's planning. Time would tell.

We discovered in Israel a unique transportation service called "Sherut." This was in essence a shuttle-taxi plying between major cities. One could buy a place in a large seven- or nine-passenger car designated to drive to a certain city. When all the seats were sold the taxi would leave for its destination—generally managing to maintain a fairly close half-hour schedule because of its popularity as a mode of travel. It was more comfortable as well as faster than the bus even though about twice the fare. Remembering our bus ride to Jerusalem, we felt the long two-and-a-half to three-hour ride to Haifa, our next stop, warranted use of the Sherut. Actually the high exchange rate for the American dollar made the rates quite reasonable.

Traveling along, my eyes drank in the curious sights. The rocky desert hills which looked so unpromising suddenly yielded terraced orchards or gardens. Leaving the hills, we noted rows of modern sprinklers now and then painting a profusion of rainbows above stalwart vegetation bearing testimony to the devoted skill and undying energy of this pioneer nation. Occasionally we found it necessary to swerve around a donkey slowly pulling a cart down the road.

In time we welcomed the cool atmosphere of sprawling orange groves, and I marveled again at the precise fulfillment of the Word of God. It was Isaiah who prophesied, "He shall cause them that come of Jacob to take root: Israel shall blossom and bud, and fill the face of the world with fruit" (Isa. 27:6). Israel's oranges have rightly been called her sun-blessed ambassadors, spreading good will in homes all over the world.

In the distance, apartment houses seemed to rise up out of wind-blown sand dunes. We were soon passing along the fertile plains adorning the glistening Mediterranean. Glancing to the right, we saw the rugged cave-pocked face of the southern extension of Elijah's Mt. Carmel. Finally, pulling into Haifa, we found a fairly modern seaport planted upon the side of the Carmel and sloping gracefully down to meet the bay. Progress and development were depicted by busy docks and thriving industry. Modern stone buildings lined the downtown streets and, standing at the curbs before them, erect like tiny little soldiers, were, of all things, parking meters!

From Haifa we ventured once again by bus inland toward Nazareth, the boyhood home of Jesus. Along the way Bible-times opened before us as we saw their primitive mode of threshing and winnowing grain. Oxen or horses were being driven round and round over the gathered harvest, tramping out the grains. We became fascinated by the farmer's picking up the threshed grain with a pitchfork and tossing it into the air, allowing the wind to drive away the chaff. This was a sight familiar to Ruth many centuries ago in this very land. It was into fields such as these she had gone to glean. My heart glowed with thoughts of her as I tried to capture something of her world.

Farther along in the hills we saw Arabs living in caves. The sides of the hills themselves had yielded to the old-fashioned wooden hand plow, etching a productive victory out of the rocky soil.

74

Crossing fertile fields, recently revived from desolation and delivered from the plague of malarial swamps, we began the ascent into the hills where Nazareth lay nestled. Looking back across the valley of Jezreel or Megiddo, I shuddered to think of the terrible war which one day will be waged there—a war worse by far than any before encountered within the surrounding hills.

I was glad to be brought back to the present by the first sight of Nazareth. It was an all-Arab village, which clearly showed their backward ways. The open shops along the narrow streets were hardly more than man-made caves. Donkeys were as much in evidence as were customers and seemed to have the same right of way! "The Virgin's Fountain" was still the city's only water source—with the added modern convenience of a conduit bringing the water from a nearby mountain spring. An ancient synagogue, perhaps the one in which Jesus had actually taught, though empty (undoubtedly for lack of a Jewish minyan—the required number of ten men for a service), had withstood the ravages of time.

We felt we had once again stepped backward in time. This was unmistakably a land of great contrasts. Within an hour's time one could travel back into the romantic, historic past, suddenly be swept into the vigorous, flourishing present, and then be projected into the prophetic future. Even though there could be found no sense of Christ the Nazarene today, still we felt a certain inspiration just to contemplate His physical presence here centuries ago.

We resumed our travel toward Galilee. About six miles from Nazareth we passed by a very insignificant little Arab village squatting on a hill along the road. There were no outward evidences today revealing that this was the Cana of Galilee which had had the honor of claiming the Saviour's first public miracle of His ministry.

We were still lost in the wonder of it all, when, coming around a bend in the road, we glimpsed below us at a distance the blue-grey waters of Galilee. Our attention was drawn to a camp through which we were passing. Rows of small aluminum huts constituted a transit camp for the multitudes of returning exiles. The many thousands of refugees returning monthly under the "Law of the Return" (an open door to the land for any desiring Jew) had to be cared for somewhere until they could be absorbed into the economic structure of the new state. Most of these had come from concentration camps or war-torn countries. Others had been forced to leave all worldly possessions behind when joining the modern exodus to Israel. Our hearts went out again to these impoverished people who had suffered so undeservedly and indescribably, and we rejoiced they were safely home at last.

A curve in the road hid them from view as we descended into the streets of Tiberias. Leaving the bus, we made our way past the busy shops in the direction of the sea. Reaching the crest of a little hill, we saw stretched out before us a placid blue Galilee. Almost rushing down to the shoreline, we felt the sudden impulse to dip our fingers into the cold, clear water. Then, quietly standing at the edge of Crusader ruins in this ancient city built by Herod Antipas, we drank deeply of the fresh air as we gazed out across the waters.

The exhilarating thrill of envisioning the mighty power of God once displayed here flooded over both of us. These surrounding naked sun-baked hills had witnessed the Man of Galilee walking across these waters victorious over the undefiable laws of nature. As a sudden breeze rippled the surface of the water sending it scurrying toward the shoreline where with one last lunge it spent itself, we were reminded of the sudden storm which had overtaken the disciples while their Master lay fast asleep. It was His voice that had calmed the turbulent waters, the same voice which had spoken tranquility and peace to our troubled souls in times past.

Along the shore we encountered fishermen stretching out their nets to dry and mend them. It had been from such as these Jesus had called some of His disciples—commissioning them to the greater task of becoming fishers of men. Our imaginations saw Him teaching the multitudes on the hillsides, feeding the hungry, healing those who were diseased, exhorting Peter to "feed my sheep."

A quiet little park invited us to rest. As we sat meditating, a little elderly Jewess came along selling bagels (a favorite Jewish bread-roll). She sat to rest beside us and soon Mike had engaged her in conversation in Yiddish. Her story was heart-rending.

A refugee, she had been left a widow with five children in Rumania. Two of her children remained behind when she came to Israel. Arriving with practically nothing, and having no permanent place for her family to live, she sought shelter wherever she could find it.

Some days she went without eating, unable to earn enough money selling bagels to buy food for her children and herself. Unable to buy new clothing, she now possessed only the clothes that covered her body.

Weeping within, our hearts again cried out in behalf of this needy people, without the comfort or help of their Messiah. And we were the more determined to break down the language barrier through learning Hebrew as quickly as possible!

CHAPTER XV

THE KIBBUTZ

WITH A RENEWED VISION OF the purpose of our calling and
feeling the great need of overcoming the language barrier,
we prepared to leave Haifa for Kibbutz Maayan Zvi. Boarding
Israel's only train at Haifa, we began our short journey into
a new life that was to prove a new world to us. The old
rickety train gave us a sense of adventure to augment our
already excited spirits. About thirty-five minutes from Haifa
we pulled into a tiny out-of-the-way station. The lettering on
the building read "Zichron Yaakov"—our destination. Descending quickly amidst the huffs of the weary engine we found
ourselves in a lovely country-like cultivated plain. To the west
we could catch a glimpse of the shining Mediterranean. To the
the east, somewhere hidden in the nearby hills of the southern
tip of Mt. Carmel, lay our home for the next few months.

We boarded the bus bound for the village of Zichron Yaakov
and were soon winding our way into the rocky shrub-dotted
hills. Suddenly, rounding a turn, the bus screeched to a halt.

"Maayan Zvi!"

The words sent a shiver of nervous excitement through my
body. Grabbing our suitcases, we stepped out onto a lonely
dirt road. The bus whirled away, leaving us in a cloud of
dust as we started walking toward the buildings in the distance.

Maayan Zvi proved to be like an oasis in the desert. A
portion of the rocky hills had been transformed into a lovely
settlement. Welcome shade trees, green lawns, and colorful
flower gardens graced the stone and frame buildings. The
view of the Mediterranean from the plateau was breathtaking.
For miles one could see the white-capped waves silently spilling

over the sandy shore which bordered green and yellow fields. We were to experience many times the almost unbelievable beauty of red, orange, yellow and rose hues splashed across the late afternoon sky as the huge red ball of sun was slowly swallowed up by the deep blue sea. No less beautiful were the sharp clear nights when the sky, studded with stars which seemed close enough to reach up and touch, hovered over us like a canopy.

Tucked away here in the hills, Maayan Zvi had developed into quite a unique little community of over 200 people. Fifteen years before, a few courageous Jewish families from Germany, Austria, and Czechoslovakia had settled here on the edge of a swampland. These pioneers lived and labored together as one family, painstakingly draining the malaria-infested swamps (not without paying the supreme price) and reclaiming the plains that separated the sea from the Carmel. Their tents eventually gave place to more permanent dwellings as their efforts with the soil prospered.

The Kibbutz (as the communal farm is called) has become an important sector of Israel's agricultural economy—a very successful means of rapidly reclaiming a desolate and wasted land. Everyone lived and labored for the good of the community and shared equally all benefits. Each couple or single individual had his own living quarters, consisting of one or two rooms used as bed and sitting rooms only. There was no need of a private bath or kitchen as all ate at the communal dining hall and used the community bath houses. Other facilities included a communal laundry, elementary school for the children, a nursery for the infants—in short, everything needed for self-sufficient daily maintenance.

The men labored in the fields or cared for the livestock, while the women handled the household chores—cooking, sewing, washing, cleaning, et cetera. Nurses cared for the babies and readied the older children for school. The children lived in their own dormitories, spending an hour or two each afternoon with their parents after the work day was completed. A resident nurse cared for the sick, and each week a doctor came to hold an out-clinic for any needy Kibbutznik.

The community governed itself by voting for an executive committee which handled all affairs. Major decisions, however, were subject to the approval of all the members.

Religiously, we found them far from the faith of their fathers—atheistic, agnostic, or unconcerned. We were at once aware of the tremendous responsibility set before us!

Social activities were frequently planned for the entire community, so that, all in all, they were quite independent of the outside world, except for the necessary economic exchange. The people of the Kibbutz supported themselves not only by living off the land, but also by selling their excess produce and using the proceeds to purchase needed manufactured items. It amazed us to see that on the limited acreage they owned, they raised a great variety of vegetables and melons in season, peanuts, potatoes, and hay. They had banana groves, grape vineyards, and artificial fish ponds, breeding a delicious carp in particular. In addition they kept dairy cows and chickens for their own needs.

Not having experienced farm life hitherto, Kibbutz life proved very rugged physically. Although Israel has made tremendous strides in development, many of the comforts we take for granted in America are luxuries not yet known in this struggling young economy. Perched on the edge of the Carmel, the living quarters for the Ulpanim (Hebrew language students) were two long frame buildings, each divided into five rooms opening onto a long veranda. Each room boasted a large window on the back wall providing a magnificent view of the sea about two and a half miles to the west. The furnishings for the three students occupying each room consisted of three cot-size beds with sufficiently comfortable straw-filled sack mattresses made in Hong Kong, one table, one regular chair, and two folding camp stools. A small wardrobe with shelves was built into each room. The lack of curtains on the window, rugs covering the wooden floor, pictures on the wall and such luxuries did not seem to matter to our pioneer spirits. The bare necessities were sufficient.

Outside our bungalow we had a faucet with hot and cold running water—hot in the heat of the day, cold in the cool of the evening and morning. Here in a bucket we were to wash the few things not rugged enough to withstand the community laundry. About a quarter of a mile hike from our quarters were the public shower houses—one for the men and one for the women. As the several showers were to accommodate everyone, I found that to avoid the crowd, I would have to shower early in the morning before breakfast. This was fine except that they did not heat the water until about 10:00 a.m. Due to the expense of electricity in Israel the majority could not afford continuous hot water.

Our rooms were clean and comfortable enough for rugged living. Or so I thought, until one day I came back from work to find our beds torn apart and our straw mattresses drying in the sun. Upon further investigation we noticed our floors were wet also with some kind of fluid. We learned the mattresses had been sprayed for bed-bugs, but I wondered later if the spraying had only moved them to the surface, for I felt I didn't sleep alone that next night!

In order to make us feel at home and give us a sense of belonging, the Hebrew teacher gave each of the Ulpan students the Hebrew equivalent for their given name. The Hebrew language has no equivalent for June, not even claiming a month of June, using their own calendar consistent with the biblical months. Therefore, to my joy, the Lord directing most assuredly, the name of Ruth was conferred upon me. Henceforth and for always I truly became Ruth—God's twentieth-century Ruth in the Jewish homeland.

Also initiating us into our new home were the ever-present snakes, foot-long lizards, multitudes of flies to plague us, and swarms of feasting mosquitoes to dodge! How comforting it was to know the Lord's protecting hand was continuously guarding us. The third day there in my devotions the Lord clearly gave me Luke 10:19: "Behold, I give unto you power to tread on serpents and scorpions . . . nothing shall by any means hurt you." I was soon to experience why He gave me that particular verse.

Early one evening, shortly after dusk, I came into my room feeling quite tired. Finding my two roommates out, I decided it was a good opportunity for needed prayer. It had become difficult in such crowded and close quarters to find times of privacy. For fear of a light inviting company, I lay quietly in the dark on my cot pouring out my heart silently to the Lord.

After a time I felt I should prepare for bed and so arose, turning on the light. Glancing at the wall above my bed I noticed a dark, elongated shape clinging to it. The realization of what my eyes were communicating to me froze me where

I stood. My one thought was that I must kill that scorpion with one blow, lest it show up in our clothing or bed later. Taking off a shoe and breathing a quick prayer, I took dead aim and struck with all my might. It dropped—dead! After it was over and full realization flooded upon me, my iron nerves melted away, leaving me shaking like a green-horn in the Lord's boot camp. That scorpion must have been clinging to the wall over my bed all the time I had lain there, and could have dropped off on me at any time! How gracious of the Lord to spare me.

As if that were not enough to initiate us thoroughly into pioneer living, we had another unpleasant encounter. Another evening several of us were walking down the path to our bungalow, and for no apparent reason, I glanced down just in time to see coiled—one step in front of us—a snake! My surprised outcry brought all to an immediate halt, and the fellows obligingly made a quick end of it. Again the Lord, faithful to His Word, protected us.

The program for the Ulpan was the exchange of teaching for working. We were required to give four and a half hours labor each morning, wherever needed, in exchange for classes in Hebrew each afternoon. The work proved both enjoyable and trying at times. There was the varied work of mending clothes, doing kitchen work, clearing tables in the dining hall, thinning corn stalks in the fields below, weeding flower gardens, and mopping floors in the nursery.

I avoided work in the kitchen as long as possible, having heard that afterwards it was usually awhile before you enjoyed your meals again, due to the unappetizing manner of preparation as well as pioneer standard of sanitation. Then one morning the job fell to my lot. Among other things I saw the fruit soup stirred with bare arms immersed to the elbows! Bugs and spoilage had to be culled from the vegetables. True to form, by the time I had finished, I bypassed the dining hall, sure my stomach just couldn't tolerate lunch that day!

Eventually I was permanently assigned to the garden, which I genuinely enjoyed having desired to get my hands into Israeli soil. There is something satisfying about being able to contribute even to a small degree to the distinctive growth of this extraordinary land. Such satisfaction would be mine in the future when passing by on the highway along the Carmel I could spot a green lawn near the top—one result of my Kibbutz labors. Now I understood some of the motives behind the individual planting of millions of trees in the land. To some it gave a sense of enduring accomplishment, to others a sign of belonging. The tree to many an Israeli is the symbol of the wandering, restless Jew who has at long last sunk his roots deep into the soil of his promised land.

That other Ruth of long ago had also gone out into the fields upon arriving in her new homeland. Perhaps she, too, worshipped inwardly as she looked out over the fertile fields, and breathed in the cool refreshing air as yet uncontaminated by the machines of progress. I felt she also must have marveled with an inner glow as she reminded herself that this was indeed the land, and these were truly the people to whom she had given her heart while yet in her native land. Yes, we belong here—she and I—brought by the God of Israel under whose wings we had come to trust.

CHAPTER XVI

MORE PERSONAL LOVE

As THE DAYS GAVE WAY to weeks we found that living in such close quarters with non-Christians gave rise to definite problems for us spiritually. Often our hearts were grieved by the worldly spirit of ungodliness to which we found ourselves subjected. There seemed to be no real concern about the blessed God of Israel on the part of any of the other students. They had lugged with them from their native countries books of many categories, but not one had brought even an Old Testament!

Finding it difficult to secure a quiet place to be alone with the Lord, I resorted to lone walks through the hills. Even physical infirmity from our lowered sanitary standard proved a blessing in disguise. Unable to report for work for several mornings, I was left alone in our bungalow for hours at a time. The blessed quietness and sweet solitude were as a balm to my needy soul, basking in the healing rays of the Word. However, later when my roommates would return, much to my sorrow, things settled back to their usual norm—an uproar!

Mike's job eventually became fixed in the banana groves, removing dead stock. Heavy morning dew, mud at times from irrigation, humid heat, and mosquitoes made this a little-to-be-desired work load. Often left alone to clear a section, Mike soon turned even this into a sanctuary of prayer and praise to the One whom he had come to love so deeply. Nearby workers could sometimes hear the off-key but joyous strains of, "You ask me why I'm happy and I'll just tell you why; because my sins are gone." Knowing the unpleasantness of the work, they could only marvel at such a manifestation of inner joy—something entirely foreign to them.

Mike did not realize the extent of this testimony until later when one of his roommates, a young Jewish fellow from London, upon parting with Mike, informed him that his most vivid remembrance of Mike would always be his singing in the banana groves. At various times Geoffrey had asked questions of Mike, invoking serious spiritual discussions which led him to admit Mike was most fortunate. During these times he truly yearned to believe too, but somehow he couldn't as yet.

When opportunity afforded itself to bring up spiritual matters with others, we were chagrined to learn that most of them confused belief with religion, Christianity with Gentiles, and truth with traditions. Because so few at first showed any real concern, we deemed it a time of waiting upon the Lord, meanwhile living Christ before the group and sowing the seed a little here and a little there.

Having enjoyed extremely active ministries at home, this spiritual inactivity began to weigh heavily upon both Mike and me. It was normal to wonder during this time just why we were there. And then the evening came when David, a lad from London, came in to share watermelon with me, and our conversation turned to the Tenach (the Old Testament). Although his mind appeared closed, I was thankful to be able to tell him of my belief in Jesus and discuss the Word for a time.

Another evening while I was reading the Tenach, Willy (from Rumania) dropped in to visit. Recognizing the black cover of the Bible, he volunteered that though he was considered well-read in the masters of philosophy, he had never read the Bible and was actually afraid to read it for fear it would influence him. After a lengthy exhortation and great persuasion on my part, he finally accepted it to read. My initial joy turned to disappointment, however, when he returned it in fifteen minutes with the excuse he just couldn't settle down to read it.

Later Mike and I separately and together were able to give Willy extensive personal testimony as well as the plan of salvation. His agnosticism made him difficult to convince but he was challenged with much to consider concerning the claims of Christ.

In God's own planning Mike was brought together with Jack, another American, who revealed a depressed, distressed spirit. Having been an alcoholic and a dope addict, Jack had sought peace in religion but had not found his Messiah, the Prince of Peace. Discerning in Mike the stability he needed, he came to him seeking help, and was given the story of Mike's deliverance from misery and hopelessness. Though almost persuaded in those moments, Jack couldn't seem to give up to to the Lord. So he left, still in his misery and, worse, still in his sins, but possessing a New Testament.

At such times we knew why we were there. But little did we comprehend all the Lord was accomplishing or had in mind. The common bond we shared in Christ drew Mike and me together for spiritual fellowship frequently. The times we could manage to spend in the Word and prayer together became a spiritual oasis in a literal desert! All of the stimuli we had known from church services, Bible classes, Jewish missionary service and meetings had remained far behind us in California. Like Moses we were walking the back side of the desert, and although we found the sweetness of His fellowship, the richness of His presence exceedingly sufficient for our souls, yet we hungered for the human fellowship of like-minded people. Then too, the problems we faced from time to time were more soluble in the light of discussion; discouragements and depressions became more bearable with sympathetic understanding and fervent intercession.

It is quite natural for deep spiritual love and respect to blossom into the warm glow of a more personal love. The Spirit of Christ in Mike had attracted me from the first time we had met. But the first realization of this more personal love for him had brought rebellion and frustration, so sure I had been that the Lord wanted me to serve Him alone. Still vivid in my remembrance were the occasions of soul anguish when well-meaning persons would tell me I should remarry, that I was too young to live the rest of my life alone. At such times a tear-stained pillow had muffled the prayers of protest, "Lord, please don't make me marry again. I want only to live for Thee here, and then to be with Thee and Doug for eternity." Along with the awakening of this new love a tremendous inner battle of loyalty to the deceased was waged, until my soul in desperation once again cried out to the Lord, "Thy will be done."

Finally, as the Lord began to reveal the broader ministry we both could have together, my heart yielded to this beautiful thing He had implanted within it. The story of Ruth became my story as the Holy Spirit wove it into the tapestry of my life, thread upon thread. And so it was left in the hands of the Master Planner to bring into reality this new life and ministry that filled my waking thoughts.

What beautiful thoughts most likely filled the little Moabitess' mind too, as she went daily to glean in the fields of Boaz. Such grace and favor as she had tasted from the hand of this valiant one, such sweet fellowship as she had shared at his table, could not have failed to stir the dormant embers of love that remained in the heart which had once loved and lost awhile.

For a time the closely guarded secret that gave wings to the toil of the day and a glow to the once heavy and lonely heart must not be revealed. Even as Ruth had cherished her secret love within, awaiting the Lord's time to make it known, so I also knew I must silently love from afar until His perfect time for fulfillment would come.

CHAPTER XVII

THE CONQUEST OF THE DESERT

OUR FIRST HOLIDAYS in the land were welcomed as a needed respite from the non-Christian atmosphere of our Kibbutz life. An invitation had been extended to both Mike and me to spend the Jewish New Year with missionaries in Jerusalem.

Eagerly we put in our morning's work time (four and a half hours of washing dishes for me) so we could leave by early afternoon. Hurrying down the hill to the station, we found we had missed the train for Jerusalem. There would not be another. It was too near the High Holy Day beginning at sundown. Such days were revered with the same strictness as the Sabbath. Adjusting our plans to meet the situation, we took the next train to Tel Aviv and caught a Sherut for Jerusalem, arriving there on the eve of Rosh Hoshana (the New Year).

We appreciated our warm welcome and were delighted to be in the company of fellow believers once again. We could not adequately express our pleasure at being able to sit down to a refined table once more. The lovely cloth, dishes, and silverware, though not lavish, were in extreme contrast to the bare wooden table and metal plates to which we had grown accustomed in the two months at Maayan Zvi. Most gratifying of all was the blessedness after so long a time of bowing our heads together and unitedly offering thanks for the bountiful blessings of our Saviour.

Prayer meeting afterwards was a special joy as we prayed for these blinded ones, slumbering on in the darkness of traditions. Mike was asked to present his testimony to the group.

The rich reward of hearing it again caused my heart to yearn for the fulfillment of its love. But I was to learn the lesson of how sweet is the peace gained when desire can be left in His hands to fulfill or withhold as He wisely purposes.

The delights of the evening culminated in the renewed, though almost forgotten, experience of getting between clean white sheets spread out on a comfortable unoccupied mattress, and nestling my head on a soft pillow. Only then did I realize I had actually missed this luxurious feeling so common to us back home.

The next morning we ventured out onto the streets to view Israel's celebration of this very holy day. Our hostess took us to a small nearby Shul (synagogue) where we could look on through an open doorway at an inconspicuous distance.

Bedecked with black Yarmelkas (the skull cap) and white prayer shawls (the Jewish robe of righteousness), the orthodox men were fervently and loudly chanting prayers of repentance and devotion to the God of Abraham, Isaac and Jacob. We were moved with compassion for these arduously striving after that righteousness which is of the law of Moses—unattainable by their works and received only through acceptance of the righteousness which is in Jesus the Messiah.

Eventually we found our way to the top of Mt. Zion, mingling with the pious crowd there to view the solemn services invoked by the blowing of the Shofar (ram's horn). Our hearts were intermittently thrilled and grieved to watch the reading of the Torah in Hebrew by these who reverence the God of Israel and yet do not recognize His Holy One sent to redeem them from the bondage of their sins. How greatly we longed to tell these, who for all their zeal could only hope for forgiveness, that in their Messiah they could know assuredly they were cleansed for now and all eternity. But because of the language barrier not yet conquered we could only turn away, sad in heart, but prayerful that somehow God, even the God of their fathers, would reveal the truth to them.

After the next ten days of penitence these so blinded by tradition would also observe the most holy Day of Atonement by afflicting their souls with a twenty-four-hour fast. Penitential prayers seeking forgiveness for broken vows and promises made to God in the past year would be followed by the reading of the Torah and prayers for the dead. The season would end with a single long blast of the Shofar announcing that everyone's fate had been sealed for another year—the acceptable unto life and blessing, the remainder unto death and judgment, according to the inscribing in God's book of life.

Our refreshing days passed all too quickly, and with some regret we departed for the drier but needy pastures of Maayan Zvi. Not many days after our return my roommates left the Kibbutz Ulpan for city life. The pleasure of a single room was short lived when, in order to conserve space, it was necessary for me to vacate my room and join two girls from Argentina who did not speak English. At first I felt like a stranger in my new quarters because of our inability to communicate. However, as time progressed, we were amazed at how much we did manage to communicate to each other in our meager Hebrew—not without pain, but succored with laughter!

One of the most indispensable qualities needed on our journey through life, and especially for the foreign missionary, is the ability to laugh in difficult situations. The reality of this was renewed to us the Friday the Kibbutzniks visited the "Conquest of the Desert" Exhibition in Jerusalem. We boarded the train at the Zichron Yaacov station below the Kibbutz to find that already there was standing room only, although the train had originated in Haifa just thirty-five minutes before. We braced ourselves for the more than three-hour ride ahead of us, realizing we might have to stand all the way, refusing to be deterred, knowing this was probably a once-in-a-lifetime opportunity. As it turned out, it was!

After another stop or two the aisle of the train in which we were standing had become quite crowded. About that time we jerkily pulled into another station. Through the window I could see what must have been more than a hundred people on the platform. "They'll never let those people in," I thought aloud. "There just isn't room." Apparently realizing the doors were not being opened, the crowd without began pushing at them. From an impulse of survival the group inside rallied at our door trying to hold it shut. Amid excited shouts and rapid chatter in Hebrew, crying and screaming erupted from everywhere; suddenly the door pushed open and in the mob plunged. Grasping hands with one of the other girls of the Ulpan we clung together for fear of being separated and left alone in the midst of this wild mob.

Others of our group were forcibly pushed into the next car like twigs caught in the fury of a river rapids. The intruders were pouring in through the windows, climbing on top of the train and forcing their way in through the door until we were literally packed in like sardines—though not as orderly! If I could have made it a few feet to the door, I would gladly at that point have given my place to another, but I couldn't budge in any direction. Hysterical children separated from panicky parents were screaming "Ema! Ema!" (Mother! Mother!). Several little Yemenite Jewesses, squatting on the floor, sick and exhausted, were in danger of being trampled underfoot. But no one would or could give an inch.

Finally things quieted down somewhat and slowly the engines began tugging and chugging their heavy burden onward toward our destination. When a little later we made a short stop at another station a couple in one of the cars tried in vain to leave the train at this their destination. Unable to squeeze out, against their wills they became prisoners of circumstances to Jerusalem!

In time we began the long slow ascent into the Judean hills. As we wound our way around the hills it seemed more and more certain on every curve that the unbalanced overload would surely tip and overturn the creaking train.

The reality of possible death brought not fear (I was ready and even desirous of meeting the Lord) but rather a sense of the utter futility in such a manner of death. My purpose for living had not yet been accomplished, and it seemed wrong to place myself (though unintentionally, of course) in such a precarious position. I knew I belonged not to myself but to Him who loved me and gave himself for me. An awareness had awakened that I must treat this body of clay respectfully as His property, which indeed it is! I realized that for the Christian to take unnecessary chances or foolishly to put his life in jeopardy was in the same category as tempting God. And where once I would have gladly welcomed death for selfish reasons, now I desired, for the sake of this unenlightened multitude, to live to proclaim and share my wonderful Saviour.

The Lord did see fit to spare us, and at long last a weary and worn people took heart at the first signs of our journey's end, and it was a thankful group who poured forth from that train.

After a reviving lunch which we had brought with us, we went to view the various displays of Israel's spectacular efforts to conquer the desert. These were truly a people from the same mold as their ancient ancestors who many centuries before them had conquered with might and ingenuity this very same land. It gave one a new sense of living in momentous times— times of the foreshadowings of the great prophetic fulfillments awaiting the coming of the King.

As the afternoon wore on a few of us decided to return to the train an hour before departure time to be assured a seat going home. To our great surprise all of the seats were already occupied and once again there was standing room only! Not having the will to go through that again so soon, unless it were absolutely necessary, Mike and I decided to pay the little extra cost to us to return by Sherut. We hurried back into town only to be met with further disappointment. With the evening of the Sabbath fast approaching, there were no more scheduled taxis for Haifa which could drop us off at Maayan Zvi. Our last hope seemed the bus. Perhaps that would be less crowded than the train. But our hearts sank when we saw the bus station so jammed we knew we could not possibly get on one before bus service halted for the Sabbath. It appeared we were forced back to the train.

Reluctantly we made our way back to the depot only to find the train loaded and the gates locked because of the crowd still trying to gain entrance. While pondering our plight we watched our transportation pull out of the station a full half hour ahead of schedule. The only thing left to us now was to take a Sherut to Tel Aviv, which we could make before sundown, and hope to locate there an unorthodox taxi driving that evening to Haifa.

When we arrived in Tel Aviv our Sherut driver accommodated us by leaving us on a corner where he said there should be such a taxi looking for passengers. We did find the needed car as well as another person desiring a Sherut to Haifa. The driver set his price, and we waited for other necessary passengers to come along and fill up the car, making his run worthwhile. While waiting, our fellow passenger who had been bargaining with another driver came and told us quietly that this other one would take us a little cheaper. Obligingly we left the first car and got into the other one. At this point the drivers began to argue. I was glad I couldn't understand their heated words!

When more passengers arrived our new driver quoted his price to us all which was now the same as the first driver's rate. No amount of reasoning could bring him down to his first quoted fee. Indignant that he had obtained our business dishonestly, we all piled out of his car. The battle was on again, both drivers wanting our business! The negotiator motioned us to follow him. Obediently we marched around the corner and down the block to be picked up by the first driver.

As we were about to start off, the second driver pulled up alongside of us, loudly unleashing his anger with accompanying vehement motions at our driver. For a few uneasy, prayer-packed moments I didn't know what was going to happen; then apparently realizing defeat, the angry driver pulled away in a huff; and with no little relief, we were off toward home.

The Lord accomplishes His purposes in all things when we seek to know and to do His will. To our joy we discovered a hungry-hearted passenger beside us. As Mike witnessed the Word and testimony it was my privilege to hold them up in silent prayer. It was already dark when an hour later we came to the road leading to our Kibbutz. Departing, Mike left the man with a gospel tract and we went on our way rejoicing, feeling it was well worth it all—after all!

CHAPTER XVIII

TO NATANYA

NEITHER MIKE NOR I was satisfied that we were progressing rapidly or developing proficiently enough in our language study in the Kibbutz, so when a resident Ulpan was to open in Natanya near Tel Aviv in the middle of October, we both made our plans to transfer. In this Ulpan students paid rather than worked for their room, board, and tuition, and considering the exchange rate on the American dollar the fee was very nominal. We would be housed in a local hotel, spend each morning in Hebrew classes, having most of the afternoons and evenings for study. This would mean that we could put our entire effort into learning Hebrew to our profit.

As we prepared to leave the Kibbutz we were thankful for a few with whom we had been able to leave a witness. Sanford, a graduate psychologist with an M.A. degree, had belatedly joined the Kibbutz Ulpan after missing his return ship to America. We were ultimately convinced that the Lord had a purpose in this, for upon hearing a Hebrew Christian testimony for the first time, Sanford indicated great interest, desiring to know more. As Mike witnessed from the Old Testament Scriptures, he listened attentively, admitting that even in America he had never heard these things. Deeply impressed with the biblical truths, his resultant reaction was revealed in his words: "I am obliged to you, Meir [the Hebrew equivalent of Mike—meaning 'one who brings the true light'], and I don't know whether to feel hopeful or discouraged!" Mike was hopeful!

Less promising was the third occupant of Mike and Geofrey's room, an emotionally disturbed young man, Hyam. At times his attitude made the atmosphere of their tiny room unpleasant if not almost unbearable. Steadfast patience and prayer eventually opened the way for Mike to point Hyam to the Messiah. Encouraged to read the New Testament, with tear-filled eyes Hyam asked, "You don't think it will make me a Christian, do you?"

Truthfully Mike affirmed, "It might."

"I would never forgive myself if that happened to me!" he ejaculated, rejecting at that point his only real help.

Having been unable to converse spiritually with my Spanish-speaking roommates, I had prayed earnestly for some way to leave a testimony with them. The answer came in the form of a Spanish New Testament supplied me by another missionary. Using Mike (who spoke a little Spanish) as interpreter, I was able to present it to Leah, who received it warmly. Her attitude assured me that she would read it, and I knew I could trust the Lord's faithfulness to impart that faith which comes by the reading of the Word.

Reassured that the Lord's purposes in our coming to the Kibbutz were fulfilled, we said our last farewell to Maayan Zvi and hired a Sherut to Natanya.

Depositing our luggage at the King David Hotel, the headquarters of our new school, we took a bus into Tel Aviv to pick up the necessary money for this Ulpan which we had individually requested be wired from home. Mike's money was waiting for him, but much to my dismay, mine apparently had not as yet arrived. My disappointment would have undoubtedly bordered frustration had I known this was to be just the beginning of a number of financial consternations. (I had no idea then that they would eventually lead me into a beautiful life of living by faith. Experience was to become a pedagogue that would write her lesson indelibly upon my mind and heart!)

Meanwhile, graciously, the Lord's constant faithfulness had not left me stranded without some provision to meet the need— once more through Mike. Because of the Lord's fore-planning he was able. to advance me enough for an initial payment to the Ulpan, assuring me a place. Word from home revealed the money had been sent and evidently was lost somewhere en route. After a month of investigation, to my great relief, it was finally located and obtained.

Natanya was a lovely little resort town situated along high bluffs overlooking the Mediterranean and boasting an uninhibited view of the coastline for miles. Gorgeous variegated shades of greens and blues, intensified by the clearness of the water, were bordered by lacy, foam-capped waves blending themselves into golden-tan sands. The fresh cool breezes were a surprising contrast to the warm temperatures of the water itself—still wonderful for swimming late in November.

Israeli city life proved to be very different from that which we had experienced in the Kibbutz. We had exchanged a sheltered togetherness for that of an independent liberty, more in accord with what we had known in America.

Strolling down the main street, it was rewarding to take cognizance of our new environment. Small but adequate facilities such as a laundromat (no more bucket washings!), dry cleaners, a variety of clothing and repair shops, stationery stores, cafes, bakeries, and tiny grocery stores would pleasantly supply our wants and needs.

We stopped to view a horse-drawn bakery truck parked in front of a store. The driver was tossing unwrapped whole round-shaped loaves of brown bread into a barrel. When one missed the barrel, landing on the sidewalk, he retrieved it, and wiping it on his sleeve added it to the barrel!

The necessity of having a suit cleaned sent Mike seeking out the dry cleaners. The pleasure of such a convenience was dampened sadly when he learned the suit would not be ready for three weeks.

When my watch needed cleaning, I happily located a watch repair shop to accommodate me. I returned for the watch several days later only to be confronted with a delay of another few days. As my repairman, an orthodox Jew, could not rewind the watch on the Sabbath it would take an extra day or two to check out the accuracy of its timing. "Patience is a great virtue" was the obvious axiom for Israel!

I was glad to take advantage of the laundromat for my washing even though the drying had to be done on the rooftop of the hotel. As in biblical days most of Israel's architecture consists of flat-topped dwellings. Looking out across other occupied rooftops the literalness of the words of Jesus was portrayed vividly before me. "When ye therefore shall see the abomination of desolation . . . stand in the holy place . . . then let them which be in Judaea flee . . . let him which is on the housetop not come down to take anything out of his house" (Matt. 24:15–17). When Jesus spoke those words nearly two thousand years ago in regard to the coming time of Jacob's Trouble, the Great Tribulation, the meaning was clearly understood. These many centuries later here in the land His Word is and will be just as meaningful and can be just as accurately obeyed.

City life was not a complete utopia in comparison to country life. We had not bettered our hot water circumstance since leaving Maayan Zvi, for the expense of heating water made continuous hot water just as prohibitive in the city. Three mornings a week we enjoyed hot running water. On days in between an electric water kettle had to suffice.

Our most difficult adjustment came when winter set in with its cold and dampness. It was somewhat of a shock to learn that none of the buildings were equipped with heating systems of any kind. The discomfort was somewhat remedied by donning more clothing. Our sense of humor rose to the occasion and rescued us from the depths of self-pity. Who would guess that underneath the denims I had salvaged from the Kibbutz, I was wearing my pajamas for added warmth? Or that tucked inside my rain boots (now worn rain or shine!) were three or four pair of socks? On colder days when I could see my breath in my room and I had to get outside and walk to keep from shaking, I was sorely tempted to go out on a hunt for some red flannels! I finally settled for a small kerosene heater which helped a little.

On the other hand, such trivial discomfort could not dampen our joy of laying hold on the language. We soon found we could converse in a simple manner in Hebrew. With progress came the realization of how great an amount of Hebrew we would have to learn to be able to express the Gospel to those who know no English. One wrong word could make such a difference. Eric, reciting in class, said he signed all of his letters with a fried egg, and bald-headed Jonah mistakenly (or was he serious?) said he combed his hair with a towel!

We were grateful to note that the tasty food was more carefully prepared and served than at our former Ulpan. Accordingly we could hope for better health. The great lack of meat in the nation in these early years (the meat shops

97

were closed three-fourths of the time) was compensated by an abundance of fish and cheese. A favorite nutritional food in season was eggplant prepared in an unbelievable variety of ways. A current joke had it that the native Palestinian girl had to learn one hundred and one different ways to prepare eggplant before she was eligible for marriage.

Most of the Israeli food was palatable—except for one delicacy, fish heads! On one occasion at the school I had been introduced to an Israeli woman who did not speak English. She seemed hungry for friendship and invited me to visit her. In order to put my classroom instruction into practice, and with the long-range view of building a friendship which would permit the sharing of the Gospel with her later, one Sabbath morning I took advantage of her invitation. She received me warmly and we spent a lengthy and profitable time conversing entirely in Hebrew.

Just prior to the noon hour as I rose to leave, she refused to let me go, insisting I stay for lunch. Out of respect for her meager circumstances I tried to excuse myself, but to no avail. Seating me with her family around the table in the living room, she hurried into the kitchen, returning with their special Sabbath fare—fish heads! I dared not, for the sake of the Gospel, offend these people. My only recourse was to pray this lunch down, bite by bite, watching my host to determine how much I was expected to consume. Following his example all went well until he plucked out the eyes and ate them! That was one step beyond all the grace that I could muster!

CHRISTMAS!!! Christmas almost here? There was nothing to remind one of that hallowed day except the cold black dates staring back from the calendar. Even a diligent search would produce not one sign of the day so extravagantly celebrated among the Gentiles. There was no evidence of remembrance throughout this land which saw Christ's birth—no manger with shepherds or wise men carrying gifts, no carols filling the air, no brightly and colorfully lighted windows, no mention of the Saviour born in the City of David. How gratifying that our knowledge of the Lord was not that of a holiday or season of the year, but as a Person bringing salvation and being salvation personified!

Since to the Ulpan officials December 25 was just another

regular school day, neither Mike nor I attempted to gather with our new Christian friends in Jerusalem. To many around us Christmas Eve passed unnoticed. We, however, fellowshipped around the Word of Him who had been born not only in Bethlehem but also in our hearts. We had jointly just received a food package from Diane and her husband of recent months, Ray, and were touched to find each item Christmas wrapped. For a little while as we gaily unwrapped the packages and then sampled the hot chocolate and cookies, we were caught up somewhat in the spirit of other Christmases.

Christmas had not always been a joyful time for Mike. Still painfully he recalled dreading this season as a child. It had been so hard to sing the required carols at school about Jesus who, he was taught, had been a traitor to his people and the symbol of much of their suffering. Mike knew his people were never to say the name of Jesus (undoubtedly in compliance with Exodus 23:13, ". . . and make no mention of the name of other gods, neither let it be heard out of thy mouth"). Therefore, whenever they came to His name in a carol, Mike would remain silent.

As he listened to the words he was perplexed. Why should the Gentiles call Him the King of Israel? He wasn't their King! No less difficult was it to face the never failing question from school mates, "What did you get in your stocking for Christmas?"

Determined one Christmas Eve not to go through the embarrassment of being different from his friends again, he entered the house and announced to his little orthodox aunt, "I am going to hang up my stocking."

She was indignant, "No, you're not!"

Refusing to be swayed, Mike insisted, "Yes, I am!"

"No, you're not! Christmas is for the Gentiles. We are proud to be Jews, and we have nothing to do with their false god. We have only suffered in that name!"

"I am and I will!" And with that he dashed up the stairs to his room.

"If you do there'll be nothing in it!" she called after him.

Within a few minutes he marched back down displaying a long boyish stocking, the end of which he tucked into the top drawer of the buffet. Surely his aunt would relent when she realized how much this meant to him, he reasoned.

Upon awakening the next morning his first thought was of the stocking. Climbing out of bed he tiptoed downstairs and through the quiet house to the living room, fearfully hoping he would not be disappointed. One glance told him the stocking was still empty! Running back upstairs he threw himself upon his bed, weeping as though his little heart would break.

Moments later he heard his aunt's voice from below "Zunale [little son], why aren't you down here for breakfast?"

Defiantly, "I'm not coming down until there is something in my stocking!"

There was a note of finality in her voice, "Then stay in bed all day! There will be nothing in your stocking!" And with that he heard the click of the back door. She must have gone back to their little grocery store on the front of the lot.

"Surely she didn't mean that. Maybe she was teasing and there is really something in it now." Refusing to give up hope he quietly climbed out of bed and ventured downstairs once again. The empty stocking was almost more than he could endure. Fleeing back to bed his sobs echoed through the house.

After a while he heard voices downstairs. Uncle Mike was talking to Auntie Toba. Suddenly the voices subsided. Then a few moments later, "All right, Zunale, come down and eat your breakfast. There is something in your stocking now." The click of the door again told him she was gone.

With a new spark of hope he hurried downstairs this time and sure enough his stocking was bulging. Enthusiastically he took it down from the drawer and pulled out some wadded up newspaper. His heart began to sink as he pulled out more newspaper, a potato, then an onion. Disappointment was lessened a little when he pulled out a red apple. In those days fresh fruit was a rare treat during the icy winters of Wisconsin. At least he could tell his friends he received an apple. And then finally wedged way down in the toe of the sock he touched a coin. When his eyes beheld the fifty-cent piece his fingers had retrieved, he knew he could face his school chums again. Fifty cents was a generous sum to a small boy in depression days. This was surely a worthy gift to brag about to his friends. Nevertheless he had learned a hard lesson. Never again would he ask to hang up a stocking for Christmas!

Dread of the Christmas season along with unpleasant memories remained with Mike until many years later when the

Saviour was born into his heart. Then that which had been dreaded was transformed into the joy that His coming to earth had been intended to bring. The once distasteful carols were now lustily sung. How deeply he desired to share this unsurpassable joy with his own people, and how grievously he bore their rejection is revealed in a letter written to his spiritual mother on Christmas Eve:

A balmy, ethereal breeze is blowing . . . a star-studded sky above . . . and in the heaven of heavens, He who was born the Babe of Bethlehem and is now our High Priest looks down upon the children of men, marvelling that some yet look up to Him and crown Him, Christ Jesus, Prince of Peace and Coming King! What noble gift God gave to wayward man in the Person of His Son! Oh that the children of men might praise Him for His unspeakable gift! ". . . a light for revelation to the Gentiles, and a glory to thy people Israel."

Yet in this very land of His people, His people know Him not—though almost two thousand years have passed since He was born, bled, was buried and broke the bands of death asunder according to the Jewish Scriptures.

My own heart is sad this evening. It did not occur to me that it would be so. A strange heaviness weighs it down. Perhaps it is because of the total lack of recognition of Him in this locality; perhaps it is because of my own memories of years when I spelled Christmas with an "X" (the unknown quotient): perhaps it is because of memories far more pleasant when I was at home —yours made mine—for Christmas! Maybe this heaviness is caused by being compelled to live this day far too conformed to the ways of this world. He would not have us so unseparated.

The carols that we sing at this season, too, are missed. There is no music in the air here—no joyous bells! When one does hear music, it is heavy with the thud of marching feet to a methodical beat that culminates not in soft words sung to a Saviour but in strident cries that give glory to man and not to God!

How long, Lord, until Thy coming? How long in which man blasphemously boasts. "Where is their god?"

How long will they mockingly say, "He saved others, yet himself He cannot save!" Ah, that even tonight the stars would be pushed aside so that the Lord of Glory might show himself Sovereign of sovereigns, King of Kings, Prince of Peace! Should He not reveal himself this eve, He will some evening soon according to the Scriptures, synchronized with His schedule. Then we shall be like Him, we shall be with Him evermore—without separation throughout endless eternity. What blessed hope is ours! "Even so come quickly, Lord Jesus!"

CHAPTER XIX

THE SCHOOL OF CHRIST

As we settled down pretty much to routine living and the exhilaration of our new circumstances wore off, a spiritual leanness began to plague me. The lack of sufficient active service to the Lord to stimulate the soul, plus the worldly and even at times ungodly atmosphere to which we were constantly subjected had gradually taken their toll in draining my cup of joy. Stripped of the outer circumstances that not only bless but also strengthen the Christian, we were left to the naked reality of our inner experiences.

The problem of loneliness I had suffered periodically through the years since my mother's death, stemming from a personal unmet need of a close love-relationship and companionship, became aggravated by the too often silence from those across the seas who had pledged themselves behind me. A "sent one" cannot know all of the loving thoughts back home that go unexpressed and can easily feel isolated and alone, and even worse, unloved by long silences. Equally so, a missionary can truly feel the strength of the prayers of those standing faithful, or the lack of them.

These times of feeling neglected and forgotten, however, deepened my understanding of what that other Ruth surely experienced. How alone she must have felt as she wearily trod that dusty road back into Bethlehem from the fields of Boaz. Cut off by distance from the life she had known and those she had loved must have left an emptiness within her. Perhaps she wiped an unseen tear from her cheek as remembrance tore at her heart. It is at these barren times the heart learns to

103

turn heavenward and the soul is exercised to seek hard after the Lover of it.

Ruth had left her lifeless idols for the fellowship of the living God. Only as we learn to release the idols of our own hearts can we know the fullness of that sweet fellowship and the joy of abundant living. The school of inner darkness and spiritual dearth was to teach me the depths of this truth. The Lord had begun to strip me of all crutches that I might lean only upon Him, and to remove everything dear that nothing might be an idol in His sight.

It had not yet been fully revealed to me that there is the danger of allowing the heart to become unduly attached to the good gifts the Lord bestows, resulting in their becoming idols which subsequently must be given back to Him in consecration.

The Lord had first taken my dearest idol, Doug, home to Himself in order to draw my heart heavenward. The joy of reunion with him and eternity together with our Lord was the mainstay in my early sorrow and resultant loneliness. It had not occurred to me that this sustaining hope and joy was actually a crutch upon which to lean.

Eventually when the wound was sufficiently healed, God had removed the crutch by turning my gaze earthward again through the love given for Mike. However, the healed wounds of having lost the two who were closest to me on earth left sensitive scars. As the weeks wore on with no indication from Mike that the Lord had done a similar work in his heart, the scars began to ache. How eagerly my heart yearned to manifest its love and have it returned. Silently, patiently, painfully, that anxious heart had to live day by day, hour by hour, crying to the Saviour alone for strength and comfort. I would learn that through such times of waiting upon Him we are brought to complete yieldedness of will.

Outwardly others saw only a quiet countenance, but inwardly there was always present the agonizing realization that Mike might wed another. Wasn't I even praying about his seeming need of a wife—a helpmeet? Prolonged fellowship together had revealed the obvious void in his life left by the negative past out of which he had been saved. My own sensitive nature recognized the instability wrought in him from having been deeply hurt, and the restlessness from feeling unattached. I was sure that the positive qualities of love and encouragement, added to his staunch devotion to Christ and his unquenching zeal for the lost, could make Mike essentially another Paul. My great longing was to be the one to provide that love and encouragement.

At the same time I knew that if it were the will of the Lord to withhold this blessing of love-fulfilled from me and if He were to grant it to another, I could accept a new heart-wound with a spirit of yieldedness. Since the Lord had taken from me those I had loved and needed most, the fear was implanted within that He wanted me to walk alone and, thus, would withhold Mike's love from me in order to draw me closer to Himself.

Meanwhile, being in such close fellowship with Mike did not always create a desirable relationship between us. There were definite times of personality conflict (seemingly normal when two lives are so entwined) when it appeared probable to me the Lord had good reason in not bringing us together, and when Mike's very facial expression bespoke his annoyance at my presence!

Prayer, fortunately, not only changes things, but it also changes people. As prayer victoriously met the situation now, I was sure mutual love would preclude future situations. Convinced of the changing power of love, these conflicts often resulted in further pain and fear—pain that he evidently did not love me now—and fear that he never would!

The impulse to run from the situation was repressed by the never completely diminished hope of "some day!" On the other hand, I knew I could end my inner turmoil by revealing my heart to Mike, thus sending him forever from me (so convinced was he that he should serve the Lord alone). As I desperately clung to the Lord, He would let me neither speak nor run—but quietly wait, building an inner strength that would later be needed.

During periods of loneliness back in the States, I had found solace in burying myself in spiritual activities. But here now I was faced without so much as this escape. I recalled my frequent prayer after Doug's death, "Use me any way You are pleased, Lord—in joy or suffering, the hard or easy way— just please don't leave me sitting." Usefulness to Him gave purpose to life. I could not face the emptiness of being shelved.

105

This activity, even though for Christ, had also been a crutch, for I had endeavored to fill the emptiness with activity for Christ rather than with the person of Christ himself. The stripping process was not easy, but the peaceable fruits of righteousness it would yield made it more than worthwhile.

Removal of the first crutch came naturally enough. Thoughts of glorious reunion with Doug in heaven no longer contained the soothing balm, nor brought the strengthening joy they once had imparted. This had been dimmed by the new beauty that filled my being when visualizing the ministry my "Boaz" and I could have together in behalf of Israel.

However, this had turned to pain as time had lessened hope and faith in its fulfillment. I emerged stripped. And there was no consolation in family or friends. No longer was there joy in the hope of death, or in the prospect of service in this life. I felt very much alone, and plagued with the thought, "What can I, a lone woman, really do?" I had already experienced the handicap and limitations to missionary service by my single status and sex. An unseen darkness had gradually descended, finally engulfing me and threatening to crush the spiritual and ultimately the physical life from me.

The deserted seashore became a haven to this anguished soul, seeking God's face and mind in the midst of His rugged creation which so powerfully evidenced the majesty of His presence. Agonizing cries could be lost in the echo of the pounding surf, while the sands faithfully hid the secret of warm tears shed freely upon them. The school of God's refining includes no easy lessons and produces no graduates this side of glory.

Without realizing it, I was grieving for my idols, trying to cling to the 'crutches' without which I could not face life. There was nothing left for me in life or death but the Lord himself, and somehow in the soul-struggle I had lost the sight of Him. A cloud of darkness hovered between us, and no amount of soul agonizing could break through. Stripped bare of spiritual graces I began to see how truly ugly and sinful the self within is before the Lord, until I came to loathe self and its power, and began to plead for its destruction. Meanwhile, groping for a way through this darkness to find again the light of heaven, I began reading *Abide in Christ* by Andrew Murray. Time would reveal that this tiny book had not been included in the packing of my trunk by chance but rather by Divine direction.

The answer began to filter through one day when the Lord anointed one portion to my heart. Andrew Murray spoke of the indwelling Holy Spirit being our link, our lifeline between heaven and earth. This stirred a chord within, bringing about a sensitivity to divine fellowship once again. Contact had been renewed by the Holy Spirit between my hungry heart and heaven. The Lord had begun a work which would soon be brought to fruition. I felt strangely that God had loosed my little vessel from its moorings (the handicapping crutches and weighty idols), and now I was beginning to sail free.

In this newly imparted victory I was able to choose the Christ life—the way of the cross. I offered myself solely to Him and asked for the lonely path—though not lonely because of the intimacy of His constant fellowship. I willed to give up to Him all earthly pleasures and desires, turned my back upon anything I could ever possibly have with Mike and chose to be completely absorbed in Him. Following this prayer of commitment came the trust that He would accomplish in me what my heart and soul had willed.

It was the very day of my prayer that the Lord began to teach me one of the basic lessons in His school of learning Christ-likeness. Often we students would practice our feeble Hebrew on each other at the lunch table after the morning sessions. I would consistently forget the gutteral sound in several words—perhaps even psychologically because it was so foreign to me and so difficult for me to master. This time I was severely rebuked for what appeared laxity to my assailant. Feeling the rebuke was totally unfair and lacking in desired sympathy and helpfulness, I voiced my self-defense which in turn was rebuffed. Inwardly I was deeply hurt by what I termed injustice, and outwardly I had shown a rebellious spirit.

The Holy Spirit immediately revealed to me that my reaction was not glorifying to the Lord, Christ's way being, "He was oppressed, and he was afflicted, yet he opened not his mouth" (Isa. 53:7a). The way of the cross is death to self— never defense of self, for the sake of self, outwardly or inwardly! This day I had felt the pressure of His molding, sweetened by a yielding spirit, in the school of humility.

One of the next lessons resulted from a bout with fear.

Shortly after gaining my new victory I was attacked by a deep-seated fear that I might lose my new experience. Fellow-shipping with Mike awakened the realization that my whole life had been undermined by fear. Again the divine Teacher spoke to me out of His Word. "For God hath not given us the spirit of fear" (II Tim. 1:7). "Perfect love casteth out fear" (I John 4:18). If we are totally committed to Him, body, soul, and spirit, surely we can trust Him who is perfect love not to allow anything adverse to come to us or touch us except that which is for His glory and our good. The wisdom and love in His withholding the good could be equally trusted. In trust lies rest from fear.

It became apparent the Lord was taking me into a new walk with Him—on a higher plane than I had known before. From the day I had yielded my life to the Lord in the hospital I had learned to pray in all things: "Please, Lord, *if it is Your will*." Now I was being taught a more elevated way. Rather than seeking His stamp of approval on my plans, it was now my sole desire to ascertain His pleasure: "Please, Lord, *if it be pleasing unto Thee.*"

My highest goal became the bringing of glory to the Lord. Everything was evaluated in the light of this and willingly accepted, even when painful to me, or rejected though desirous to me, in accordance with this goal. Herein was the key to victory—receiving all things as from Him alone, and desiring to please Him first and foremost with no regard to self-pleasing.

As a result of sharing with Mike my new experiences and lessons learned in the school of *Abiding in Christ*, his spiritual appetite was whetted. Borrowing Andrew Murray's book, he immediately became convinced of its truths and also sought to enter into this life of practical holiness. A prayerful and obedient student, Mike had imparted to him daily new spiritual graces in knowledge and experience. Our sharing together each day of new gleanings in holiness became rich blessings and challenges to us. Our spirits were being knit together in a bond of fellowship that could not help but renew within me the desire and hope that this relationship might be lasting. Walking the "way of the cross" together did not now seem inconsistent with my recent choice of Christ alone, as our relationship was so completely centered around Christ, and of such spiritual benefit to one another.

Just at this time one of the young women students, Miriam from London, came to Mike for advice and assistance. Feeling the problem called for a woman's insight too, he asked permission to bring me into the consultation. As we worked together with her and sought to lead her to Christ, we were both made aware of God's wisdom in using man and woman together. Seeing things differently (as men and women do not think alike) they complement each other, providing a good and even necessary balance.

I was beginning to appreciate womanhood perhaps for the first time. From childhood I had almost resented being a woman, convinced that men were more privileged than women. Now the Lord was showing me firsthand the beautiful place of woman as a helpmeet. Instead of resenting my sex, I saw I should live womanhood to the fullest that God intended and herein also find the joy He intended. Unfortunately this refreshed to me my previous problem concerning Mike. To keep my desire toward Christ first, I had to constantly lay "us" on the altar of sacrifice, binding my offering with strong cords of prayer that it should remain fixed.

Christ, in turn, opened to me the precious truth of His heart, broken because of unreturned love. I was learning in the school of Christ truths that cannot be revealed to the soul apart from comparable experience. "That I may know him, and the power of his resurrection, and the fellowship of his sufferings" (Phil. 3:10). The height and depth were yet to be realized.

CHAPTER XX

THE FUNERAL AND VICTORIES

IT WAS TRUE! My new-found joy was fading. Fellowship
with Christ was not the same vital reality it had recently been.
According to the Lord's schedule, it was time once again to
extend the stripping process. Withdrawal of the brightness of
His intimate fellowship resulted in my prayerfully probing
within, seeking a cause. The Holy Spirit began to uncover
conditions heretofore unrecognized by me.

In answer to my earlier prayer for destruction of the self,
the searchlight of the Spirit of God swept into the dark crevices
of my heart revealing the roots of the sin nature inherent in
us all. To an honest facing of fact the fruits of this evil root,
though subtle, were readily discernible: pride of dedication
and zeal; desire for the admiration of Christendom; a self-
sensitiveness, not wanting to be hurt; self-pleasing, wanting
my desires satisfied; self-love, and more contained in the
self-ego.

The ugliness of unveiled self in His holy presence cast me
—woeful and helpless—upon my face before Him, bringing
me to a spiritual crisis. Could even the Lord himself pull me
out of the depths of this horrible pit? It seemed more reasonable
to snuff out this ugly self-ruled vessel than to attempt to
remold it.

The terrible awareness that I was less than nothing, filled
with uncleanness in His sight, crushed and drained me emotionally until physically I could not leave my bed. For nearly
twelve hours through a dark night, a tremendous struggle
ensued as I pleaded with the Lord either to slay me or deliver

me. I could not live another day in this body of death. By early morning it was clear that death was the only answer, death of the self-ego. Drawn to the sixth chapter of the book of Romans, on my knees before Him, I read that we were crucified with Christ and raised to newness of life. I knew this was my standing before the Lord, but not my state. The only reasonable solution lay in a funeral—my state must be brought into accord with my standing.

Reading on in Romans seven I saw Paul's struggle as my struggle between the unholy flesh and the indwelling Spirit of holiness. Romans eight revealed the victory to those who walk after the Spirit and not after the flesh. I pleaded with the Lord to nail this Ruth to His cross and by His power to keep her there crucified, and to remove everything good and bad from me that stood between my soul and His fullness. This included my love for Mike. The Lord brought to my attention the part that my longing for the beautiful life together with Mike had had in usurping the fullness of His fellowship in my soul.

In desperation I cried out, "Lord, if it means taking my very heart and cutting it out of me and casting it into the depths of the sea, please do it! Take my love for Mike, that You gave, and slay it that it may never come between us again."

Abraham and Isaac came before me and I felt I, too, had been asked to offer my Isaac. That cherished love, precious gift held dear, which had been received from God, must be given back to Him. At the same time I knew I dared hold no hope of its being restored to me as Isaac was to Abraham, for then it could not have been a true yielding.

A quiet hush filled the room, bringing peace and with it a deep abiding sense that there had definitely been a funeral in that room that morning. The Lord had heard and answered my prayer and now the future lay in His hands. To me was left only this minute, this hour, this day to live as He directed and in His strength. The days that followed brought forth the "peaceable fruits of righteousness" manifest in a new sweet and gentle spirit, and a rich abiding victory.

Circumstances remained unchanged. What had changed was my reaction to them. I did not cease to have emotions or desires, but these were no longer self-centered or self-controlled. My precious Teacher had showed me that my very soul, the

111

seat of my emotions—my feelings, desires, my will, all, including the subconscious mind, must be purged, cleansed by His Spirit of holiness. The entire vessel must be sanctified or separated unto Him, recognizing no ownership but His.

I now saw distinctly the difference between dedication of one's self to the Lord and the yielding of the "ego." When I gave my life for service at Doug's death and prayed, "Lord, I'll do anything You want, serve, suffer, anything, but please don't leave me sitting," I really had given Him my life to use but had not relinquished the inner self. Feeling I could bear anything the Lord purposed for me except inactivity, I had held that reservation. Now I knew a higher plain. "Lord, if it pleases Thee to shelve me, to leave me sitting, then Thy desire is my will, my very life. Whatever pleases Thee, pleases me." Rather than the fleeting refuge of busyness for Him, I had found the blessed shelter of himself wherein is complete satisfaction. No longer should there be disappointment—rather everything received as His appointment.

As the soul is purged and the self is crucified, Christ can be formed in us. It becomes He who lives His life out through us, bearing forth the fruits of His Spirit—love, joy, peace, long-suffering, goodness, gentleness, faithfulness, meekness, and self-control. Then no matter how the battle rages or the winds blow we are steadfast, unmoveable vessels, manifesting stability and peace in contrast to the weak and failing past efforts of self. Herein I found great victory.

On my knees silent before God, listening rather than pleading, the purging process was working and opening my understanding. The Holy War of Satan's battling against the Lord, trying to usurp His glory and lordship, with earth the battleground, became a vivid reality.

Everywhere is seen the conflict between the two opposing forces of good and evil, light and darkness, holiness and sin. Our lives knowingly or unknowingly are caught up in the struggle, either engaging positively on God's side, or aiding and abetting His enemy by negligence or willful choice.

My every thought or deed, decision or choice must be evaluated in the light of bringing glory to the beloved Son, thereby defeating His enemy. I now knew Satan not as much my enemy as His.

I was learning to pray, as well, that Satan might not be

able to touch us in any way, lest in doing so he score a victory against Christ through us. For was it not in this way that sin entered the world? Satan deceived Eve that he might thwart God, usurping His place of lordship, His glory. In disobedience to the known will of God, Adam and Eve had committed the same sin as Satan (Lucifer then)—that of exalting the self-will above God's will. Mankind, created dependent upon God became independent of Him. To remain so meant to side against God and automatically be counted on Satan's side.

It is only as we go back to the place of utter dependence and complete obedience that we can truly please Him. This constituted the life of the Son upon the earth that pleased the Father in heaven. The Son did and said only that which was revealed to Him by the Father. His will in the body of human flesh was in complete harmony with the Father's. I, too, in order to please and glorify the Lord, must seek to live always and only by the indwelling Spirit in complete dependence upon and obedience to the Lord.

This reached down even to the menial everyday things which to me came to include even the alarm clock. If I was to live this life of utter dependence upon the Spirit, it must be according to His schedule. I could trust Him to enable me to meet any and all engagements which were His will for me, being confident that any missed were not therefore in His planning, only in mine! In the months and years ahead I was to find His faithfulness more secure and constant, more exacting, than any alarm clock could ever be.

No less dependent upon Him was my financial status. Word had arrived from home that my reserve was gone, leaving me from the human standpoint "broke"—without even funds to get home! It was a blessing that I could not know the school of struggle yet to be faced before I would graduate into the life of living totally by faith. Certain lessons are learned only through experience, the bitter experience of taking things into one's own hands rather than waiting and trusting in the Lord.

In the ensuing days a greatly disturbed Miriam often sought our counsel. She admitted having laughed at us four months previously because of our belief, but through the precious working of the Spirit of God, in her time of need she recognized in us the peace and joy she lacked. When first pointed to Christ as the answer to her serious difficulty, she had exclaimed, "But I can't go to Him! I'm a Jew!" Now as she hungrily listened to our witness she showed a simple childlike belief in the presentation of the Scriptures. God's future plans for the nation of Israel under King Messiah's reign thrilled her. No less intense was her emotional reaction to the eternal fate of the unbeliever. Emphatically she expressed her dread of the sentence of eternal hell, and her desire not to end up there. Only one thing seemed to hinder the yielding of her heart to the Lord—a strong desire for vengeance upon one who had betrayed her.

Circumstances necessitated her return to London. As time drew near for her departure she came to visit me. At the close of a three-hour session she knelt beside me as I prayed for her, expressly petitioning the granting of strength to relinquish what had become an iron barrier to her. She arose not yet born again, but as we parted for what we thought would be the last time in this world, she went forth with a New Testament in her hand and hope in her heart.

Mike had spent the night at a Kibbutz with other missionaries dealing with an interested young couple. Information came to him concerning Miriam's situation which he felt would help to settle her heart. Knowing she was scheduled to leave Israel within hours and not knowing how to reach her, he committed it into the hands of the Lord. He left the Kibbutz in the morning asking the Spirit to control even every second of his life. Within minutes after reaching the highway he was able to flag down a passing Sherut. Stepping in, to his great surprise there sat Miriam! After imparting the helpful information, he inquired of her what she was doing about Christ.

Her answer was encouraging, "I'm praying to Him and asking Him to do what has to be done."

Six days passed and business took me to the customs office in Tel Aviv. As was now my daily practice, in my morning prayer I asked the Lord to guide my very steps that day, living His will out through me moment by moment. Within a couple of blocks from the bus station, I came face to face with Miriam who had missed her original flight and was rescheduled for one on the morrow! Within moments it was plainly evident she was still not yet born anew.

For forty-five minutes, as traffic buzzed and pedestrians passed by around us, I was thrilled once again to encourage her to yield herself to the Lord.

After departing from her, I met a missionary friend from Jerusalem. Walking along together I told her of Miriam. My heart was stirred again for Miriam as my missionary friend revealed some things I felt would be beneficial to her. While praying that somewhere in that city of nearly 400,000 Miriam and I might be brought together again, I was startled to hear behind me: "So we meet again!"

Recognizing that the Lord was indeed at work, I made plans to meet with Miriam after lunch for further conversation. Thus in the warm afternoon, strolling along the beach, I again opened the Word to her.

In response to the Holy Spirit's wooing, Miriam's heart began to yield up its stumbling stone. The desire for salvation seemed momentarily to supersede all other emotions including vengeance. When we parted for the last time in Israel, it was with her promise that she would go to the privacy of her room and ask the Lord to enable her to turn to Him, holding nothing back. Kneeling before the Lord would be difficult for her to do for fear of being seen, but she realized she must allow nothing to stand in the way. To my sorrow word from London several weeks later revealed she still could not testify of a changed life. Our consolation now lay in intercessory prayer.

More and more we comprehended the importance and place of such prayer. When we often found our mouths closed in witness, our hearts turned to intercession that He would do in these lives what we were unable to do. The ministry of the Saviour at the right hand of the Father today is intercession. As we yield to His living His life out through us, we, too, will become intercessors.

To become effectual we must attain this spiritual height the same way as He. We may weep over Jerusalem as Jesus did, but this compassion is not intercession. Following His steps we must enter into our Gethsemane to pray, "Not my will, but thine. . . ." Having done this we must take up our cross and follow Him even unto death—the death of the

115

flesh—ultimately to be raised unto newness of life. In our resurrection life we ascend in Christ into the heavenlies, and there in the presence of God, our Father, we can intercede with a pure heart and will. The mind of Christ is revealed to such a one and the resulting effective prayer moves the hand of God.

The Patriarch Jacob stood out before me. As he wrestled with the Angel of the Lord, he determined to persevere to a blessing. It did not come for all of his determined effort— until the strength of the flesh was subdued. The permanent crippling of his flesh would always remind him that the power was of God, and the price of the blessing costly!

The deserted orange grove next to the school became my prayer closet at recess during classes. Lifting my face into the brisk stimulating wind, or bowing in the quiet hush of seclusion, my soul was stirred and warmed before Him, while the communion of intercession was made and my soul rewarded.

The words of Boaz to Ruth echoed back across the centuries. "The Lord recompense thy work, and a full reward be given thee of the Lord God of Israel" (Ruth 2:12). Ruth was now enjoying the fullness of her reward in His glorious presence. Turning heavenward, facing toward that vast expanse of blue, one could be caught up in the hope of His sudden appearance or lost in wonder at the glorious sunsets which magnificently revealed the shores of the eternal city. How my soul longed to tread them—now so familiar to her. However, my days of gleaning in the whitened harvest fields were not yet completed. The need of much labor turned my eyes back again to the needy fields.

CHAPTER XXI

SOWING THE SEED

THE OUTWARD RESULTS of our new spiritual experience did not pass unnoticed by the students. The inner joy and peaceful rest manifested in our faces prodded many questionings. Some came to Mike, "What has Ruth been doing to give her skin such a glow? Has she been sitting under a sun lamp?"

Of me they inquired, "What do you use for your complexion to make it so clear and radiant?" Acknowledging the fact that we manifested something wonderful which they could not boast possessing provoked some to jealousy and to discovering our secret.

David was one of the first to come to us. He revealed he knew without our telling him that we had a story to tell. He listened intently as we both told him of our faith in Christ and His marvelous workings in our lives. David surprised us by testifying of a belief in God and His Christ, but revealed confusion as to who Christ really is. Mike and I, not unlike Aquila and Priscilla of ancient Ephesus, expounded the way of God more perfectly to this modern-day "Apollos." David, like so many Jewish people, seemed fearful of losing his identity with Israel and his heritage by stepping out clearly for Jesus Christ. Would that they could see they lose nothing and gain everything, as the Book of Hebrews so clearly teaches! All of biblical Judaism was fulfilled in Him, and to receive Him is only to let go of the shadows and pictures to lay hold of the reality.

Our new walk in the Spirit had opened Scripture to us in

a new way. I now understood the wood, hay, and stubble of I Corinthians 3:12–15 to be that which man in his human flesh and strength can produce—not necessarily bad but temporal. Man can plant a tree and produce wood; a seed, and produce hay and stubble. Knowing full well now that only what the Lord himself, the Eternal One, produces through us would be eternal, we dared not force the door of witness but chose rather to wait upon His openings. These came in marvelous ways.

One morning in regard to going into Tel Aviv to pick up some money, I debated as to whether I should do some chores before or after the trip. Seeking to know the Lord's mind, I was suddenly impressed to leave immediately for the bus station, not even waiting to eat breakfast. I understood the Lord's planning and purpose when I met Eda, an elderly student, also on her way to the bus station. I was aware that Eda was fervently Zionistic.

As we took seats together on the bus, I inwardly prayed for the Lord to accomplish His will in our being together. Almost immediately she asked a few questions that opened the way for a strong witness. Without restraint or fear I was able to relate my own testimony in some detail.

"Does Mike believe similarly?" she was curious. Her lack of antagonism encouraged me to present Mike's story of glorious deliverance, plus Old Testament proof passages concerning Jesus the Messiah, garnishing it all with future prophecy. It was surprising to learn she had attended, according to her own words, "wonderful meetings among the Quakers in Philadelphia."

No less fruitful was Mike's bus ride from Tel Aviv back to Natanya a couple of weeks later. Sarah from the Ulpan was also returning and invited Mike to sit next to her. The widow of a deceased rabbi and sister to a rabbi of thirty-two years ministry, Sarah inquired as to Mike's occupation in the States. When told it was Hebrew Christian work she immediately asked, "Are you a missionary?" The Lord enabled Mike to give his testimony intelligently and in Christian love. When he had concluded she remarked, "Your story is not new. You see, I am on the faculty of a Methodist University in the States, but I do not believe as you do." Perhaps the Lord was watering seed already sown, which through fervent prayer would later blossom into eternal fruit.

118

Dora did not receive the Word as graciously. She expressly desired to hear from Mike's own lips the story of "one who really believes" as she had never before had such opportunity. Dora, who had been a chemist until Hitler changed her life and sent her through the furnaces of an earthly hell, posed profound questions which Mike answered from the Bible. The tortures she had seen and suffered had destroyed her belief in God. Refusing to believe the Word, and having had her curiosity satisfied, she closed the door to any further witness. Our hearts ached for her, but found a little consolation in the power of intercessory prayer.

Others came questioning, and precious seed was planted until antagonistic students brought pressure to bear on the teachers. This resulted in Mike's being called in and ordered not to speak of that Name again among the students in the Ulpan. It was almost as though we were reliving the book of Acts! Hoping to keep the door of utterance open he asked, "Isn't there religious freedom in this land?"

To which he was told decisively, "There is. But not in this Ulpan."

The Lord has His ways and though we were compelled to comply with their wishes, the Word still went forth in various ways to many, among whom was the teacher of the class. Mike described the incident in a letter home:

This morning in Hebrew we had an exam. While waiting for the second part, which would be given in some fifteen minutes (we were forbidden to look at our books), I took from my pocket Dr. Feinberg's pamphlet "Is the Bible God's Word or Man's?" and began reading it. Then boldly but calmly I took out of my pocket my small Bible and began reading the seventeenth chapter of Leviticus. My teacher came by, stopped, and asked what I was reading. I showed her, pointing her to verse eleven, "For the life of the flesh is in the blood: and I have given it to you upon the altar to make an atonement for the soul." She remarked she didn't like it and started to walk away.

Perhaps prompted by the Holy Spirit, I picked up the pamphlet, pointed to Dr. Feinberg's name and told her that he was a personal friend, one of my professors, a fine American Jew. She asked permission to read it. Gladly did I hand it to her, later to add Max Reich's tract, "If the New Testament Is Not True, What Then?"

While writing the exam, I looked up and was shocked to see her reading the latter! A bit later she returned both. I remarked that she read hurriedly. She said she read the latter and only half of Dr. Feinberg's. She made no comment, did not seem concerned. Of course you will add your prayers to mine that this will prove to be a soul who is to be delivered.

Springtime in Israel is wonderfully contagious! The hibernation of winter is past; everywhere the soil bursts forth in resurrection life. The hills and valleys display their joy with a profusion of gaily colored wild tulips, poppies, anemonies, daisies, mums, and many other varieties familiar only to the botanist. Patches of deep reds and yellows and purples carpet the drab browns and greys of previously barren fields. The exuberance of nature fills the air with a song, and you feel it is good to be alive and to be in Israel.

A little ragamuffin dog abandoned near our hotel had attached herself to me. One day while following Mike and me to school, she reminded us of Mark in the Book of Acts who had accompanied Paul and Barnabas on their missionary journey. From that time on we found ourselves referring to her as Mark.

Her spunky nature and decided attachment to me soon won her way into my heart. After a bath (leaving her a little white fluff-ball) she took up residency in my room and became an enjoyable constant companion wherever I went.

Mark and I shared the joy of the land by long excursions through the countryside, strolls in the park, or frolicking in the sand along the beach. We loved the walk along the road skirting the sea. It was so inspirational in its beauty that it became to me an Emmaus Road as I talked with the Lord.

When school ended about seven weeks later, I found I could not keep Mark with me, as I was so unsettled and she would hinder my freedom to minister. The Lord supplied a fine home for her, but the heartache of separation left another scar— she had become such a part of my life and heart.

At the same time Mike left for Jerusalem to room with a

Hebrew Christian young fellow from Germany who needed spiritual help. The cessation of rich fellowship we had enjoyed in recent months, plus the lost companionship of my little pal, left me feeling depressed and very much alone in the natural sense.

However, the Lord revealed purpose even in this new sorrow. On my way up to Jerusalem the following day by Sherut, I rode with a woman whose whole family, including her husband, had been killed by Hitler. It suddenly dawned upon me clearly why the divine purpose of my life had been made up of one heartbreak of separation after another. I had been sent to a tragically brokenhearted people. How else could I understand, genuinely feel compassionate toward them, fellowship in their sufferings? Our Saviour himself had suffered in body and soul even as we do, enabling Him to succor us perfectly. This then is the way of the Lord—and God's way is perfect!

CHAPTER XXII

DOORS CLOSING

WHEN THE END of the Ulpan was drawing near, it had become essential to determine the will of the Lord for my next move. My Hebrew was not adequate for the technical lectures at the Hebrew University, nor would it be for several years. Financial support coming in was rather meager and had to be taken into consideration as well. My heart's desire was still to be one of the people, to live among them as one of them—not only as a missionary to them. These were a people who needed love and understanding, not just proof texts and sermonizing! They had been so offended by many who had falsely claimed the title "Christian" that the stigma "missionary" by now had built up insurmountable walls.

Realizing this made it difficult not to think that one of the best ways to become one of the Jewish people would be to marry one. My love for Mike had been offered upon the altar of sacrifice, and I would not take it back myself, even though I knew that now for the first time the Lord could safely bring us together in marriage. There would not be the danger of my putting him before the Lord as I had Doug. By His grace this test had been victoriously passed! Meanwhile, however, I could not take this possibility into consideration. The Lord would have to take the complete initiative if we were to be brought together.

When I met Rachel it seemed the Lord was opening a new door for me through her. Rachel was a young Hebrew Christian widow, who had lost her husband in the War of Liberation which gave birth to the new state of Israel. She was less than twenty-one years of age when Israel gained her costly independence. Having been born of an American father, even though in Palestine (so called before the division of the land by the United Nations in 1948), Rachel could claim United States citizenship by applying in the U.S. before she reached twenty-one. Therefore, wanting to give her unborn child the privilege of an American heritage, she had made her way to the States.

When she arrived in New York she had no idea of its immensity. Comparing it perhaps to Tel Aviv she decided to board a bus and go sight-seeing. It wasn't long until she realized she was hopelessly lost, and presenting her plight to a nearby policeman was taken to a police station. Upon learning she was from Israel and that this was her first time in the United States, the officers decided to initiate her into something typical of the American way of life. Taking her to a popular eating place they ordered a hot dog for her. Knowing what dogs were she was horrified! Before she could voice her protest someone put down in front of her a red bottle with a label which she read as "cat-sup!" It was sometime before they could convince her that neither of these American favorites had anything to do with dogs or cats!

One day Rachel came upon an evangelistic street meeting geared to the Jewish populace. Her curiosity stopped her and shortly she was arguing with the Hebrew Christian spokesman. Unable to defeat his arguments on the spot she left, determined to prove him wrong and return. After studying and searching the Bible, looking for proof against his declarations, she returned asking questions. Soon convinced that Jesus was the Messiah and Saviour, she received Him for herself.

Rachel remained in the United States several years after her son was born, becoming grounded in her new faith. Eventually, compelled by love to her own people and country, she returned to Israel to spread the "Good News." She had found a wonderful ministry in teaching grade school down in the Negev (desert) in a Moshav (a cooperative small land-holder's settlement).

As Rachel ministered to the children she prayed and saw doors opened to witness to the parents through them. She encouraged me that I, too, could get a teaching credential after two years of training—and a similar door of outreach to the people. It seemed sensible to go down and look over the possibilities.

The three-hour ride by bus from Jerusalem with Rachel was, as always, enjoyably adventurous. Driving down through the Philistine territory of Bible days prompted my curiosity to search out the vale where David slew the giant Goliath. If the mute hills could speak, what tremendous tales of valor and miraculous victories in behalf of Israel would they relate?

The ever present abundance of boulders and rocks everywhere brought to mind David's metaphor, "The Lord is my rock . . . in whom I will trust" (Ps. 18:2), and gave it new depth of meaning. In a sense the strength of the rocks had become Israel's foundation as they have been gathered and formed into shelters and fortresses. It was sad, I speculated, that she lacked the firm foundation of her Cornerstone long ago rejected—consequently to become a stone of stumbling to her.

Such wanderings into the past were periodically interrupted when I was jarred back to the present by a very realistic twentieth century! It never ceased to amaze or amuse me to see a little farmer board the bus with a live turkey under each arm, a duck tied to a rope, or a gunny sack full of live chickens. No one seemed to mind the presence of the livestock. There was an understanding, sympathetic spirit among these people— a pioneer spirit of togetherness that was building a nation out of the rocks, and weeds and sands of a land long ago forsaken— but never forgotten.

Suddenly, as if in the midst of nowhere, the bus slowed to a halt. "Moshav Sharsharet," announced our destination. Descending from the bus I glanced over the dry, brown countryside, dotted with the green desert shrub denoting recent winter months, and a distant harvest already yellowed by the desert sun. The air was warm and fresh with the fragrance of spring.

About half a mile in the distance I could see the simple wooden buildings of Rachel's orthodox Moshav home. Taking a firm grip on our luggage, we began trudging up the long roadway, stopping now and then to rest our hands. At the edge of the community, as we stopped to rest, we noticed a group of orthodox men, including the rabbi, standing outside one of the humble homes. Knowing the family, Rachel immediately recognized there was a Brith (a biblical circumcision on the eighth day) being celebrated. She quietly told me to pick up my bags and walk quickly past them not as much as glancing in their direction and not stopping even if my arms fell off under the strain, as this would greatly offend them. (Strange women should not be around such an affair!) Obediently, I followed at her heels, not daring to look left or right, praying for the strength to make it, all the while ignoring the pains of blisters beginning to form on my hands.

My first day observing school was most revealing. Rachel had to teach three different grades in one small room and with practically no teaching aids. Again I was faced with the need of proficiency in the language if one is to be able to teach without great disorder and confusion.

Sharsharet is located just north of Beersheba and across the fields from the Gaza Strip which is faintly visible in the distance. Because of frequent Arab infiltrators from Gaza (which had become the jumping-off point for Egyptian border raids), it was necessary to sleep each night with a rifle ready to fire standing against the wall for quick accessibility. My third night there, after retiring, we were attracted by the noise of a couple of trucks and noticed lights criss-crossing back and forth across the fields. We knew there was trouble and surmised that infiltrators were suspected. We learned the next morning that our guess was right and that there had been twenty-five guards standing by rather than the usual two. (Such incidents were to continue until Israel's Sinai Campaign two and a half years later would finally put an end to these raids from Gaza.)

Things in the land had been very tense since the massacre on Scorpion's Ascent in the Negev the previous week. A bus traveling between Beersheba and Eilat had been waylaid by Arab infiltrators, and eleven passengers had been shot and killed in cold blood. Feelings were high and Rachel felt sure Israel was on the verge of war with the surrounding Arabs again. Almost daily gunfire along the Jerusalem Corridor and the border south of Jerusalem added to the unrest. In less than a week there would be Jewish retaliation in an Arab village across the border south of Jerusalem. Perhaps Israel and Jordan were as close to actual war as they had come since the early days of statehood.

Within a short time a strong lack of peace and a deep

restlessness in my soul bore witness to my spirit that this was not the Lord's place of service for me. Only after returning to Jerusalem was my peace restored, so I decided to remain there at least temporarily, seeking prayerfully the knowledge of His will so eloquently expressed in Paul's prayers: "... to desire that [I] might be filled with the knowledge of his will in all wisdom and spiritual understanding" (Col. 1:9).

It was necessary to return to Sharsharet a few days later for some luggage and books which I had shipped down there but which had not as yet arrived at the Moshav when I decided to return to Jerusalem. I could see the Lord's purpose in the delay when I returned to find that the night before they were delivered, Rachel's floor had been flooded by a broken pipe. If they had been there they would have been caught in it and my books and other things most probably ruined.

After spending the day with Rachel we headed for the highway that I might catch the 4 p.m. bus. Rachel feared we couldn't make it in time with my heavy suitcase and box, so she summoned one of the men of the Moshav who had a horse and cart nearby. It turned out the wagon was being used to haul manure fertilizer of which there was abundant evidence, but there was no choice if I was to catch the bus! So gingerly we climbed aboard, carefully seeking the least offensive spots. And then, as though to vex us, the horse headed out across the fields, responding to the driver only by going in circles, until finally in desperation he climbed out of the wagon to lead the horse down the roadway. Thankfully, and none the worse for wear, we managed to reach the highway just before 4 p.m.

Saying "Shalom" once again to Rachel, I sat down on my suitcase to wait for the bus to Jerusalem. As I waited, I watched the sun disappear behind the buildings of the Moshav, and dusk begin to descend over the land. By 5 p.m. I decided there wasn't going to be a 4 p.m. bus to Jerusalem. I would not be able to get my luggage back up to the Moshav by myself, neither did I dare leave it alongside the road unattended the length of time it would take to go for help. Looking out across the deserted barren fields in every direction, I did not relish the idea of sleeping by the highway all night either.

Desperately I prayed for a bus to come along—any bus, going anywhere! If I could just get back to civilization! Perhaps I could even get to Jerusalem yet tonight, but if not, anything would be better than being stranded alone in the desert.

Finally (oh welcome sight!) a bus appeared around the bend in the road. Eagerly I flagged it down. As it rumbled to a stop, a couple of men jumped down and grabbed up my luggage for me in true Israeli hospitality. Thanking them I turned to the driver and asked in my most polished Hebrew, "Where are we going?"

Recovering from obvious astonishment he answered, "Tel Aviv." With a word of approval I paid my fare and we were on our way.

Earnestly I beseeched the Lord that we might arrive in Tel Aviv before the last bus scheduled for Jerusalem. As always, the Lord showed himself gracious, and when we arrived I was able to transfer to a bus bound for Jerusalem. The Lord even provided a very kind newspaper gentleman to assist me with my cumbersome luggage.

The usual three-hour trip from Sharsharet to Jerusalem had stretched into five and a half, but joyfully and gratefully a very weary Ruth crawled into bed in Jerusalem that night!

Thus far I knew what was not the will of the Lord for me— but what was? More and more it seemed impossible to do a work alone. Several incidents had shown me that a young, lone woman could not minister safely and effectively. The unsaved know nothing about the compassion of Christ within us for a lost soul. So often our love and concern is misunderstood or misinterpreted. I found age made no difference, as in the case of the elderly widowed father of one of our friends at the language school. I thought his kindness was that of a father toward a daughter until in his broken English one day he told me of his love for me!

Then there was the time I came to the realization my friend Mrs. Silverberg was trying to make a match between her bachelor cousin and myself; and again when Willy's obvious advances had to be squelched when we were in the Kibbutz. There was no doubt that my single status and youth were a definite hindrance to independent work.

127

Still there was no clear leading to connect myself to any active organization in the land at this time either. This would bring me under the stigma of missionary, another handicap. The missionary is evaded by the populace and unofficially black-listed by the government.

It had also become increasingly clear that to do a truly effective work for the Saviour here in the land, one would not only have to be well-versed in the modern Hebrew but also the biblical Hebrew, and in all the writings of the rabbis throughout the centuries in which so many of the Israelis were well-versed. (Our witness thus far had been almost totally to English-speaking Jews.) It would necessarily take years to become a proficient worker. The more effective way would be the raising up of Spirit-filled leaders among the Israeli believers themselves. However, the cost to them in various forms of persecution, from physical abuse to loss of employment, apparently discouraged the needed growth.

As I pondered the obstacles I wondered, "Could the Lord be closing the door to me here in the land and leading me back home where there is a wide-open door of access for me to serve actively among the Jewish people?" Surely the Lord would soon make clear His will, for my finances were fast running out. Apart from divine intervention it would be necessary to return home at least long enough to put my finances in order. There was enough left to pay one month's rent at the WMCA Hotel—but not enough for a second month.

My heart was buried deep here in the land, but reason and closed doors told me it was more important to be where the Lord could freely use me, and most of all to be where the Lord wanted me. I could not escape the constant heart yearning for the wonderful ministry I had envisioned that Mike and I could have together, which would also be at least a partial solution to many of the obstacles I faced. The hunger for companionship and like-minded fellowship strengthened the yearning.

Zvi's humble quarters, which Mike was now sharing, consisted of a two-room abandoned Arab house constructed of stone on the edge of no-man's land. One room had a stone floor, the other only dirt, and was meagerly furnished with a table, three stools, and two steel cots with straw-filled mattresses. A small one-burner kerosene stove was used for heating and cooking. The lack of hot water made bathing necessary at the YMCA nearly a mile away.

Convinced the Lord had led him there for the sake of Zvi's soul as well as those of surrounding Jewish neighbors, Mike could share these very uncomfortable living conditions with praise. And the purposes of the Lord were not for Zvi alone. Mike recorded: "Philippians 4:19 took on new depths this a.m. Sometimes we need to be without in order to be within—without comforts and material surpluses to be within His will. He will always supply what we need. Sometimes we need to go hungry, need to be without, for our spiritual welfare."

Situated only a few meters from the Israeli-Jordanian border, they were constantly aware of an Arab sentry posted just across the border, some twenty yards away from the house. Each time Mike or Zvi carried the garbage out to its receptacle, the sentry took position behind his machine gun to remain there until they disappeared into the house again. Needless to say, with the many border incidents between Israel and Jordan, I continually prayed for their safety.

Our infrequent meetings on the street or at a Bible class, prayer meeting, or church service at one of the missions were always a source of mutual blessing and thanksgiving. It seemed Mike, as well as I, missed the wonderful times of fellowship we had known at Natanya. Could the warmth of love he emitted at these meetings have a deeper source than just Christian friendship? It came as a surprise to me to learn that he, too, was seriously seeking the will of the Lord concerning returning home in a couple of months. The lack of freedom to evangelize was disturbing to his spirit. Like the Apostle Paul, because of the deep inner constraint born out of compassion for his brethren, he could not be fully content unless active for Christ.

In this beloved land we could not knock on doors to witness for Christ or stand on street corners passing out Gospel tracts. Radio time was not available for the preaching of the Gospel of Jesus Christ. Very few Jewish people dared be seen entering a church or known place of Christian worship for fear of being marked and then persecuted. Without years of language study, the opportunities to touch a soul here and there would be sorely limited. Mike felt his thirty-eight years, plus the shortness of time to get the Gospel out, might warrant his return to America where he could be totally active and immediately effective among the even-more-numerous descendants of Abraham.

As for myself, I was strongly sensing a door behind me swinging shut, as. the voice of the Lord was clear before, "This is the way, walk ye in it." If the Lord were leading me home, temporarily or permanently, there could be a wonderful opportunity through slides to create a prayer interest and burden for Israel. It would be wise for now to spend some time traveling and taking pictures, meanwhile praying the Lord would either open a door to remain or clearly close the door behind me.

With this as my aim, when opportunity presented itself to cross into Jordan at Easter time with four missionary friends, I felt I should go. Permission to cross into Jordan from Israel and to return again was granted Christians and Gentiles only · at Christmas and Easter, that they might visit the holy places of their beliefs. This would be my only opportunity. However, there was one problem. It was already 12 days past the deadline for making application for clearance across the border and re-entry back, and only five days before the crossing date! But I was not without hope. The Lord had opened doors for me before!

My going forth to the American Consulate was previously bathed with much prayer. Undoubtedly due only to the Lord's foresight I already had in my possession a passport picture which was required with the application. The Lord granted favor in the eyes of the official and even though past the deadline, my application was accepted and sent—however, with the understanding that it might not be accepted at this late date by Jordan. (Jordan investigated each application carefully in order to weed out any possible spies using this means to enter their country.)

The next step was to secure some American dollars as my Israeli money would be worthless in this Arab state which officially refuses to recognize the existence of the State of Israel. Mike came to my rescue here.

When I was told two days later that the Arabs were considering my application that very day, I went to the Lord in fervent prayer and received assurance I was going across.

The next problem confronting me was the renewal of my Israeli visa which was due, that I might be able to re-enter Israel. This had taken weeks in the past (I had only two days before my friends' scheduled crossing on Good Friday), and there was even the possibility of refusal. The last time Mike had obtained his visa renewal in Natanya, he was almost refused and warned not to actively propagate Christianity. Several other missionaries recently had been forced to leave the country because of just such refusal.

The Israeli government is not opposed to the presence of Christians in the land, but intensely so to any evangelizing of the Jews. They have struggled so ardently for their Jewish homeland, they cannot allow elements to arise which they believe can mean persecution and suffering to them. This stems from a misunderstanding of the difference between Gentiles and Christians. Their much suffering has been at the hands of Gentiles, not Christians, as they believe. We who are born again truly love the Jews because our Saviour is a Jew, and we feel a debt of gratitude to those who gave to us and preserved for us the Word of God.

There was no doubt in my mind that I was on the consulates' black-list of missionaries by now, so again I sought the Lord to prevail—and prevail He did! Reluctance gave way to affirmation when I revealed to the consulate official I would probably be leaving Israel by the end of the sought-for three-month extension. I left rejoicing in another victory, also wondering if this was another indication from the Lord that I was to turn homeward. It seemed doubtful they would consider extending my visa again, except of course by divine Providence.

By Good Friday morning my clearance had not yet come from Jordan. Nevertheless, by faith in the Lord's miracle working, and encouraged by the obstacles overcome thus far, I took my papers necessary to present at the border for crossing and headed for the Generali building for my re-entry permit. It was disheartening to find myself at the end of a long line. It was obvious it would take half the day. Just at this moment one of the girls who was crossing in our group appeared with a friend of hers, a man of influence. In minutes what would have taken hours was wondrously accomplished. Breathing a prayer of thanksgiving and praise, we headed for Mandelbaum

Gate—the one legal place of crossing from Israel into Jordan.

Only one obstacle remained. With much prayer and trembling, I presented my papers and waited almost breathlessly to know if my name was listed as having been cleared by Jordan. One by one my four companions heard their names called. Mine was not there! But surely it would come through any minute. The Lord would not have miraculously brought me this far to close the last door in my face. I was asked to step aside. My companions joining me, the five of us stood earnestly praying for much grace and favor in the eyes of this Arab official. I tried to look as Christian and harmless as possible, glad my dress was very much American, and trusted the Lord would cause them to know I was not a spy! Moments later I was asked where I intended to stay in the Old City.

I replied, "The English mission's Christ Church," fully aware they did not know I was coming; but two of my companions had made reservations there, and I was trusting the Lord to provide for me there as well. Satisfied, he told me I could go on through and they would let me know when my name cleared. Once again the Lord had done the "exceeding abundantly," and every door had swung open before His power.

Stepping through the invisible Mandelbaum Gate and crossing past the barbed-wire of no-man's land, we came to a street lined with Arab shops. Just ahead we could see the huge ancient walls of the Old City Jerusalem, weather-worn stone upon stone, towering majestically into the deep blue sky. We gazed in excited wonder at the old Damascus Gate, recalling the tremendous events it must have witnessed. It was through this gate a very proud and zealous Pharisee named Saul had passed on his way to persecute the Jewish Christians in Damascus. Several years later this same gate had seen his humble re-entrance, this time as a zealous Jewish Christian himself. Somewhere on the road that stretched out behind us toward Damascus, he had met the glorified Christ, and not only his life and name were changed but also Paul's very being itself.

And even more noteworthy, it was through this very gate that the Lord of creation, humbled in the fashion of His creation, carried His cross—the instrument of death for Him, but of life for us. If these stones could cry out, what praises they would utter! Our hearts sang with the Psalmist, "Lift up your heads, O ye gates; and be ye lift up, ye everlasting doors; and the King of glory shall come in" (Ps. 24:7).

Stepping through these mammoth gates, we were in a sense immediately swept back two thousand years in time. We felt as though we had stepped back into the very pages of the New Testament.

CHAPTER XXIII

THE OLD CITY

WITHIN THE CITY WALLS we met with a bustling eastern culture of another world, one which perhaps would not seem as foreign to Paul and the early Christians as to us. Passing down the crowded cobblestone street, we were unable to read the Arabic signs posted above shop entrances or displayed in windows. The few modern tourist gift shops seemed inconsistent, interspersed with the little open markets of produce, hand-woven articles or crockery, and various other dark stalls and shops. Upon sight of American tourists, the educated merchants enjoyed displaying their learning as well as their wares. Distinguished above foreign sounds, "Cheapest place in town," penetrated our disbelieving ears!

There was a danger of being separated by the jostling throng or of finding ourselves in the pathway of a donkey obediently carrying its burden. Now and then we would see a man as burden bearer, carrying a heavy piece of furniture strapped to his back or bearing a tremendous load of boxes, et cetera.

We were saddened to see the poverty that must accompany non-progression and lack of education. The children had developed the art of begging as well as dogged persistence. Centuries-old houses had been built into the very walls of the city, or jumbled together upon the remnants of still older dwellings throughout the city, forming dark and narrow corridors. A timid child would occasionally disappear through a mysterious doorway or peek through a high-grated window— evidences of a dwelling back in the darkness.

Along the twisting passageways we made our way up a set of stairs, past David's ancient Citadel, finally to locate the Christ Church. My joy was complete when informed they could accommodate me as well as my companions, a crowning indication to me of His definite will for me to be here.

After an enjoyable lunch at the mission church, laden with cameras and film, we sought to hire a taxi to take us the five or six miles south to Bethlehem. The countryside was lovely in the soft shades of spring. Rounding a curve in the road, we came upon an old quarry with stonecutters patiently forming building bricks from rough stones with hammer and chisel.

Traveling on we passed a small caravan of burden-bearing camels led by an Arab astride a donkey. It was a common sight to see Arab women in their contrasting dark or brightly colored gowns walking along the road, skillfully balancing a large sack of greens or grain, or a pottery jar of water upon their heads. About two miles from Bethlehem we came upon the monument which has declared for nearly forty centuries the undying love of the Patriarch Jacob for his beautiful Rachel. Our hearts were touched by this remembrance of Jacob's love and loss.

The little town of Bethlehem, glistening in the sunlight, was set upon rolling hills, facing terraced vineyards and olive groves. As we entered the city, my heart thrilled to think of that other Ruth arriving in this very town with Naomi at the end of their long, difficult journey. Inwardly moved to sentimental tears, my mind reviewed her story. It was here she found rest and love in the heart and home of her Boaz, and within these gates she bore Obed, the grandfather of King David. How fitting that David's greater Son, the future King of Israel in whom that nation will one day find rest and peace, should also have been born in this City of David.

We entered with the Good Friday pilgrims, stooping through a small doorway into the Church of the Nativity. The huge austere church built by Constantine the Great was a typical old Roman basilica. Beneath the church in a warren of underground passages can be seen the smoke-blackened cave walls of the traditional birthplace of Jesus. As there are a number of ancient houses built over similar caves in the limestone rock in Bethlehem (still used as stables today), it is very likely

135

such a one did provide shelter and privacy for the Great King's arrival into this world. Aware this could possibly have been the very location, we found it an empty shrine.

Our enjoyment was turned to sorrow to see poor unlearned peasants worshipping with kisses stone statues of the Crucified One, and ragged ones laying gifts (costly to them) at the feet of lifeless images. We inwardly groaned to tell them of the living Christ whom we worship with adoration and praise, but alas—the language barrier! We could only pray that in their sacrificial devotion they might somehow hear the Word of the Spirit and have Him born into their hearts.

Outside again, we wandered along the streets and upon investigating a huge stairway, stumbled upon a large open Bedouin camel market. Never in my life before had I viewed firsthand such poverty and filth. Amid loud arguing, everything was being sold or bartered from what appeared to be goats' milk in canvas bags to camels. We felt a little sick as we turned away.

Our continued excursion took us to the roof of the Church of the Christmas Bells—so named for their pealing forth each Christmas a memorial to His birth. From thence we could view most of the city. Turning eastward we looked across the flat roofs of Bethlehem to the Shepherds fields where the shepherds were watching their flocks the night the angels heralded the birth of the long-promised and awaited Messiah. Just beyond them lay the brown and yellow fields once owned by Boaz. The vocabulary of man cannot express the well of feeling that bubbled up within my heart, silently overflowing with praise and thanksgiving for such a gracious privilege.

The Ruth who had become so much a part of my life had walked that dusty road leading out of town and had meekly, but bravely, gone into those fields to glean. Could this strange inner assurance be the Lord impressing me through this privilege, "Even as her heart's desire had been fulfilled and her life made complete by her Boaz, even so you, too, will know the completion of that which I have begun in your heart"? Later as we drove out through those fields, my eyes devoured the scene, seeking to lock within the memory of heart and mind that which these eyes might never view in this life again.

Returning to Jerusalem that evening, we watched the Roman Catholics re-enacting the events of what we call Good Friday.

A number of priests had carried an image of the crucified Christ down the Via Dolorosa (traditional street of sorrows, or way of the cross), chanting in Latin as they went, a great throng crowding about them. Arriving at the ancient Church of the Holy Sepulchre (built over the Catholic traditional site of sacred Calvary and the garden tomb), with much ceremony they wrapped the blood-stained image and laid it in a small marble-lined tomb. The inside of the huge windowless, cave-like church was lighted only by candles and torches, whose flickering cast eerie shadows on the walls. We noticed a damp, musty odor of decay.

The great crowd had pressed in and reverently stood watching the mass being chanted, patiently awaiting their opportunity to gain merit, according to their teaching, by showing their devotion. In time they came weeping with emotion and with trembling fingers touched the tomb or kissed the image, all the while praying fervently. Many burned candles at the shrine, perhaps in behalf of deceased loved ones. Again we wept within to see those, so blinded by the fallible traditions and teachings of man, leading the blinded multitude.

Leaving this darkened place (both physical and spiritual) we walked up the Mount of Olives in the light of a full moon and looked back across the Kidron Valley to the dim lights of the Old City. Our hearts thrilled to the words as we softly sang "The Holy City": "Jerusalem, Jerusalem, lift up your gates and sing, Hosanna in the Highest, Hosanna to your King. . . ." And then our hearts grew quiet in the retrospection of how He wept and prayed over this city. Beholding it, as we were doing at that moment, He had cried out in desire to gather her unto himself as a hen does her chicks, but she would not. A little later He knelt in the shadow of her great walls and earnestly prayed, in spite of His agony, the Father's will be done, even for her sake. She didn't know the Son of God had visited her!

Reentering the city we found the previously crowded streets now nearly deserted and frighteningly dark. On a back street we passed by a bakery where they were baking bread for the next day. Stopping, we watched the bakers place the flat cakes by means of long-handled shovels into heated stone ovens. Delighted with an audience, the bakers offered us a tasty sample of their finished product. Further along, although the shops were closed, we discovered a falafel stand still open on a corner. Hungry, we indulged ourselves, to discover them a little different from the Israeli falafel, though very tasty and even hotter! I purposely did not look to see what they were composed of, having learned that over here sight can spoil the appetite!

Saturday arrived bright and early for five eager sight-seers. Again hiring a cab whose driver would serve as guide as well, we headed north into the area of Samaria. We traveled through countryside nicely cultivated even though the crudest methods were still employed. We were startled to find complete disregard of the biblical injunction not to yoke the ox and ass together. Even so, this very unequal team (apparently a result of necessity) pulling a wooden hand plow somehow managed to accomplish the task.

In Samaria, the modern Nablus, we were taken to the ruins of Herod's Palace where the daughter of Herodius danced for John the Baptist's head. The desolation of this once-glorious capital of rebellious Israel's kingdom, erected in rivalry to Jerusalem, was a present testimony of her judgment for disobedience to the Lord God of Israel.

Approaching the ancient well of Jacob, which had withstood 40 centuries of time near the foot of Mt. Gerizim, we thought of the time Jesus must needs go through Samaria. Traveling this desert on foot would certainly warrant the need of rest and quenching of thirst. It was here He had purposely come to speak to a needy Samaritan woman, "Whosoever drinketh of this water shall thirst again: but whosoever drinketh of the water that I shall give him shall never thirst: but the water that I shall give him shall be in him a well of water springing up into everlasting life" (John 4:13, 14). And here today beneath a little Greek church, we found refreshing drink for body and soul as the fresh sweet water, still flowing in the well, spoke to us of the everlasting water within springing up eternally.

Turning southeast we traveled through miles of parched wilderness inhabited only by a few Arab nomads as evidenced by a few black Bedouin tents pitched here and there, with the only sign of life a nearby tiny flock of sheep or a few camels. Eventually we approached the excavation of the ruins of ancient Jericho. Our eyes gazed upon a jumbled pile of mud bricks on a foundation of stone that once in orderly fashion had fortressed Israel's enemies. These very ruins today declared the truthfulness of the Word of God, for they reveal that something of a miraculous nature occurred in their destruction. We were told that scientists state they fell in the opposite direction from which they should have fallen had this occurred by natural phenomenon.

In nearby modern Jericho we discovered the potter demonstrating his unique art of molding by hand exquisite pottery on the potter's wheel as it sped round and round. We were reminded of God's illustration through Jeremiah, likening the Lord to the potter and Israel to unyielding clay. We saw in it an object lesson to us, typifying God's hand upon us—molding, forming, smoothing, that we might become vessels of honor and beauty, of His making. The stubborn, unyielding clay lay in broken pieces at the potter's feet. Our hearts cried out to be spared a similar fate spiritually.

Our continuing journey led outside of Jericho to Allenby's Bridge, spanning the muddy Jordan. This river, on a serpentine course, covers nearly two hundred miles over an approximate ninety-mile area and drops from 685 feet below sea level at the Sea of Galilee to 1290 feet below sea level upon reaching the Dead Sea. Picking up much soil along its rapid descent, the sparkling blue Jordan that flows out of the Sea of Galilee becomes a muddy-grey Jordan that empties into the nearby Dead Sea. We thought back in Scripture of Elisha's order to Naaman, the leper, to bathe in these muddy waters, and could understand his hesitancy! And to the extreme contrary, the willing desire of One greater than he who was baptized of John perhaps in this very area!

In this world of opposites the beauty of the intensely blue Dead Sea at first glance seemed contrary to its name. This huge cauldron of chemicals, made so because of the lack of outlets from it and the unending burning desert heat upon it, is one of the wealthiest spots in the world. A close examination revealed no marine life of any kind in or around it, no sea shells, fish, water plants or weeds, and we knew it was well named. Oily little waves were playfully lapping at the pebbly beach. At the water's edge we dipped in our fingers that we might taste this salty sea and discovered it more bitter than salty.

Turning back toward Jerusalem we reflected thankfully on the great part that England's General Allenby had had in Israel's becoming the Jewish State it is today. This man who had learned to pray for the Jew and the restoration of Israel at his mother's knee was himself used of the Lord to begin to answer those prayers. In December of 1917 this praying General was enabled to lead an invasion against Jerusalem and to capture it without firing a single shell on the city itself. Thus came to an end the Turkish rule of four centuries, putting the Holy Land in the power of a country sympathetic to Zionism.

This was the first step in conjunction with the then recently issued Balfour Declaration, which revealed the British Government's active intention to aid the Zionists' aspirations of establishing a national home for the Jews in Palestine. Even though it took another thirty years of struggle and battle for this hope to be fully realized, this seizure had laid the foundation.

We noticed we were climbing steadily as we wound our way along the old Jericho road toward Bethany. We passed a sign informing the traveler in English and Arabic that he was at sea level and were astonished to realize we had just climbed nearly 1290 feet from the Dead Sea in a relatively few miles!

Surrounded by brown-domed, vegetationless hills, the desolate, seldom-traveled road could make us easy prey to bandits on horseback. The parable of the good Samaritan took on new reality for us. It was on this road from Jerusalem to Jericho that a man fell among thieves, was stripped, wounded, and left half dead, later to be befriended by the Samaritan. It wasn't encouraging for us to know that even today bandits at times swarm down upon lone travelers along this road. We were indeed thankful for the secure sense of His protection round about us.

Literally climbing out of the torrid Jordan valley, nearly four thousand feet in less than twenty-five miles, we welcomed the first evidences of the olive trees of Bethany in the distance. In Bethany we were taken down into an empty, dusty cave, traditionally an ancient Christian church built over the tomb of Lazarus, whom Jesus called forth from the dead.

We were somewhat amazed to have to buy candles to

use for lighting upon entering the dark cavern, only to have them collected at our exit to be sold again to the next visitors!

Although one can seldom feel positive about such biblical locations, our hearts nevertheless were stirred to recall again this marvelous miracle of resurrection power. And if this were not the very site that witnessed His messianic authority, it was at least somewhere within this little village.

Journeying back through the Mt. of Olives, we visited the beautiful little garden of Gethsemane where Jesus spent a portion of His last evening before the Cross. Within its walls we stood under the shadow of an aged olive tree of tremendous girth, so old it must have grown here in Jesus' day. Still fruit-bearing, these trees stand as a memorial to the willing sacrifice He made for us. From thence our short jaunt back into Jerusalem ended all too quickly—and with it a wonderful day of retracing many of the travels of our wonderful Lord.

In the early evening one of my companions and I decided to do a little souvenir shopping. So off we went through the narrow, winding streets, looking for a shop we had taken note of earlier. Pausing in front of one of the shops, we noticed four Arab women huddled in what appeared to be a heated discussion. Standing off to the side was a very meek, dejected-looking Arab man. The scene gave every indication of one of the decisive disadvantages of polygamy! Unquestionably this poor Arab had long ago discovered it is not always joyous and beneficial to have four wives! I couldn't help but chuckle inwardly as we turned away.

Locating the shop, we spent quite an interesting time viewing and evaluating merchandise. We found it necessary to calculate the Arab price into American dollars in order to determine if the article was worth the priced amount. Our English-speaking Arab salesman was trying his best for a profitable sale. At one point when I was deep in calculations concerning a certain article, he continuously chattered an unceasing sales pitch in my ear! Automatically, trying to arrest his interruptions, I answered, "Ken, Ken!" ("Yes, Yes!" in Hebrew).

Immediately his tone changed, "Oh, you want to speak in Hebrew, do you?" and off he went into a fluent Hebrew! I stood as though glued to the spot—tensed, afraid even to look up at him!

Completely ignoring his outburst in Hebrew, hoping he would think I didn't understand and all the while praying to the Lord for help, I pondered whether to run or to cry out, "You can't touch me; I'm an American citizen!" Glancing helplessly at my companion, I saw in an instant he didn't know what to do either.

Then as suddenly as the storekeeper had started his obvious tirade, he quieted and said in English, "So you have been on the Israeli side—how long? As a tourist?"

Before we could say much he went on, "Well, I hold nothing against the Jews. I used to have a shop over there and some of the Jews were my best customers, until I had to flee and could not return. I still have property and relatives over there."

We knew how the Arab leaders had told their people to flee, promising they would soon return, not knowing that Jewish strength and later the United Nations division of the land would make the return for many impossible. We nodded sympathetically and hurried to make our purchases. Within a few minutes we were out on the street again, lifting our relieved hearts heavenward in praise and thanksgiving for the Lord's protecting hedge about us, and inwardly determined never to slip with the Hebrew again.

CHAPTER XXIV

EASTER AT THE GARDEN TOMB

EASTER SUNRISE SERVICE at the garden tomb, near Gordon's Calvary outside the present city walls, was scheduled for 4:30 a.m. We had greatly looked forward to the experience of arriving at the garden tomb early, before the rising of the the sun, as the two Marys and Salome did that first resurrection morning.

Rising while the city still lay hushed in sleep, we quietly made our way through the dark, chilly streets to Damascus Gate. Glancing at our watches by flashlight, we saw it was ten minutes before 4:00 a.m.—time enough to go for two of our companions staying at a mission on the Mt. of Olives and to return to the garden by 4:30. To our complete astonishment we were confronted with a closed Damascus Gate guarded from without! We had not been aware that we had been locked up within the city each night. At first we were disheartened. Would we be able to get to our destination by 4:30 with this delay? Lifting our prayer to the Lord and our voices in request to the guard, we rejoiced to hear the gates slide open and free us at 4:00 a.m.

Hurrying together with our companions who had been waiting for us, we arrived in the early dawn at the garden. How precious to watch the sun slowly rise over the broken-off hill of Mt. Calvary, the place of the skull, and spill its glorious light over onto the gray tomb, gradually dispelling all darkness. Our hearts swelled within us as our voices jubilantly sang forth, "He arose, He arose, Hallelujah Christ arose!"

Then together, saints by His grace, we broke bread, remembering Him until His coming again.

A little later what a precious privilege it was for us to walk into that sepulchre, very possibly the exact one where He was laid, and behold its beautiful emptiness. There were ledges at the foot and head of the grave—possibly where the angels had sat. We sat down, too, and read again the accounts of the resurrection. Meditating upon those sacred events recorded in the twentieth chapter of John's Gospel, I could visualize grief-stricken Mary coming to the tomb early that morning. Knowing the soul-agony of the total loss of the one held most dear, carried me back in feeling to her experience, her world. Captured by the inspiration of the moment I saw her:

The small frame was bent as though she carried the weight of the world upon her shoulders. The agony of the past few days had left its mark upon her frail body. The once rosy cheeks were unnaturally thin and sallow, emphasizing high cheek bones. The pain-filled eyes could not seem to see the cheerfulness of the first sunbeams dancing their way over dew-soaked blades of grass. Even the playful little gusts of fresh morning air could not lift the dejected chin. She could not see the beauty of the morning, so dark was the night in her heart.

The others were gone now, and the sudden quietness of the countryside made her feel very tired. A cloudy mist filled her eyes, and the storm that had been gathering suddenly broke forth in a gush of tears. As though she could bear the burden no longer, she sank to her knees.

Choking sobs drifted out upon the morning air, and the pitiful form shook as though all of the anguish in that lonely heart must break the body. All the hopelessness and distress that had come down through the ages seemed to be gathered here in this one aching heart.

Almost as suddenly as the storm within had broken forth, it subsided. Weakly she pulled herself up to peer again into the empty sepulchre. Tired, swollen eyes beheld two white-robed figures sitting where her Lord had lain. Her senses, dulled by the agony she felt within her breast, could not perceive the meaning of the presence of these white-robed figures. To her tired brain the soft angelic voices almost seemed to come from another world. "Woman, why weepest thou?"

Empty eyes stared straight ahead. Slowly her lips fashioned the words, "Because they have taken away my Lord, and I know not where they have laid him."

Absorbed in her grief, she slowly rose and turned from the tomb. Mist-filled eyes faintly perceived a form standing before her.

Again the words echoed in her ears. "Woman, why weepest thou?"

A faint hope stirred within her tortured breast. "Sir, if thou have borne him hence, tell me where thou hast laid him, and I will take him away." Humbly she dropped her eyes to the ground, fearing the answer.

". . .Mary. . ." There was only One whose voice contained such tenderness! Its very tone quickened the faint hope within her and sent new life and strength surging through her body.

Quickly lifting her face her eyes once again looked into the Master's. The lifeless face became radiant with joy. The tired body became erect, and a new light shone forth from the once empty eyes.

"Rabboni! Master!" Suddenly the dark night was over; dawn had broken through. She had found her Master, and He was alive!

Though centuries later, the hearts of us who also had found the living Master rejoiced with her. Contrary to the normal experience of this life, rather than bringing pain, hopelessness, and depression as a place of death and separation generally does, this tomb brought sweet joy and hope to our souls. We did not look for even one of His bones, for even as the Scriptures declare in Psalm 16:10, His body did not see corruption. The hollow emptiness of this place proclaimed anew to us the triumphant message of the angels of long ago, "He is risen!" The full meaning was comprehended by us in His own words, "Because I live ye shall live also" (John 14:19).

We climbed up Gordon's Calvary. In a way it seemed significant to find this hill still a place of death, being occupied today by a Mohammedan cemetery. It is believed by many to be the actual scene of the cross because of the face of the skull clearly etched by nature into the side of the hill, giving this place the ancient name of Golgotha, "the place of the skull" (John 19:17). We felt that our feet were treading upon hallowed ground as we climbed the altar of Calvary where the

Victim became the Victor over our sins and death.

Going back into the city, we made our way through the congested, narrow streets and along crooked, dark passageways toward the southeast corner, eventually emerging upon what at first appeared to be an immense stone-paved park, with only a small area given over to grass and trees. Small tufts of grass or weeds here and there forced their way up between the blocks of stone, which were once trod by the feet of the Aaronic priesthood and other pious Jews in days when Solomon's Temple, and later Herod's reconstructed temple, had stood here in all of their grandeur. This tiny hill, known to Abraham as Mt. Moriah, where God spared Isaac from sacrifice, later to become the threshing floor that David would purchase for the building of the temple, had remained essentially unchanged from apostolic days after Titus' destruction of the Temple in 70 A.D.

Near the center, erected over the rock believed to have upheld the burnt-altar in the courtyard of the Jewish temple, is the Moslem shrine, the Dome of the Rock. Entering in, we exchanged our shoes for the required mosque slippers which would not contaminate the oriental rugs of this sacred shrine with particles of the outside world. A flight of steps led beneath the sacrificial rock to a cavern, where a channel cut into the rock for drainage of the blood of the Levitical sacrifices could be traced.

We were shown a flagstone which gives a hollow ring when tapped. Our curiosity, as well as that of many others before us, was whetted concerning what might be found beneath. For reasons of their own the Moslems consistently refuse to permit an investigation of what some believe might possibly unearth the ancient Ark of the Covenant or other Temple vessels mysteriously missing after the destruction of the first temple.

Stepping back out into the brilliant sunlight, we turned eastward toward the blocked up Golden Gate facing the Mt. of Olives through which we felt sure Jesus had made His triumphal entry into Jerusalem just preceding His crucifixion. We marveled at Ezekiel's prophecy concerning it, "Then said the Lord unto me; this gate shall be shut, it shall not be opened, and no man shall enter in by it; because the Lord, the God of Israel, hath entered in by it, therefore it shall be shut. It is for the prince; the prince, he shall sit in it to eat bread before the Lord; he shall enter by the way of the porch of that gate, and shall go out by the way of the same" (Ezek. 44:2, 3).

Even as God had said, this gate today stands blocked up awaiting the time when Israel's Messiah shall stand victoriously upon the Mt. of Olives from whence He ascended into heaven. It is reserved for the resurrected David (Jer. 30:9) who shall be made a prince among the regathered sons of Israel (Ezek. 34:24).

We thrilled to contemplate how soon this might take place. Before that, however, another Temple must one day grace this very area, the Temple in which Antichrist during the time of Jacob's Trouble will place his image to be worshipped. Only the withholding hand of God, in conjunction with His schedule, has kept the rebuilding of that Temple from being a present reality.

We recalled that during the War of Liberation, the Israeli Army was marching toward the Temple area ready to take it, when their attention was diverted elsewhere momentarily leading them away from the area, not to have the opportunity of capturing it repeated at the time. Subsequently, with the dividing of Jerusalem, access to the area by Israel was denied, and would be until her recent victories, apparently in God's foreordained time.

From a good source we had heard that the blueprints are already drawn up for the rebuilding of the Temple and various parts of its construction as well as the furniture it will contain have been prepared and made ready for the given time. I remembered learning that the orthodox section in New Jerusalem has a school to teach young men of the priestly line how biblically to perform the animal sacrifices. The stage is indeed prepared and set!

Leaving the immediate Temple area we wandered down a narrow winding lane, and turning a corner, discovered the ancient wailing wall. This was believed to be the only fragmentary remains of the Temple wall when it was destroyed by the Roman soldiers led by Titus. Through the centuries until the division of the land in 1948, Jewish people had come to this wall to bewail the fact that they had no temple at which to make their sacrifices, and to plead with God to send their Messiah and deliver them from Gentile oppression.

Many believed that the Lord's compassion had never completely forsaken these stones. Some had written prayers on scraps of paper and stuck them into the crevices between the stones, while others in anguish of heart and soul had beaten their fists against the wall until the smooth stone had worn away, leaving the imprint of their mourning.

It was tragic, we reflected, that they had not yet come to understand that God had permitted the destruction of the Temple because there was no longer need for the animal sacrifices! They were once for all fulfilled in Jesus Christ. And when they as a nation do finally receive Him as their long-awaited Messiah, He will deliver them from Gentile oppression. We longed that He might hasten the day of Israel's redemption.

One evening at the Christ Church I picked up a commentary on the book of Ruth, and opening at chapter three began reading. It spoke of Ruth's need of rest in a home of her own. The settled feeling of having put down one's roots brings cessation of restlessness to the spirit and a sense of belonging as nothing else does. It so perfectly described my need! I read on of the love of Boaz for her, and his reluctance to be assertive about it. The author surmised that there must have been a light in his eyes for Ruth that Naomi saw. I wondered if the Lord were speaking to me? Could the warmth and light sometimes in Mike's eyes when we were together have the same source, love?

Our four days in Jordan were all too quickly behind us. Reluctantly we tore ourselves away from cherished Bible places and headed back toward Mandelbaum Gate. As we approached it this time, I wasn't concerned as to whether my name had cleared with Jordan, even though I had heard nothing from them. My trip across had been accomplished, and I now possessed a number of exposed color films of many of the holy places. However, my name was on the list this time. So, without further complication, we stepped over an imaginary line, leaving behind the world of yesterday, and greeted "Shalom" to the world of tomorrow.

CHAPTER XXV

JOURNEYINGS OFTEN

WITH JORDAN TUCKED AWAY securely in my unforgettable memories of past experience, the inactivity of the present renewed my problem concerning the immediate future. Circumstances rendered it mandatory that I soon ascertain the will of the Lord regarding remaining in Israel or returning home. My reason and logic pointed back to the United States and an active ministry, but my heart was so completely lost to this land and people it was difficult to think in terms of leaving without the hope of returning in the near future.

Continual beseeching prayer, in the attitude of a heart completely surrendered to His will, ascended heavenward that He might reveal His perfect plan and by His Spirit lead me accordingly. Time, in view of eternity, plus the great need to propagate the priceless Gospel, was too precious to allow it to slip away, lost to eternal dividends, merely to satisfy even a proper love. Nor did my finances at this point permit the possibility of an indefinite stay.

In the midst of my contemplations, I was invited to travel across Europe with three other missionaries who were leaving the land at the end of May. With the exchange rate on the American dollar, the cost to go home by way of Europe would be approximately the same as to fly home directly. If I were to return home soon, this perhaps would afford me the once-in-a-lifetime opportunity of a wonderful experience which I would not dare to attempt alone. My restlessness of spirit within began prodding in that direction. Unless the Lord opened a place and work for me in the land within the next several weeks, joining them appeared the wise thing to do.

Meanwhile, when a more immediate invitation was extended to join a two-day tour through the northern part of the country, I was glad for the further opportunity to acquire color pictures. Later it would be fully evident that this was of the Lord's directing in preparation for a ministry in the States.

Seven of us piled into a well-seasoned, time-worn station wagon one crisp morning and headed for Tiberias, stopping at each significant place along the way to capture it on film. Vibrant fellowship around the living Word and stirring testimony fed an inner hunger which many hours spent alone had created.

Arriving at Tiberias late in the afternoon we searched out a place to appease our physical hunger. Choosing a restaurant on the lake shore we enjoyed a fish caught in the waters of Galilee, amazingly called "Peter's Fish."

Later in the evening we sought out the crest of a nearby hill overlooking the dimly lighted Tiberias below us. Aware of the lost multitude out in that darkness, our hearts were moved with compassion. The car became a sanctuary of prayer as we each in turn beseeched the Lord to open a way for the Gospel of Christ to shine through the darkness of those unenlightened souls. And we felt assured that much was accomplished in behalf of slumbering Israel that night.

One of the members of our party, a Hebrew Christian businessman from Dayton, Ohio, sponsored a radiocast to the Jews of that area. Desiring a unique and colorful background effect for the making of a tape to be released later on his program, we rented a boat early the next morning and rowed out on the Sea of Galilee. We had just finished recording song and testimony on tape, when the sea began to roll. Quite suddenly a blast of wind had swept down from the surrounding hills upon the waters, surprisingly like we had read of in the time of Christ. The resulting choppiness of the waves tossed our helpless little boat to and fro. Now we could comprehend the suddenness of the storm which had alarmed the disciples centuries before. And it was to this same Jesus to whom they had turned that we also turned for help! Centuries later, though unseen, His presence was just as real and His power still as dynamic. We did not hear the words, "Peace be still," but just as suddenly, as though we were reading the account rather than living it, all quieted down again. The winds and the waves still obey His voice, and we rejoiced to experience His power in this land where multitudes had once marveled at this Almighty One.

Resuming our journey northward, we found lush green hills in the upper Galil lavishly displaying an abundance of wild flowers. Not far from a gay field of bright red poppies, we gazed across the waters of Lake Hule, the waters of ancient Merom, to the faintly visible snow-capped Mt. Hermon in the distance. We saw the beginnings of a water project, which would tremendously help to quench the insatiable thirst of both Jordan and Israel's arid land, but sadly destined to wasteful delay by a pernicious hostility against Israel even though it was to Jordan's own detriment and defeat.

Our return trip took us into Haifa where we visited a Christian children's home. The children, so responsive and eager for attention and love, captivated my heart. Could this be a place of service for me—helping to teach and train these little Jewish ones, with an outreach to those around? The possibilities warranted my seeking the mind of the Lord concerning this. Accepting an invitation to return for an extended visit might reveal the answer.

Our brimful hearts spilled over in song the last miles of our journey homeward. While we sang the miles away, dusk turned to night as we began the ascent up into the Judean hills. How adeptly the Psalmist had declared, "As the mountains are round about Jerusalem so the Lord is round about his people . . . forever" (Ps. 125:2). Rounding one of the last curves before entering Jerusalem, our eyes caught a glimpse of the lights of the Holy City flickering in the distance. Unitedly we broke forth in our favorite, "Jerusalem, Jerusalem, lift up your gates and sing; Hosanna in the Highest, Hosanna to your King!"

Left alone again with time on my hands because of want of spiritual activity, the restlessness which for a while had been dormant, was back to plague me. In contemplation of various possible activities, I could not escape the inner sense of feeling so incomplete, so inadequate, so handicapped alone. Everything within me intensely yearned for what to me was so obviously the perfect answer—the fulfillment of being a help-meet to Mike in the Jewish ministry. As the Lord had not been pleased to fill my inner lack and need in any other way, I allowed myself the hope that He intended to satisfy this longing with fulfillment.

Often when presenting my case in detail before the Lord, I sensed a peace and joy in this conclusion, and at such times by faith I presumed to consider us as betrothed by God until He should bring us together or show me otherwise. During one such height of faith while passing by a shop window, I was greatly attracted to a simple but lovely silver-plated set of glass holders. The urge to buy it as an Israeli memento for a wedding present for Mike and me was so strong I could not resist.

Greatly elated over my purchase I hurried home with my precious possession held snugly within my arm. Having passed through the front door of the YMCA, I turned toward the elevator to come face to face with Mike. He showed no visible notice of my unusual surprise and was warm and sweet as always. Inwardly I chuckled, not daring to tell him my little secret—that the package held so lovingly within my arm was our first wedding present! I was sure he would like it as well as I.

Later I was to learn that for some time he had been praying the Lord would give me a husband, so convinced he was of my need for a companion and protector. Many who have traversed this path before have learned through experience that one should be careful how he prays! It is not uncommon for the Lord to use the invoker to answer his own petition!

Days of decision were drawing near. My rent was nearly due at the "Y" and my financial status still left me with insufficient funds for another month's rent. In His perfect timing the Lord undertook for the immediate need by opening the door for me to accompany a couple of missionary ladies on a trip to Nazareth on the very day that my rent terminated.

Then upon returning to Jerusalem I consummated plans to accept the earlier gracious invitation to visit at the children's home in Haifa. Two missionaries from Jerusalem were driving there with a one-night stopover in Tel Aviv en route.

This proved beneficial to me in that I was able to claim at the American Express a check which I had been anticipating from home. Was it significant that this would cover the major portion of my boat ticket through the Mediterranean if I were to leave with the missionaries going through Europe? The door appeared definitely to be opening in that direction.

My days at the children's home in some ways proved very rewarding. Though working with the little ones was enjoyable, it did not challenge my mind or spiritual life. Hence, I soon became aware that it was not satisfying that deep inner need within my soul to be used of Him in His place. Within a few days the still small voice within had spoken, "This is not my place of service for you, either." Restlessness began to creep in and I knew it would soon be time to move on again.

While at the home I met Diana, a seventeen-year-old Jewess from Baghdad. Her story was heartrending, as is generally true of the majority of the Israelis. When she was thirteen years of age her aunt and cousins were leaving Baghdad for the newly formed state of Israel, by an Israeli plane sent to transport freely any Jews desiring to emigrate to the new state in accordance with the Law of Return. They pleaded with Diana's family to accompany them. But her family, prosperous in business, felt they could not at this time in life give up everything, only then necessarily, to start all over again in Israel.

When Iraq agreed to let her Jews go to Israel, she refused to allow them to take out with them anything of value, including jewelry, watches, pens—even top coats! Then all their property and goods left behind were confiscated by the government.

The cousins who were close to her begged Diana to go with them. She wanted to accompany them, not understanding that for political reasons there could be no return from Israel to this Arab country.

The afternoon arrived for the scheduled airflight to Israel. Diana had been napping as was their custom, alongside her mother. Quietly without awakening her, Diana slipped away and hurried to the airport with only a few belongings, thinking she would be back in a few days. Her mother, upon awakening, found Diana gone and hurried to the airport but only in time to see the plane airborne and her child thus torn from her life.

After Diana arrived in Israel and learned that she could not return to her dearly beloved mother, the realization of what she had done flooded upon her. And to add to the heartbreak there is no mail interchange between Israel and Iraq since the Arab countries, as much as is possible, refuse to recognize or acknowledge Israel's existence.

When Diana learned I might be returning to the States, hope of contact with her family was born anew in her heart. She beseeched me to be an intermediary for correspondence between them, and I gladly agreed. How greatly they must have longed for word of her these past four years. They had been dark, lonely years for this child separated from mother love, except for the salvation she had found in her Messiah. Here at the children's home this little Jewess had found the Hope of Israel.

During my stay at the home, Israel celebrated her sixth birthday. It was thrilling to see the expressed joy of this ingathered people who for so long a time had been strangers and exiles from their God-given land. For two evenings the streets were literally filled with wholesome gaiety and celebration. All vehicles were at a standstill in the main part of town. Everywhere was the joyous sound of singing and one could barely press his way through the throng of folkdancers. Until the darkness of the night was absorbed by the rays of the dawn the Horah, which has become as much a part of Israel as her national anthem the Hatikva, was danced in the streets.

The height of the celebration was the impressive Independence Day parade. Herein was displayed a tremendous show of Israel's military might, the pride and strength of this pioneer people with an unquenchable spirit.

As darkness fell, ships in Haifa harbor fired bright rockets into the black sky above. In my mind they represented the brightness and hope Israel had brought into the darkened lives of so many oppressed, suffering, homeless Jews. Their joy now, as well as their sorrow, was mine to share. Deep within it was painfully real how very difficult it would be to say goodbye to this land I had learned to love so dearly.

More and more I was sensing that door behind me closing and the inner assurance that the Lord's way, at least for the present was leading back home to California. The Lord, knowing my heartbreak in departing, gave consolation to my spirit, "Delight thyself also in the Lord and he shall give thee the desires of thine heart" (Ps. 37:4). He seemed to be saying, "Trust Me. This is my perfect way for fulfillment." Also I was becoming convinced that I had to find that inner satisfaction, the sense of belonging in a work, and rest in companionship, before I could truly be lastingly content anywhere.

As I thus began to formulate my return plans, my financial importunity had to be faced. There was only enough money for a boat ticket through the Mediterranean to Genoa, Italy. There would have to be money for the trip through Europe and the crossing of the Atlantic. I was convicted about asking anyone but the Lord for my needs since He had led me into a walk of total faith in Him. After praying and waiting upon Him, He had not moved hearts to supply my need. At the time I could not understand, but would later learn His purposes in withholding. (There were further lessons in faith to be learned!) Finally I concluded as the time drew near that the only thing I could do was to draw on an investment I had made with an uncle at home. And so instructions were sent home for my receiving of the necessary amount before our sailing date.

My last days in Israel were days of sweet sorrow. As one who is about to be parted indefinitely from one who has captured his heart, my eyes absorbed everywhere the wonderful sights that bespoke Israel to me, and I tried to commit as much of it as possible to memory. This would later bring hours of pleasurable recapture when my heart would ache for this lost love.

Fleeing again to "my book" I took courage from my biblical namesake. When the little Moabitess knew her days in the field were approaching an end, she too had faced an unknown future. As she looked across the once yellow fields now left almost bare by the reapers, she must have wondered what lay in store for her. She had so enjoyed the times of fellowship with Boaz in the field. Would their paths cross again? Could she but know that the leaving of the fields was to culminate in the fulfillment of her heart's desires, she surely would not have felt so reluctant to leave.

For me the assurance within that He doeth all things well, and that He had my future also planned His perfect way, brought emotional stability.

As an added consolation there was a new assurance that

CHAPTER XXVI

SHALOM ISRAEL

MY LAST WEEK IN ISRAEL was at hand. The weather was warm and balmy, especially pleasant in the Galil, where one could enjoy wooded hills and terraced valleys, babbling brooks and tall palms, the bleating of sheep and the song of birds.

Gladly I had accepted as from the Lord an invitation to spend a few days with one of the missionaries with whom I had recently crossed into Jordan. Elna, a nurse at the Scotch Mission Hospital in Tiberias, had made arrangements for another missionary friend and me to occupy a room in the nurses' quarters.

The pleasure of fellowship during balmy evenings spent on Elna's balcony overlooking the inky sea was augmented by the beauty of a huge yellow ball of a moon which appeared to rise up out of the eastern side of the sea, painting a silvery path across it. Psalmist David had so eloquently expressed the testimony of creation to the Creator. "The heavens declare the glory of God and the firmament sheweth his handiwork. Day unto day uttereth speech and night unto night sheweth knowledge. There is no speech nor language where their voice is not heard" (Ps. 19:1–3).

Awakening at 5:30 in the morning, we were amazed to find the sun was already high. We breakfasted on the balcony, enjoying the contrasting blues of sea and sky, benefiting to the utmost from the warm, clean morning air. The serenading of our little winged friends bore testimony to their enjoyment of God's creation also. A little later strolling leisurely down by the sea, I felt I understood why the Son of God had loved it here so well. Still present was a rugged, naked beauty and a marked peacefulness not as yet marred by progress or commercialism.

Swimming in the cold fresh Galilee was most refreshing after the afternoon's torrid heat. One afternoon, hiking down past the scanty ruins of Magdala, birthplace of Mary Magdalene, we stopped to visit at the YMCA. Built beside a little cove fed with bubbling hot springs, it proved an even more delightful place to swim—especially in the warm moonlit evenings. After one such pleasurable evening our gracious host offered to escort us by motor boat back to the shores of Tiberias. It was difficult to determine whether it was the cool spray of the water upon the balmy air, or the thrilling sensation of sailing up that silvery path flowing down from the giant moonball in the heavens before us that sent a little chill up my spine. At that moment it would have been easy, beckoned by a visible Saviour, to have stepped out upon that shimmering sea, expecting it to hold me. And I knew without question that He was beckoning me to step out upon the uncertain future before me, made sure by His undergirding power and lighted by His radiant light from heaven.

My financial situation had not improved except for a gift that enabled me to meet my last expenses in the land and ship my trunk home. Even though I fairly plagued the American Express office, the money from my uncle had not as yet arrived the very day of sailing. How distressing it could have been had I known of a conversation just that day back home. My uncle was on the telephone calling mother, "When does Ruth need the money I am to send?"

Mother's answer set things in motion, "Today!"

"Then I had better wire it immediately!" But of course it was already too late to be received by me before sailing. Nonetheless, the inner conviction that my plans had been directed by Him and that I was to be on that ship, prompted a step of faith that might have appeared foolish in the eyes of the world. Knowing that as the Lord guides He also provides, I dared to board ship with one American dollar in my possession.

I knew the money was available to me, but why it had not come I could not understand. On my last trip to the American Express in Tel Aviv, just hours before sailing time, I left instructions for any money received for me to be wired to the

American Express in Genoa, Italy, my port of call. Now it was in His hands alone!

It was impossible to hold back the tears as I said "Shalom" to Eretz Israel (the land of Israel) in my heart. I knew, the Lord willing, I must someday come this way again. A vital part of my love and prayers—even of my very heart—would always belong to her, and I would forever cherish the precious eleven months I had been privileged to share with her.

A group of our missionary friends surprised us at the dock, desiring to send the four of us off with God's blessing. Among them was Mike who was also due to leave Israel in about two weeks. He, however, planned to fly directly to London, arriving there before I. His plans also included calling on Miriam, who as yet had not experienced re-birth, to be followed up by my arrival in London soon after. Mike had agreed to check my post office box in Jerusalem and leave any mail for me that might possibly arrive after my departure at the American Express in London. I was unaware that this was going to be the means of a special blessing for me there.

Ann, whose destination was New York, had received a farewell card from some of her Christian friends in Jerusalem. Along with their signatures each had included a Scripture reference. Irene, also from the States, was reading off the references as Ann looked them up in the Bible. She unintentionally quoted First instead of Second Thess. 3:1, and Ann read, "Wherefore when we could no longer forbear, we thought it good to be left at Athens alone." The humor of the error was enjoyed by all as we teased Ann that she had better beware of getting left at Athens alone. It might not have struck us as funny had we then known what was to occur in Athens! But in the end we would appreciate the Lord's obvious sense of humor.

Just before 9 p.m. our little Italian steamer weighed anchor and set sail. As we moved slowly and unobtrusively out of Haifa harbor, we lingered on deck for a last, longing view of our beloved Israel. How beautiful did the lights of Haifa appear, studded, as it were, on the side of the Carmel like a multitude of brilliant diamonds on a dark velvet setting.

CHAPTER XXVII

THROUGH THE MEDITERRANEAN

THE SEA WAS CALM AND QUIET and we slept well, perhaps from emotional exhaustion as much as anything, our first hot night out upon the Mediterranean. The next morning we dropped anchor just offshore from the ancient isle of Cyprus. Learning it was to be a two-hour stopover we went ashore by motor launch at a cost of fifty cents per person.

Looking over the semi-desert terrain, so like the land of Israel, it was difficult in this peaceful atmosphere to visualize the inhumanities 53,000 Jews had suffered here up to six short years ago. Refugees from Hitler's inferno forced to exist in camps in Germany long after the war was ended for want of a place to go, seeking a chance to live again, had tried to emigrate to Palestine during the years between World War II and Israel's declared statehood. Because of the extremely limited immigration quota allowed into British Palestine, multitudes sought to enter illegally. When apprehended they were forcibly deported, some back where they had come from, many to barbed-wire detention camps on Cyprus. Here they found themselves in some respects under conditions no different from that which they had fled in Germany. Imprisoned by their friends, some were to languish here for months and even years awaiting the rebirth of their beloved nation.

We felt inward anguish to remember the atrocities enacted against this people, first by her enemies and then by her friends, for the express and unhappy crime of having been born a Jew. We took up Isaiah's cry, Israel has indeed suffered double for her sins! How different it could have been had she received her Messiah when He came to her the first time.

By our second day at sea, satanic suggestions of fear and doubt concerning the future began to press in on me. What would I do if the money were not waiting for me in Genoa? My present reserve had been reduced to fifty cents by now! Faith struggled to the surface and reasoned, "Surely if the Lord has brought me this way, then He will not fail me in Genoa." The enemy does not surrender easily. The seeds of worry cast upon my mind were now more vulnerable because of the fresh pain of giving up the land that I loved so dearly. What of the future upon returning home? Would things be any different or any better there than in my beloved Israel? As of now there was no definite indication of His plan for me and the future looked dark ahead.

Victory lay in trust—at this time blind trust, and the promise of the Word. Isaiah 45:2, 3: "I will go before thee, and make the crooked places straight . . . and I will give thee the treasures of darkness, and hidden riches of secret places, that thou mayest know that I, the Lord, which call thee by thy name, am the God of Israel," spoke comfort and encouragement to my soul. I was asked to live only one day at a time and today the path was clear before me.

Ruth 2:18 stood out clearly in my reading, "And she took it up, and went into the city: and her mother in law saw what she had gleaned and she brought forth, and gave to her that she reserved after she was sufficed." Following in Ruth's footsteps I, too, was now leaving the fields in God's planning possibly in order to share with my mother-in-law the much that I had gleaned from my Boaz and his field, Israel!

Perhaps to encourage my heart that I was of a surety in the center of His perfect will, He brought me in contact with a twenty-two-year-old Jewish lad from Athens, Greece. It was obvious that Micki was a troubled boy with a hungry heart. Relaxing on deck while watching the lush green hills emerge out of the glassy sea along the Turkish coast, our conversation was easily turned to a spiritual discussion. Upon learning of my belief, he questioned me concerning the difference between Judaism and Christianity.

Here and there one could glimpse a few isolated houses nestled back among the trees on the hills. Picturesquely a peasant with a few sheep appeared along a pathway just visible in the distance. Inspired by the conversation and the scenery, we spent a profitable four hours discussing spiritual things, employing mostly Hebrew and English. At one point, when all efforts had failed to bring to his understanding the meaning of the righteousness of Christ, which we must have imputed to us to stand before a Holy God, the Holy Spirit brought to my remembrance the New Testament Greek word for holy. Immediately a light of understanding crossed his face, and ground was definitely gained.

Unfortunately, Micki's scientific mind and errant teachings were a stumbling block to his believing in miracles or accepting the Bible as the Word of God. He reminded me of the intellectual and philosophizing Greeks whom the Apostle Paul had encountered in Athens.

The following day we put in at Piraeus, the port city near Athens. Before disembarking Micki did accept a Gospel of John in French (supplied by one of my companions), promising to read it through ten times, all the while asking the God of Israel to show him the truth. Content to rest my case in the powers of the living Word, my prayers followed Micki as he departed, and I earnestly hoped to meet him again—on those golden shores of eternity.

When we learned the ship would be nearly two hours in port, Irene and I decided to go ashore and take a train the few miles into Athens to sight-see. We were impressed with a bustling, thriving city, the modern influence of the Western world set in contrast alongside the ancient culture of the Eastern world so familiar to us by now.

We just missed one return train, but felt unconcerned as we had already learned the ship never sailed according to schedule. Arriving back at port, Irene was sauntering a little ahead of me as we passed along a crowded wharf. I noticed someone said something to her but thought nothing of it, until suddenly she turned and called, "Hurry!" and with that broke into a run. Following closely at her heels, as we came out onto the dock I saw our ship slowly beginning to pull away. The gangplank alongside the ship was already about two feet in the air! The steward who had been frantically watching for us ran down the elevated gangplank and grabbed us by our hands pulling us onto the steps at the last possible moment. Looking back as we climbed up to the deck, we were startled to see the distance between us and the dock widening rapidly!

After catching our breaths and apologizing for the anxiety we had caused, we suddenly remembered Ann's mistaken verse, ". . . to be left at Athens alone." The joke was not on Ann but on us! Had the Lord been trying to warn us of our near plight? Or was it one of those marvelous displays of divine humor? How thankful we were for His overruling love, and how good the ship felt beneath our feet!

Our voyage took us through the four-mile-long Corinth Canal, sliced out between rock mountains. As we sailed out into the Gulf of Corinth, we could faintly perceive evidence of old Corinth on the distant shore where Paul preached centuries ago. It was a special blessing to remember his ceaseless zeal for his own people dispersed among the Gentiles. Oh, that the Lord would raise up more Pauls among the Jewish exiles today!

It was night when we passed between the toe of Italy's boot and Sicily. The latter, set ablaze with light, was beautifully triumphant over the surrounding blackness. In the inspiration of the moment, we broke forth with hymns and were happy to be exuberantly accompanied by a Swedish Christian group aboard.

Two of our party, Margaret, who was returning to Switzerland, and Irene left us at Naples on our fifth day at sea. Their plans were to rejoin Ann and me in Florence, Italy, within three days. The following afternoon Ann and I were glad to say Shalom as well to our little Italian ship, having been on the verge of sea sickness from the pitching and rocking caused by choppy seas the last two days. With a mixed sense of fear and hopefulness we headed at once for the American Express office in Genoa. What a relief and joy to find my money waiting!

CHAPTER XXVIII

A STRANGER IN EUROPE

EVERYWHERE THERE WAS STILL evidence of the severe bombings Genoa had suffered during World War II. In spite of the presence of destruction, the tourist could not miss her great pride in being able to boast the birthplace of Christopher Columbus, or her glorious past as the Mediterranean's once principal city. The presence of trolley cars, numerous neon signs, and large, modern deparment stores, so foreign to the Near East from which we had come, reminded me of America and made my departure from Israel more of a reality to me.

My heart yearned to turn and flee back to Israel. However, the still small voice within reminded that for the present there was only a closed door in that direction and no matter how intense the impulse, I must not turn back but press on in the direction of His leading. A quiet assurance underneath gave renewed stability and peace, the strength to go on, to ignore the heartache which backward glances brought. It seemed my lot in life was always to give up that which I loved most. I hoped this might be the final test to prove my love for Him supreme, that He would see fit to entrust me with possession of the loves of my heart. I had determined that never again by His grace would I ever allow a love for anyone or anything to become an idol in my life. I had clearly learned that though there is a special sweetness poured into the soul from a heart wound inflicted by His love, there is only sour bitterness excreted from the heart broken by self's assertions and demands.

The next day Ann and I departed by rail for Florence, arriving several hours later in a spring downpour. Missionary friends of Ann's welcomed us. After a time of refreshing and fellowship, our hosts took us on a tour of this very fascinating historic center of the arts. We gazed with due respect upon the tokens of her famous past and people: Michelangelo's David, paintings by Leonardo Da Vinci and Raphael among others, and the unexcelled bronze doors of Ghiberti, pronounced by Michelangelo as worthy to be the gates of paradise!

With a feeling of solemnity we stood before the very spot where Savonarola, a Hebrew Christian, was burned at the stake for his open stand against ecclesiastical corruption. We were informed that lack of religious freedom persists to this day, making Protestant missionary activity difficult, quite comparable to the situation we had experienced in Israel.

Ann was not able to resume her travels homeward immediately, so when Irene and Margaret, who had rejoined us by now, announced they were going on to Venice, I decided to accompany them. By late afternoon we had arrived in this city of canals and bridges built on the gulf of Venice in the Adriatic Sea. Leaving the train, we caught a "bus boat" for the San Marcus Square, popular with pigeons and tourists alike! It was soon apparent to our aching feet that the mechanical age had hardly touched Venice, whose populace moved about by foot or by boat!

Looking beyond the old, dirty exterior of this musty-smelling city whose narrow streets crossed and recrossed its winding canals, we found it uniquely quaint and romantic. Margaret spoke enough Italian to enable us to make our way about with ease. Through inquiry we obtained rooms for the night in the tidy home of three pleasant spinsters, who seemed very odd, though perhaps no more to us than we to them!

In the evening we took a ride around the darkened city in a gondola. Finding our way to the ghetto section, we attended a Sabbath service in an ancient synagogue, which surprisingly boasted some forty Jews in attendance. Our hearts ached for these yet oppressed outside their land and without their Messiah. We rejoiced that Margaret, because of her Italian, was able to witness to one of the Jewish women.

Perhaps it was because of the dark waterways between the buildings confining one to the city, as well as the lack of open sunny fields, green trees and soft grass, that caused us to feel that Venice was pervaded with the feeling of oppression and darkness. The contrast to our next stop, Switzerland, was beyond expression.

Leaving the dank, deteriorating old world behind, we traveled into the Alps with their breathtaking beauty of sweeping green valleys, surrounded by majestic, rugged mountains, lifting their lofty white peaks into blue heavens above.

We fell in love with the charming little villages and towns with their flower-adorned chalets and romantic old castles. It was gratifying to our womanly instinct to find everything, including the streets, kept so clean and tidy. Margaret, at home in her native Switzerland, became our very capable guide to an enchanting world.

Forever after, Switzerland would be to me the peace and quiet of a deep-set valley bed or a sunny plateau surrounded by rocky walls and distant dazzling pyramids covered by eternal snows. In memory would linger the ride in a suspension cable railway to the foot of the stately Jungfrau, an inspiring hike through pine woods and flower-dotted mountain meadows, and the sensation of being at the base of what reminded us of a giant teacup as we encircled the green little village of Lauterbrunnen to view its lovely waterfall.

Reluctantly we turned away from the magnificent Alps and after crossing the placid blue waters of Lake Thun boarded a train for northern parts.

In Berne, Margaret and Irene bid me farewell and departed for Zurich. Plans were for Irene to meet me several days later in Paris while Margaret went on to her home in Switzerland. I felt duty bound to go on alone to Frankfurt, Germany, in order to execute a promise made to one of the missionaries in Israel before I had left.

The three-hour ride alone to the Swiss-German border, where I would change trains, passed quickly as I was caught up in the enjoyment of the never ending array of scenic beauty.

The train departing for Frankfurt was so scheduled as to give me a four-hour wait-over. Checking my bags at the station, I spent the time looking over the city and experiencing my first glimpse of the Rhine River which divides it. My imagination was stirred as I recalled that my Jewish great-grandfather had lived somewhere along the banks of this river in Germany before emigrating to the United States. I

166

shuddered to think what might have been had he and the family remained in Germany.

It was cold and dark by the time I arrived back at the station to board the train again, only to find it late. After awhile, weary of standing, I perched on my suitcase to wait what seemed an eternity. Sitting there in the cold, I watched the hands of the clock slowly move around its stolid face once—almost twice. Alone in a strange country on an almost deserted platform late at night would have been most frightening if it had not been for the assurance of my Father's protecting love and care.

At long last a trainman beckoned me onto a coach in which I found myself the only passenger. With the clickety-clack of the wheels echoing in my ears I settled down to try to get a little rest the remainder of the night.

In a short while the German customs official, swinging a lantern, passed through my car. Addressing me in German he rattled off that which was completely unintelligible to me. When he finally stopped it was with a sense of futility that I could only reply in my language—apparently just as unintelligible to him—"I'm sorry but I can't understand you." To add to the frustration he only rattled back in German, to which I could only reply in English! From previous experience of passing through customs I felt sure he was asking if I had certain articles in my possession. I was equally as sure I had nothing of concern to him, but how to communicate through this impregnable language barrier? Finally, as a last resort, he pointed to my suitcase, which I opened for him. A quick look spoke volumes, convincing him that all was in proper order, and I was passed through German customs without further ado!

Somewhat relieved and tremendously thankful, I settled back again, praying for continued safety and rest.

However, frequent disturbance by the train conductor, as well as my uneasiness at being alone, allowed me little sleep. The first rays of dawn were greatly welcomed and soon after them the first sights of Frankfurt.

Outside the train station I located a policeman who spoke a little English and gained easy directions to my destination. There I found a gracious welcome as I was received out of love for our mutual friend in Israel.

Recently this home had become a refuge for a young girl deserted by her husband. Although she had not as yet found the comfort and peace of the Saviour, she was earnestly seeking help. With my hostess acting as interpreter for us, it was my blessed privilege to share with her the testimony of His grace and comfort in my life. This gave further purpose to my trip here alone and made the difficult night on the train more than worthwhile.

My mission accomplished, I spent the rest of the day sightseeing in Frankfurt and then purchased a ticket for Paris for the next morning. I was not desirous of another night journey! Extremely weary, I retired early that evening. Suddenly at 5:30 a.m. I was awakened out of a sound sleep by the Lord. Hurriedly I dressed, packed and headed for the station, arriving ten minutes before departure. The Lord had not once failed to awaken me in time to meet my schedule since Natanya days when I had turned my dependence from the alarm clock to Him!

The twelve-hour ride from Frankfurt to Paris was long and comparatively uneventful, that is, until we reached the Paris station. Upon arrival, before I could decide my next move, an aggressive red-cap had suddenly grabbed up my bags and hurriedly made his way through the crowds to the front of the depot. Not knowing where to go, by the time I had gotten my bearings and retrieved my bags I had obviously incited the wrath of one red-cap who apparently had missed his opportunity of gaining another tip from another passenger.

Evidently not taking into consideration that he had voluntarily swept away my bags without waiting for solicitation, he burst forth in what I interpreted from the tone of it to be a sound tongue lashing. Bewildered at his French tirade, all I could do was to offer an apology in English and tip him for his services. Realizing the futility of further conversation, he turned and went off muttering to himself.

After obtaining the address of the YWCA I endeavored to board a bus in front of the depot. I was puzzled at first when the bus refused to open its doors to me until I saw it circle and stop across the street. Hurrying over to the proper bus stop, I was again refused entrance and motioned to the other end of the bus. Finally, breathless, and a little embarrassed, I accomplished my purpose, and upon boarding the bus really had to chuckle at myself when I was handed a pamphlet entitled, "To travel by bus and underground like a Parisian."

It was already dusk when I found the YWCA and inquired for a room, only to be told all of their rooms were filled. However, upon request, they graciously gave me the address of a French Christian organization within walking distance. Stepping out onto the darkening street, I quickly made my way to the new address, breathing a prayer with every step, reminding the Lord of my need not only of a room but also of protection and clear guidance.

After locating the correct number it was necessary to make my way down a dark hall and up a dark stairway. By this time it was with some feeling of apprehension that I knocked on the door. It opened to a brightly lighted room with voices of gaiety drifting in from another room. A friendly reception somewhat restored my confidence but left me still in need. No vacancy!

Where to turn now? Understanding my difficult situation as a stranger to Paris, they kindly took it upon themselves to locate by telephone a bed for me at a Girl's Guide Hostel across the city. And then in a further spirit of Christian love they provided me with an escort who took me by Metro (subway) to within walking distance of the Hostel. This time my every step was a prayer of thanksgiving and praise. Once again my heavenly Father had wondrously worked to provide for His needy child.

With a new day and a new burst of energy, I sought out the Cunard Lines office to verify their having received a pre-paid reservation for me on the Queen Mary from London to New York. Along with my request for the money which I had received at Genoa, I had also sent instructions to my uncle regarding obtaining the Queen Mary reservation for me. My efforts were met with disappointment. Not wanting to have to spend another three weeks in Europe alone, and in order to hold space on the next sailing, seven days hence, I put a substantial deposit on a ticket to be refunded should my prepaid reservation come through. I estimated this left me just enough funds, if handled carefully, to see me home to California.

Making my way to the American Express, I welcomed reunion with Irene. Then together we set out to see Paris.

I had discovered from the beginning that the pedestrian

took his life into his own hands whenever attempting to cross any of the busy streets. Traffic laws seemed completely disregarded, and we were amazed there were so few accidents among the uninhibited drivers!

Names which we had previously only read about in history books or in the newspapers became a reality before our eyes— the river Seine, the Eifel Tower, the Arch of Triumph, et cetera.

In spite of my ceaseless activity, Mike was often in my thoughts. If his schedule had not fluctuated from the plans he shared before I left Israel, I knew he should have arrived in New York about now. Did he ever think of me as I so often did of him? Was he content to feel our close relationship which we had known in Israel was a thing of the past? Would we ever meet again here on earth? The answer to these questions remained alone in the knowledge and planning of the Master Engineer who held the blueprints of our future!

A light rain had dogged our footsteps all the way across the continent, so much so that after bidding farewell to a grand Paris we were already acclimatized for the wet voyage across the English Channel. Through fog and drizzles we could only faintly perceive the white cliffs of Dover just before docking in Folkstone, where Irene and I parted company once again. Since her schedule included a trip to Hastings to visit relatives, I traveled on to London alone.

CHAPTER XXIX

LONDON

MINDFUL OF MY LIMITED FUNDS I once again sought out the YWCA for lodging. They could accommodate me for three of the five nights I was scheduled to spend there. This would give ample time to locate, with the Lord's direction, another shelter for my last two nights.

Miriam's voice was warm and friendly on the telephone. Delighted with the prospect of a friend to whom she could show her beloved London, she arranged to meet me for the evening.

In a short time Miriam's familiar figure emerged from a crowded bus at a nearby corner. Within moments I knew she had not yet been born again. It grieved me to find her actually cool toward spiritual things, though I realized perhaps my sole purpose in being here at this time was to stir up the embers of conviction and whet her spiritual appetite once more. She did not try to hide the fact that she desired a solution to her disturbing problems at home.

Miriam had fresh news of Mike. He had been in London just the previous week and had spent an evening with her before sailing for New York. Her news of him only served to stimulate an inner hunger to see him once again. It seemed decades since we had said "Shalom" in Israel, though in reality it had only been eighteen days. Unceasingly my heart craved that rest and sense of completeness which I could only know in the companionship and home of my Boaz. So strong was the desire that it had become second nature to me to look in everything and everywhere for signs from the Lord that He meant to bring my seed of hope to fruition. Even so, it startled me when my eyes first caught sight of the advertising slogan at that time prevalent on many of the London buses, "Insure the future with Pearl." The difference in spelling didn't weaken the inner glow radiated by the thought or quench my heartfelt reply, "Yes, Lord, gladly would I insure the future with Perl!"

The next morning a check at the American Express for the possibility of mail which Mike might have left for me on his sojourn here was unrewarded. In the afternoon Miriam took me to her home to meet her grandmother with whom she lived. I soon saw the basis for some of Miriam's problems. There was little, if any, real love in that home. Because Miriam, an only child, had not fulfilled her family's hopes and plans for her socially, she had become the target of their animosity. I felt relieved for her as well as myself when we resumed our sightseeing excursion. Seated atop a double-decker city bus, Miriam unburdened her heart to me, seeking advice and understanding. This gave opportunity to present the born-again experience all over again as the only adequate and sure answer to her needs.

It had been drizzling most of the day and finally the cold and wet drove us to seek shelter inside. Miriam chose for us the Strand Corner House Cafeteria where the food was good and the surroundings pleasant for further conversing. It appeared many others had the same idea; nonetheless we found places at a table for four which was later vacated to us alone.

Seated across the table from me, Miriam was earnestly seeking help, pouring forth questions which apparently were contributing to the block hindering her salvation. As we lingered, engrossed in discussion, a young couple eventually took the empty seats alongside of us. Much to my surprise and delight I noticed they each bowed their heads, offering a silent grace. Certain they could not help overhearing our conversation, and if Christians, easily discern my dealings with Miriam, I was encouraged to believe they would be holding us up in silent prayer. Before long they began repeating Scripture verses to one another from the Navigators Memory Course packets which I recognized before them on the table. Miriam also noticed this and in a low voice asked of me, "Do you think they are born again?"

I replied, "I can't know definitely, Miriam, but it is usually a sign when people memorize the Bible as they are doing."

For a few minutes she mulled this over in her mind until her curious nature overcame any sense of discretion and she suddenly blurted out, "Excuse me, but are you Hebrew Christians?"

My first reaction was puzzlement as to why she had inserted the word "Hebrew" in addressing them, feeling it would bring confusion; but I was suddenly taken aback to hear the young fellow reply, "As a matter of fact I am!"

David had recently been saved at Billy Graham's London Crusade, and subsequently met Nancy, a Gentile Christian, in the Crusade Choir at Harringay. Fellowship had blossomed into romance, and they were now engaged with the joyful anticipation of building a Christian home together. Miriam was very much impressed with their testimonies, and all thought of time faded into the background as the three of us together encouraged her to come over on the Lord's side. When the lateness of the hour finally demanded attention, before departing, Nancy, having learned I was just passing through London on my way back to the States, earnestly desired that I have dinner with her at her hostel the next evening. I welcomed the prospect of further fellowship.

As I lay on my bed that night listening to the steady patter of the rain outside and pondering the events of the day, I marveled again at the Lord's perfect ways and exact timings, basking in the rich reward of blessing in being used of Him. It could only have been divine direction that placed David and Nancy at our table in the large cafeteria that night, and for a manifold purpose yet to be unfolded before me!

The following morning a trip to the Cunard office revealed the arrival finally of my prepaid ticket, making it possible to finish my booking on the Queen Mary sailing on the 17th, three days hence. I was informed at that time that I could not collect my refund for the deposit made in Paris until back in the States. This would make my financial reserve sorely limited, but with the Lord's help, if I were careful I would make it.

Having heard of the wonderful work of the Hebrew Christian Testimony to Israel Mission in London from Mike and from some of their workers whom I had met in Israel, I greatly desired to visit the work. A telephone call resulted in an invitation to attend their prayer meeting in the afternoon. Their obvious love for Mike, who had been with them the previous week, opened their hearts to me at the mention of his name. It was sweet to carry with me continuously the remnants of the gleanings from his field.

As we shared prayer burdens I related my dealings with Miriam and the events of the previous evening. Again the miraculous working of the Lord in beautiful dove-tailing was in evidence! One of the workers knew David, had lost contact with him, and had been concerned about him.

They took Miriam immediately upon their hearts in prayer and promised to follow her up after my departure. The mission was to have a definite part in her future.

In the evening I joined Nancy at her hostel for dinner according to plan. The young people were warm and friendly and anxious to make me feel at home. When Nancy learned of my need of lodging for the next two nights, she took it upon herself to seek a room for me there at the hostel. Arrangements were made to bring my luggage the next day. My cup of gratitude overflowed in thanksgiving for my heavenly Father's provision which never fails!

After a simple and adequate dinner, Nancy was anxious to introduce to me something of her world, and thus became a gracious hostess and escort to London's famous West End. As any first-timer to London, I was obligingly impressed with the magnificence of the eleven-hundred room Houses of Parliament situated on the edge of the Thames, as well as the famous Big Ben, and Westminster Bridge.

We stopped for a warm cup of tea on the South Bank of the Thames. As we relaxed, enjoying the beauty of the night lights reflected on the dark waters before us, Nancy bared her heart to me, revealing a serious problem that threatened to envelope her future. Her youthful face and entreating eyes expressed the spiritual immaturity of a babe in Christ and an earnest plea for big sisterly advice and assurance.

The Lord's intricate pattern of purpose in our meeting was being revealed as He enabled me to minister to the spiritual needs of this one who had been used of Him to minister to my physical needs. The fellowship and testimony which I could gladly share proved a strengthening force through Nancy's trial and testing.

More time spent with Miriam gave insight into the depths

of her inner struggle. She indicated sincere desire to experience the new birth, but seemed unable to yield her deterring obstacle to the Lord. Her parents had failed to teach her proper parental discipline through the years, resulting in her present difficulty of yielding to any superior. I was encouraged by her honest heart, however, and because of it felt assured she would eventually be saved.

I awakened the morning of my last day in Europe with that sense of anticipation that accompanies the knowledge that this is a somewhat special day—actually the twenty-fifth anniversary of my entrance into this world. I wondered what new (perhaps a birthday) blessing the Lord might have in store for me.

A fascinating London lay at my feet, and I could not leave on the morrow without having taken advantage of its bidding. The early part of the day was spent in watching the colorful changing of the guard at Buckingham Palace, the trappings of England's previous glory, and then visiting the memorials of her notable ones in Westminster Abbey. Later, a thousand years of crowded history paraded before me in the Old Tower of London and St. Paul's Cathedral.

Realizing there might be word from Irene concerning her arrival in London, too, I was prompted in the late afternoon to make another visit to the American Express. I had become aware that when crossing streets I had to watch myself carefully, for it was so natural to look only in the wrong direction before stepping off the curb! Did one ever get used to cars and buses being driven on the wrong side of the street? Making my way carefully I arrived at my destination.

Much to my surprise a check brought forth a letter from Mike overlooked the previous time. There was a certain witness within my heart that it had not been missed by accident, but rather according to the loving planning of the Lord. This was my special birthday blessing from Him, as He alone was aware how hungrily I yearned for word from this one who had come to mean so much to me.

Eagerly absorbing every word of victory and praise, I tried to read between the lines for some indication of his interest in me. My soul rejoiced for the wonderful opportunities he had had with several in Israel just before his departure. Then, last but not least, it encouraged my heart to read that he was frequently remembering me and my ministry in prayer. How involved his thoughts of me were, or when and if we would ever see each other again I did not know, but somehow there was again a peaceful assurance that the Lord would complete what He had begun even as He had for Ruth the Moabitess.

What had seemed the summation of a beautiful friendship for her had proved instead only the closing of a chapter. I felt content for now to leave it all in the hands of the Author of this twentieth-century version of Ruth being written into my life.

My attention was brought back to the reality of the present with news of Irene's arrival from Hastings that evening. As this was to be my last night in London, Miriam joined me in meeting her, and as it turned out, her unsaved sister-in-law at the train station.

Strolling along from the station to No. 10 Downing Street, Cleopatra's Needle, and other points of interest of which a royal London seemed never to run short, Irene and I found opportunity to witness further to these hungry souls. When time came for our final parting late in the evening, it was regretfully "Shalom" once again to a still unsaved Miriam. And yet there was consolation that the dying embers of conviction and desire had been stirred up and fanned into a new flame which I prayed would not quickly cool off. To help feed the coals, I arranged for Miriam to contact the Hebrew Christian Testimony to Israel who would befriend her, taking up where I had left off. Surely it was only a matter of time until she would yield herself up to the life-giving Holy One who was wooing her so tenderly.

CHAPTER XXX

GOOD-BYE, EUROPE

It was still cold and grey outside when I suddenly awakened out of deep sleep. Glancing at my watch I saw it was 5:30. This would give ample time for breakfast and fare-wells before catching the seven o'clock train for Southhampton. I hurriedly dressed and packed. Since I had been sleeping until about 8 a.m. each morning here in London, I was keenly aware of His faithfulness in meeting every need—even that of my being awakened on time!

Nancy and I felt a mutual sadness as we fixed breakfast together, realizing that was to be my day of farewell to Europe, to England, to each other. Our acquaintance had been of short duration, yet during the past three days our hearts had been knit together in Christian love. After a time of warm fellowship in prayer we hurried off for the station. It was all we could do to keep from weeping, our friendship had come to mean so much. It made one appreciate anew the glorious future we have before us where there will be no more parting and believers will be together forever with Him.

As the train carried me away from London, my mind reflected upon the wonderful working of the Lord through me and for me, as well as in me, the past several weeks through Europe. His constant hand upon me was so clearly evident that I could not entertain a doubt that it all had been in accordance with His planning and I was truly in the center of His precious will. I would need this confidence as I neared home. Even though I did not know what the future held, I

177

felt a renewed confidence in the One who holds it in His hand. My soul, greatly encouraged, felt at peace as we pulled into Southhampton by 9:30. After passing through customs, I turned my back to a continent I had called home almost a full year, one I had learned to love and appreciate, and boarded the mammoth Queen Mary for New York.

Because of my late reservation, plus the bulging tourist section, I had been assigned to a lovely cabin-class cabin along with two others. May had boarded the ship at Southhampton also. In becoming acquainted she revealed she was a dancer in a stage comedy, and indicated herself to be a very nervous, insecure young woman with a hungry heart. It was easy to testify of my experience in Christ, so obvious to her was my quiet poise in the presence of her fearfulness. She readily admitted envy of my peace and rest in Christ, but was not ready as yet to commit herself to Him.

Our other cabinmate made her appearance later that evening after we had crossed the English Channel and taken on board more passengers at Cherbourg, France. That evening in the cabin as we conversed nonchalantly about our travels and destination, Helga's quickened interest in my having come from Israel began to arouse my suspicions. All of a sudden her last name which I had seen in passing on her suitcase flashed through my mind and I knew I was right! I rejoiced that the Lord had placed me together with a Jewish cabinmate!

For the next five twenty-five-hour days as we sailed with the sun, the voyage became to some a contest between the rolling sea and physical stamina. We noticed our table in the dining room was a little less utilized after a day or so. The seat across the table from me was occupied by a reticent Jewish lad from Israel who spoke little English. The significance of his lack of fluency occurred to me only later when I remembered he generally pointed to the menu when ordering at mealtime. We blamed the "ailment of the sea" for his leaving his plate half empty oftentimes and his failure to appear for a meal or two. That is, until the last day out when we were presented the menu for the special "Captain's Dinner" to celebrate our last evening at sea. The gaiety of the occasion made everyone a little more talkative as we expressed our choices. Suddenly we realized our Jewish companion, who asked us what turkey is, could not read the English menu! Then I realized why he had always ordered by finger! In my meager Hebrew (I could not remember the word for turkey) I explained it is somewhat like chicken. Relief and understanding lit up his face and he made a knowledgeable choice that night! Always afterwards I would wonder whether his half empty plates were a result of seasickness or of ordering with a finger.

One afternoon in the ship library an elderly Jewish couple came and sat at my table. I couldn't help but notice when the little gentleman took from his pocket an envelope from which he poured the five U.S. coins. He seemed to be studying them, apparently trying to ascertain each one's value. Breaking into his meditations I inquired in Hebrew if he spoke Hebrew, to which he replied, "Ken."

At first his attitude was hesitant—seemingly suspicious of my friendliness. I realized again how the Jew so often suspects a motive behind friendliness because of the hatred and persecutions he has suffered. But as we conversed in Hebrew his expression relaxed and he responded warmly. I learned that he and his wife were being brought to America by a son in New York, and he was trying to learn the value of American coins. As I told him each one's value as compared to Israeli money, his face displayed his gladness and he nodded understandingly.

Such incidents served to quicken afresh my yearning for that land I had come to love as "home." It was necessary to seek to maintain a yielded attitude and not allow rebellion to rise in the form of exercising my own will in making plans about returning again. The unknown future would often stretch out before me as a dark and empty chasm. But when the monster of depression seemed ready to pounce upon and devour me, I would quickly run to the Lord, my strong tower and sweet refuge, and there find strength to continue on. Or when heartache seemed nearly unbearable and the flesh would want to question "why?" the words of Job would echo and re-echo in my mind, "Though he slay me, yet will I trust in him." Then victory would lift the dejected chin, divine love soothe the inner ache, and renewed trust strengthen the will to follow on.

Once again there were encouraging opportunities to witness. Dinner table conversation one evening opened the way to relate Mike's testimony to the young man seated next to me.

179

He listened eagerly as I told him of the abundant life that Christ had come to give. Before parting that evening, he promised to read the Word of God for himself, indicating a true desire to find the joy and peace of salvation. Further witness to him the last day and a half at sea failed to bring him through the door of salvation, but precious seed had been sown with the promise that God gives the increase.

Along with such blessings there was also further training for my work among "my people." In visiting in the lounge with two young women, I found them warm and friendly until I mentioned I was returning from Israel. Their looks evidently betrayed their thoughts, for their expressions appeared to say "Oh! A Jew!" Moreover their changed, cooled attitudes bespoke volumes of their feelings. I was experiencing what my people suffer in a world that makes the word Jew a stigma. Choosing rather to remain in the camp of my beloved, rejected ones rather than spare myself, I did not reveal that I was not a Jewess—feeling that if they could not accept my people, they had rejected me as well!

As for my Jewish cabinmate, we rarely saw each other except for a few minutes each morning and evening in our cabin. Though I had prayed fervently day and night to be used with her, there was no opportunity to speak of spiritual things. Meanwhile on each possible occasion I tried to convey warmth and love to her. This proved profitable when on our last afternoon at sea the Lord brought us together. I was standing on deck enjoying the warmth of the sun when Helga came along. "So we finally meet outside our cabin!" she ejaculated.

And thus began a long and friendly conversation in which she revealed a heavy heart because of a wayward son. The Lord enabled me to tell her of my belief in Jesus as the Messiah and to quote some Old Testament proof passages. The Word, augmented with personal testimony of what the Lord had done for me, clearly touched her. And yet I felt that my friendliness and love for the Jews and Israel had probably counted more than even my words with her. She indicated a deep-seated hunger for a sympathetic and understanding ear and seemed to be responding to the love I had tried to show her. More fully than ever I realized that catching Jews requires precision casting and wise and subtle fishing!

CHAPTER XXXI

HOME

Long Island was already visible on the horizon by 6:30 a.m. After a hurried breakfast I spent our last hours aboard ship on deck watching New York's outline slowly enlarge and become distinct as we approached it. Police patrol boats and ferries scurried by as we quietly and respectfully slipped past the vigilant Statue of Liberty. I had to go almost half way around the world to see her—but at long last here she was in our own front yard!

Inwardly a sense of aversion was awakened by the first sight of the "bee-hive" Long Island Thruway. There was good reason to dread being caught up again in the whirlwind atmosphere of the fast-paced United States. I determined then and there, if possible, not to lose the spirit of relaxation that the Eastern way of life had taught me in Israel. I believe that the accelerated life we live in America tends to cause one to lose sight of the deeper values of life.

Our ship docked about 10 a.m., and with farewells and customs behind me, I stepped ashore and out onto the hustling, traffic-jammed streets of New York. How alone I felt in this huge sky-scraper city—so different from my visit here a year ago. The joy of anticipation then was in direct contrast to the sorrow I felt now in being back. Conviction that I was in the center of His will was my sole consolation.

Taking cognizance of my fast dwindling funds (no helpful exchange rate here in the U.S.!), I knew I would have to fly out of New York within a couple of days. It proved a little distressing to be told all immediate flights to San Francisco were booked up. My only recourse would be to book a flight to Chicago and pray I would be able to remain aboard on to San Francisco. My meager money supply left me no choice, so with much prayer to the One who had faithfully brought me thus far, I booked passage for Chicago in two days.

Having been blessed by rain all the way, it should not have surprised me in the least when I awakened the next morning to a warm, humid summer rain. First I set out early to visit the American Board of Missions to the Jews. The fellowship I gained there served to refresh and stimulate, alleviating somewhat the heavy-heartedness I felt in being back.

Next, contacting Diane's sister who was working with the United Nations, I accepted her gracious invitation to a tour of the U.N. Building, and afterward a firsthand view of Radio City and Times Square at night.

Everywhere the spectacle of bright lights and the noise of advertising or pleasure dens shouted, "Vanity!" The crowd is following after the glitter that tarnishes by morning and eventually ends with the crumbling and bitter waste of rust. My eleven months in a land struggling for existence and building with a purpose made me very sensitive to this contrast.

When I awoke the next morning I was content to be leaving New York and beginning the last lap of my journey home. After paying the hotel bill, I looked down upon the meager seventy-five cents left to see me to California. Again my prayers earnestly ascended, "Lord, please enable me to remain aboard the plane in Chicago. You know my need." And well I knew that any stopover in Chicago, no matter the length, would have to be spent right at the airport. At this point it was a blessing not to need fear that the Lord would be displeased with repetition. Reminding Him of my need had about become a daily ritual!

Soon after the plane set down in Chicago, I was greatly relieved to learn my seat was cleared through to San Francisco. No long cold hours or nights in the terminal! Taking advantage of the few minutes alloted before resuming our flight, I hurriedly sent off a collect telegram to my dad and brother, informing them that I would be arriving at the San Francisco airport at 8 p.m. that evening. It was sent off with another petition to my heavenly Father that He would enable them to drive the ninety plus miles to meet me.

Some hours later, with mixed feelings, I stepped off that plane into their waiting arms. The Lord had wondrously undertaken for me all the way, and it was a blessing to see their joy at my homecoming. But though I rejoiced to see my loved ones again—down deep inside I could not ignore a gnawing ache. As we drove home together to Sacramento, I was sorely aware that my heart was definitely no longer here in the States but back in Israel where I had left it.

And now that I was home, what...? What did the Lord have in store for me here? And what of Mike? Where was he? Would our lives be interwoven again, or when I sailed out of Haifa, did I sail out of his life as well? Would the Lord have woven my life so closely to my namesake's without completing the tapestry? He being the Author and the Master Planner, I could only wait upon Him. "My soul, wait thou only upon God; for my expectation is from him" (Ps. 62:5). Now with the Apostle Paul I was learning to pray for patience with joyfulness! (Col. 1:11).

Meanwhile it seemed imperative to get the message of Israel's needs across to others and solicit prayer for the salvation of her people—my people—by means of slides wherever possible.

Part III   SEEKING REST

CHAPTER III of RUTH of the HOLY BIBLE

CHAPTER XXXII

EN ROUTE

MORE THAN HALF A CONTINENT AWAY a brokenhearted Mike Perl was making his way toward California. Reflecting on recent happenings, he found much comfort in putting into practice Paul's "B Formula"—Be anxious for nothing, Be prayerful for everything, Be thankful for anything—found in Philippians 4:6.

It is never easy for a person to be harshly turned away by his own family. Could his mother's recent attitude have resulted from disappointment at his unchanged stand upon return from Israel? She had hoped that going to Israel would bring him back to Judaism. If she knew and believed the Word of God, she would have known it could only strengthen his faith in Christ, the Messiah of Israel. He couldn't feel sorry that he had tried to witness to her because of his deep concern for her eternal welfare. Her reaction had been explosive. The stinging words still rang in his ears: "There's the door. Get out! As far as I'm concerned you are no longer a son of mine. You are dead and buried! And don't ever come back. Don't even come to my funeral. I don't want it contaminated!"

He had remembered his Saviour's love that rose above violent rejection. Filled with overflowing grace, as he turned away, also rejected, he could gently say, "Remember, Mother, it is you who has cut me off. I'm not cutting you off."

His sisters unrelentingly had stood with his mother against him. "It is better if you don't ever come home again. All you do is cause trouble when you do!"

The words of the Messiah came to him forcibly, "Think

187

not that I am come to send peace on earth; I came not to send peace, but a sword. . . . A man's foes shall be they of his own household" (Matt. 10:34, 36).

The apostle Paul had promised, by inspiration of the Holy Spirit, that God's peace would keep his heart and mind. Even so the Word of God was living and active in Mike's experience, and he did possess the peace that passes all understanding, yes, and rises above all misunderstanding (Phil. 4:7).

If his family could only taste of the joys of salvation and dedication to Christ that he had tasted! Their lives were so blighted in comparison to the fullness and the riches so freely bestowed by Him.

Sweet, soothing, healing joy again flooded his soul as he recalled the blessed experience which had been his just a few days earlier on his way to Michigan from New York. The Chevy he had purchased in New York from a Christian man was performing nicely. Driving along early in the morning his attention was alerted by a lone, dejected-looking figure walking alongside the highway. This could be an answer to prayer! Had he not prayed before starting out that morning that the Lord would send him a rider to whom he might witness, and that he would be where he could easily be picked up on the highway? Quickly noting that there was no traffic coming from either direction, Mike pulled over to the side of the road just ahead of this forlorn figure. The young fellow had seemed quite surprised, but had gratefully climbed into the car.

Mike soon learned that his dejected passenger, just released from the armed services, had lost all his money in an unhappy experience in Chicago, and was now hitchhiking to his parents' home in northern Minnesota. Having been by-passed by cars many times, he had given up hope of a ride. By the time Mike arrived on the scene, because of feeling that all the chips were against him, he was entertaining the thought of suicide.

In a spirit of love and compassion Mike presented to him God's remedy not only for every adverse circumstance, but also every disparaged life. He listened quietly, thoughtfully, as Mike told him of Christ's straightening out his life for him through the new birth. "No life can be so messed up, so hope-less, as to be beyond a new start in Christ. Have you had this new birth?" Mike glanced at his silent companion.

"No, I haven't," came the pensive answer.

188

"Would you like to be born again? Right now? Have a new start in Christ?"

The answer was as spontaneous as it was definite, "Yes, I would."

Mike was elated. "Then, I suggest we pull off the road right now and have a word of prayer," he proposed, already looking for a possible place. A little side road at hand offered itself conveniently.

Turning off the highway they slowed to a stop on the side road. Instinctively glancing around, Mike's gaze was instantly halted! "Look!" he said pointing out a church-sponsored sign almost directly in front of them.

The words stood out boldly, "YE MUST BE BORN AGAIN" (John 3:7). The working of the Holy Spirit could not be denied, nor His wooing spurned.

The Lord's hand was tenderly upon them as two young men bowed their heads and hearts, the one escorting the other into the Kingdom of God. Once again all the angels of heaven were caused to rejoice over a repentant sinner come home! And a recently disheartened soul felt a new lease on life, a new hope for the future. Soon testimony to spiritual birth and new life overflowed as this new babe, with a changed countenance, declared, "Now I feel clean inside." The rest of the journey that day was spent in joyous fellowship around the Saviour.

Looking back now as he drove along toward California, Mike couldn't help wondering if the Lord had given him this blessing in order to strengthen him for the heartbreak to which he had been headed at home. Through these meditations the Holy Spirit was speaking peace and comfort in the midst of sorrow.

Unknown to him at the time, the Holy Spirit was also directing his path. Since he was almost as far south and west as he could get from northern Michigan on the highway he was on, Mike decided that as soon as possible he must map out the rest of his journey in order to be sure of finding the shortest good route. Taking advantage of a stop in Steamboat Springs, Colorado, he checked out on a map the best route to Southern California.

At first he was a little unhappy to see he must remain on this central highway all the way to California before turning south. Picking up a mileage card with listings in relation to his present position, his eye caught the name Sacramento listed. Strange feelings stirred within as the thought gripped his mind, "Does my route necessitate going through Sacramento?" A check of the map brought an affirmation.

"That is Ruth's home. More than likely she is back by now," he mused. "What does all this mean? Is the Lord showing me Ruth is the girl for me?"

On his way again many thoughts raced through his mind, his speedometer speedily clicking off the miles between him and Sacramento. Again he recalled a conversation with his mother in Michigan.

"Haven't you found a girl yet you could marry?"

He had realized her thinking behind her question. Perhaps a Jewish wife could help straighten him out—turn him back to Judaism! Ignoring the implication, he had answered that there was one he thought he might consider marrying. He had hesitated, remembering her plea of some time before that he not marry a Gentile. "But she is not fully Jewish—only partly so."

His mother's answer had taken him by surprise, "Well, if she could make you happy, marry her!"

Encouraged, he had told her a little of Ruth, trying to evaluate his own feelings in doing so. Then had come the serious thought, "Maybe she wouldn't have me!" As this thought now again penetrated the glowing anticipations which had been building up within him, he felt an awareness awakened of one of the probable reasons the Lord had guided him along this route. "I'll stop over in Sacramento a day or two and look for a sign from Ruth—if she is there—that she might be interested in me." The thought of further rejection at this point seemed too painful to take a chance upon it.

Another hitch-hiker appeared on the scene and Mike could not by-pass an opportunity to speak to someone for Christ. This man was not as ready to receive the Saviour as the previous one. After a time of seed-sowing the conversation turned to other things.

The thoughts next uppermost on Mike's mind came to the fore. Here was an opportunity to consider aloud the possibilities of Ruth's being a suitable helpmeet for him, and to gain someone else's opinion. Presenting Ruth's background, her calling as a missionary to the Jew, zeal for the Lord, and spiritual desires as compared with his own, Mike was almost startled to hear this stranger next to him boldly state, "She sounds just the girl for you. I think you should marry her!"

The hours added into days. Finally on a Sunday afternoon with a sense of nervous excitement, Mike caught sight of the sign for which he had been eagerly watching—SACRAMENTO CITY LIMIT.

Locating a telephone he tried to reach Ruth, but to no avail. Next he sought out the address of the house her mother-in-law had occupied, only to find she had moved. Bowing his head he turned to his Guide for help, "Now what, Lord?"

Into his mind came the answer, "Diane and Ray Stocking." After looking up their address, with renewed hope he made his way to their apartment. His knock on the door brought the sound of footsteps from within.

The door, opening slowly at first, was suddenly thrown open wide with a jerk. "Mike!" Joy beamed from Diane's face. He couldn't have wished for a warmer welcome. Ushering him in and making him comfortable she could hardly contain her excitement. "Do you know where Ruth is going to be tonight?"

"No." His face asked the question.

"At our church showing her slides of Israel!"

Diane.had been the first Ruth had secretly confided in regarding her love for Mike. She had hardly needed to be told. Having known Ruth so well, she surmised it almost as soon as Ruth herself realized it. Because she had been drawn to Mike with admiration from Biola days, Diane was thrilled to contemplate the Lord's bringing Mike and Ruth together.

As soon as possible Diane was on the telephone. "Ruth, you will never guess who is sitting in my rocking chair!"

Knowing Diane as I did, the gleeful note in her voice could mean only one person. "Not Mike!"

"Yes. He couldn't find you folk so he came to us. Of course he'll be with us this evening to see your slides!"

As our friendship was renewed that evening it was reminiscent of Israeli days to share again the joys and tears, the thrills and heartbreaks that had transpired for us both since our Shalom at Haifa Port six weeks earlier. The days Mike spent in Sacramento were wonderful days of spiritual refreshing for two kindred souls unified by experience and the Spirit. Neither of us seemed sure of the future—only that we were

191

following the leading of the Lord as best as we understood it for the present.

Hoping for some indication from Mike of a more personal love for me, beyond that of a Christian big brother, was destined for disappointment. I dared not presume that his sweetness and warmth, though radiating love, was beyond that of Christian fellowship. Under such circumstances I could not, would not, openly reveal the fullness of my heart, lest in doing so it be crushed again and our beautiful relationship ended.

The fact that Ruth of long ago had revealed her feelings to Boaz first did not affect my thinking. I knew I would not dare to speak first unless positively led by the Holy Spirit. Even Ruth had not acted of herself, but had been directed by Naomi.

Meanwhile, not having received the definite sign that he was looking for, and in the face of possible rejection, Mike could not bring himself to speak. Departing from Sacramento, heading south for San Bernardino and home, he was still to wonder if Ruth was the helpmeet the Lord had chosen for him, the fulfillment of a long-time heart's desire for a wife, a home, and family. Or did the Lord intend, as he so long had thought, for him to remain a bachelor for the sake of the Gospel? The long journey home gave much opportunity for further pondering and prayer.

In the weeks that followed, meetings to show the slides of Israel began to fill my time nicely. Financially the way opened for me through my dad who advanced me the money to buy a projector and screen. I was sure I could shortly pay him back with the love offerings which were often given to help my ministering in this way. My brother insisted I use one of his credit cards to purchase gas and oil for my car, enabling me to get to the meetings. Everything appeared fine, but unknown to me I was beginning to get entangled in a financial web which eventually would teach me a tremendous spiritual lesson and prepare me for my future life and work.

I had the strong conviction that my financial dependence was to be entirely upon the Lord, that I was not to ask for or solicit offerings or funds in any way for my meetings. He would touch hearts to give as He was pleased and I could count on His faithfulness. At the same time it did not seem inconsistent to me to borrow from my dad and brother to get started in this ministry—but the Lord was to teach me what utter dependence upon Him means—and I was to learn, the way of all flesh, the hard way!

Since it was necessary to go to Los Angeles to collect the money I deposited with Cunard in Paris, I scheduled my trip to coincide with the July Watchman Upon the Walls Club meeting. Much to my joy Mike came over to Los Angeles for the meeting as well.

It was wonderful to fellowship together at the club once again. Looking around the room brought back many memories, particularly that first meeting nearly three years ago when I first heard Mike briefly give his testimony and was so impressed, but didn't meet him. It seemed unbelievable that the one whose testimony thrilled me so that night could have come to mean so very much in my life.

At the close of a thrilling and stimulating meeting, Mike suggested we meet as he wanted to discuss some things with me. I gladly consented, brimming with curiosity and elated that he desired further fellowship with me.

Lingering over a cup of coffee, with the din of voices and the banging of dishes in the background, I listened as Mike described his contemplations for a future ministry among the Jews of San Bernardino. He envisioned among other things an extensive tract ministry by mail and a radio broadcast directly to the Jews of the area. The vision of such a work was stirring to both of our hearts, so hungry were we to be active in reaching the Jewish people for the Lord.

His words surprised and thrilled me, "This is where you fit in. In the event and time that the Lord opens such a work to me I will need a secretary."

I tried not to react overly enthusiastic or to reflect the thought that flashed through my mind—it really isn't uncommon for a man to marry his secretary!

As we talked on, the atmosphere around us was enveloped in the warmth and glow of love. A tender look now and then momentarily melted away my inner strength, and I could sense a definite emitting of love from spirit to spirit. Much later I would learn of his struggle within that night—trying to ask me to be his wife—yet unable to bring himself to do it. The evening would have ended so much differently if he had known how eager I was to say yes! However, the Lord's time was not yet, for we were both to have more training in His school of preparation. More threads (some dark and sombre, some bright and gay) must be interwoven into our lives before the beautiful tapestry of Ruth and Boaz could be completed.

CHAPTER XXXIII

TRIALS AND TESTINGS

BACK AGAIN IN SACRAMENTO, in spite of the fact that the Lord was blessing the ministry of the slides in various ways, discouragement and the old unsettled feeling began to enter in once again. It brought a measure of satisfaction to pour out my soul in behalf of Israel through the message of the slides, to be used to stimulate prayer and concern for Jewish needs, but my ultimate burden was to reach the lost ones personally with the Gospel. The lack of open doors to the Jewish community and the problems created by my being a lone young woman had to be faced all over again.

No one else so understood my position or yearnings as did like-minded Mike. It brought no little consolation to be able still to pour out my burden to and solicit prayer from him through correspondence. Early in August Mike read:

"The Lord is still blessing through the pictures, but the future remains closed to me. Several other doors have closed and there seem to be no openings. Have you heard any more concerning the work you told me of in Los Angeles? It is getting to the place now where I must make a move. My family wants me to get a secular job here and settle down. However, God has called me to the Jews, and I can hardly settle for anything else. Surely if He has so called He must open some door in that field. And as I wait upon Him He will make all things clear and open the door of His choice. . . .

"I seem to be back in the same circumstances that brought

me home from Israel—a call to the Jews, but the lack of a work to work at and restlessness because His place has not yet been found. Your effectual prayer concerning this is deeply appreciated."

It proved a time of testing for both of us, as his answer revealed:

"Your uneasiness (for you are not restless, is my opinion) is a major concern to me, Ruth. Remember how we criticized dear Mary for waiting upon God for fifteen years before coming to Israel? Could it not have been that she was in the very center of His will during said period? Rees Howells, the intercessor, waited upon God for ten months for the go-sign to begin building the college the Holy Spirit had clearly conveyed to him should be built! Satan is striving to fill the hearts of the good and the wicked alike with rush, an aching need of incessant activity which shall leave no time to hear God's voice, or know what His Word reveals for these last days. God gives quietness. The atmosphere of His presence is always peace. While one walks with Him, he can quietly meet a great deal that seems defeat. God's work is done perfectly only when the soul ceases from its own work.

"It would be possible for me also to be uneasy about the little activity in my own small ministry. But is it little to wait upon God? Is it easy to know that others could easily accuse one of even doing nothing? Is it fear for the heart to say, 'Wait thou upon God though the waiting be days—months! —YEARS!'? How pleased must be the grieved heart of the Lord Jesus to see the few trusting Him to work and to do according to His perfect schedule—that self might not in any way appear upon the scene. . . .

"Please pray for His will in my own life. At any hour a door of service might open that would take me into the Tennessee, Virginia, Kentucky hills to work there. Expenses would be provided to get me there; work would be in conjunction with a brother who in truth lives by faith and has lived to see the Lord bless his ministry in beautiful results. But what about my own call to my own precious people? Maybe there are so few Jews to be saved that the Holy Spirit would have us to work among the Gentiles, trusting Him not only to lead us to those few Jews whom He would graciously save through us,

196

but also to keep us praying properly (based on our period in Israel) for His own people."

The days came when hidden tears spilled over onto the vacuum cleaner or into the dishwater, giving vent to the increasing heart-cry that so wanted but durst not ask "Why?" Keeping house for Mother who was working surely wasn't the intent and purpose of a Bible college degree. This couldn't be what the Lord left me on earth to do—nor the end of my precious calling to the Jew.

On the other hand, if I could not work alone among the Jews, perhaps I should look to the Lord for another field of service. Many areas were pleading for help. Then again the vision of the ministry Mike and I could have together brought consolation, renewing my hope and patience. Fervent prayer and seeking the Lord's mind brought times of assurance and optimism concerning my calling to Jewry. Such times were also shared with Mike:

"May this find you rejoicing, even as this servant, in the sweet renewed assurance of His calling to the neglected, unloved, brokenhearted, precious souls of Israel's rebellious sons. Assurance has come that previous doubt was merely testing. Praise His name for the privilege of being used of Him to snatch tortured Jewish souls from the brink of eternal condemnation. Oh, might many be washed in the blood of the Lamb! That all of Israel might be covered with the blood before the death angel passes over! Since the time of Jacob's Trouble is to be concentrated particularly upon the Jews, surely they must have an especially fervent, Spirit-filled witness in these last days that all who would might escape. Would we turn away from them because this is a hard work? Even Paul—the minister to the Gentiles—went always to the Jew first. It is not recorded he ever said he would give his soul's salvation if possible for the sake of the Gentiles! If we are praying that He will increase the remnant, can we not by faith wait upon Him for it?

"How great was my amazement that you were thinking of leaving your call to your own people. Here the same spirit was working in me, but when you wrote you might go into another field to labor, my heart cried out to God, 'Don't let Mike leave his call; his ministry is to his own; his testimony

197

is so needed among them!' and my soul was comforted only in such praying."

As I prayed for Mike and his ministry I could not help but include my heart's yearning to be a more vital, intimate part of his ministry to Israel. At these times with a sense of utter dependence and great boldness I would remind the Lord that if He didn't work in Mike's heart to bring us together, it could never happen. The workings of the Lord are often beyond us, and I did not then know His aim in leading me to reveal my spiritual love and concern for Mike late in August:

"Hardly am I able to come before Him without lifting you and that which concerns you into His holy presence. I heard a message recently on I Samuel 23:16 and was reminded of our relationship in Him. How great is my joy even to consider being used of Him to strengthen your hands in God— because of God-given love. I Samuel 18:1."

The Holy Spirit revealed to him as he read that this was more than a sisterly-brotherly love. Taking the matter to the Lord in prayer, his heart was assured that he could have Ruth for his wife. The beautiful fulfillment of a desire that had been his through the years was now his for the asking. But with this assurance also came what was to be a supreme test for this Jewish man. The Lord's words to his spirit were clear, "You may have Ruth as your wife, but I have a work I want you to do for Me alone that will take you far from here. Will you give up your Ruth and marriage, your heart's desire to do My pleasure?"

Mike knew this meant, for now, stepping through that door open to him in the hills, and possibly eventually to the ends of the earth. Only the soul that has fully tasted the goodness of the Lord after years of spiritual dearth and famine can offer back to his Redeemer the sweetest earthly morsel ever offered within his reach. Without regret, but not without pain, his heart, along with the girl he loved, was laid upon the altar of sacrifice, the gift of love to the One who first made the supreme sacrifice of love for him. The letter that followed to Ruth revealed the Lord's new leading in his life:

"His will for my own life has been made indelibly clear, praise His Name. To reach such knowledge came the application of Matthew 19:12 in prayer to be made a reality to me

198

by His Spirit. Then continuing in prayer, the Lord made clear, because of the smallness of the remnant, His will for me to go through 'Samaria'—to the Gentiles. In doing so He assured me that He would contact Jewish souls through me, even some to be saved.

"On August 17 I met Mac, one of three directors of a small corporation that manufactures ceramics bearing Scripture verses. Mac told me of a group back East with whom he is connected and of their search for a person who knows a little something about Israel, the Jew, and prophecy. He seemed to think that I could be this person! When asked my opinion I promised to pray about it. Mac replied he would contact the men in the East to learn if they were still interested.

"Ten days passed, then word came from Mac that 'the men in the East would be happy to have you.' By that afternoon it was easy to say yes. Territory covers four states. To reach those who are inaccessible by car it will be necessary to go in by horse or by foot. There will be preaching, teaching, and reaching to do. None of the meeting houses have electric lights; some have seats, others none! The area is demon infested and lawlessness holds sway. There is a radio station broadcasting twelve hours per day, and some city work in which no doubt Jewish souls will be met.

"They hope it will be possible for me to remain at least three months. We all agree that only the Lord Jesus knows whether it will be hours, days, weeks, months, or years. Acts 1:8 is a reality to me except that it is difficult at this time to determine whether it will be in person that the 'uttermost parts' will be traversed or whether it will be via the wings of intercessory prayer. On the other hand, personal ministry even unto Israel is more strongly anticipated! It is impossible to give further details. For your intercessory prayers enough has been said."

As I carefully and prayerfully pondered his words, the reality of what this meant in my life became painfully real. Not only was the door now closed for the ministry in San Bernardino that would include me as secretary, but also it was apparent the Lord was moving him out into a ministry completely exclusive of me.

The same stinging waves of pain and sorrow flooded through me that I had once before experienced when the one whom I had loved most on earth was torn from my mortal grasp. The Spirit of God spoke to me clearly from Mike's reference of Matthew 19:12. I knew now that Mike did love me, but had given me up for Someone he loved dearer. There was no rebellion mixed with my grief, for how could I be jealous of or ever want to intrude upon such pure love for the One I, too, loved first and foremost? Nor was the source of that love inoperative now. When the Lord inflicts pain (often necessary for our conformity to His dear Son), He also tenderly pours into the wound the oil and wine of His divine love, the active soothing salve to the soul.

My conclusion as to how this affected the story of Ruth transpiring in my life was recorded in a note to Diane:

"I have put down my pen and closed the book. Only if God takes up the pen to rewrite the ending can it ever come to pass, for my part of the story has ended. It ended like this: Boaz's heart was so filled with God there was no room for Ruth. Ruth will never stop loving Boaz and will always carry a thorn in her heart, which every once in a while pricks it, only to let a little more tenderness and sweetness flow out to a hurt and bewildered world. At times I shall bask in the warmth and fragrance of my wonderful, precious love story, but no one shall ever know, for this is a garden into which no other presence can enter with me—except the precious presence of One whose very being adds a sweet fragrance to it.

"Even as I wrote this it seemed as though someone said— but God already took up pen in hand and finished the story —the 'Book of Ruth.' That sounds sweet but only God can convince me now. For Diane, I feel such a sweet resignation to His will and the Lord is so precious. His very presence is more wonderful than a thousand Mikes, and my desire is toward Him. He is my Portion in the land of the living."

However, my sorrow was not solely for my own loss. What of his sorely needed testimony to our precious lost Jewish ones? So few see the need or are concerned enough to try to reach them. The varied results of Mike's letter were reported to him nearly two months later:

"Your letter of September 7 brought into my life one of the greatest trials of my experience and with it one of the most glorious victories He has been pleased to give. My heart was crushed that you had seemingly turned away from the precious lost Jew, but with it came a sweet submission to His sure wisdom and guidance, even though understanding to me was lacking. Your words that perhaps there were so few Jews to be saved that you could go to the Gentile and trust God to lead you to the few Jews of your ministry kept echoing in my mind. My heart echoed back—'then perhaps I should go to China where the needy are receptive and I can live a useful life until He calls me home.'

"The impression was so strong that I wrote a letter to Bob Hammond's mission requesting application blanks. This took place Saturday afternoon of the 11th. That evening my aunt told me that Bob Hammond was speaking in Turlock (nearly eighty miles from here) Sunday evening. We made plans to go so I could have personal contact with him. Sunday afternoon my statement to Mother that 'perhaps there were so few Jews to be saved that I could go to China' was stopped short by the Spirit of God, who rebuked clearly, 'Who are you to say there are so few Jews to be saved: I have saved Me 7,000 who have not bowed the knee to Baal!'

"However, God was doing something which I could not then clearly see, so the impression remained to go to Turlock. Upon arrival there Sunday night, we were told that Mr. Hammond had been there in the morning and someone else would be speaking. My deep-seated peace resulted in a complete lack of disappointment and in its place, a mysterious joy. The message, to our amazement, was on Elijah calling down the fire from heaven. I had expected to hear about China, but I heard about Israel!

"But for the first time the Lord was testing me concerning Israel, the Jew, 'Ruth'—everything connected with this ministry. The awakening was astounding that it had cost me nothing to go to Israel, as my heart had preceded me there long before my feet ever touched Israeli soil. The cost to go to China was real, to a people and land after which my heart did not thrill. The Lord was asking, 'You went to Israel because of your love for the Jew. Will you go to China because of love for Me—for love of Me alone?'

"The choice was real and mine to make. It was clear I could have my ministry to the Jew, my heart's desire, but spiritual leanness; or go to China and have Him and the blessedness of giving up all for Him and Him alone. What decision could be made? On my knees with broken heart and floods of tears, for nearly four hours Monday morning, my heart cried out as in Israel, 'Lord, take this beautiful thing, this love, Israel my Isaac, and cast it far from me lest it stand between me and Thee.' "

I could not add in my letter to Mike that I knew this must also end my beautiful hope of a Jewish ministry together with him, and the total fulfillment of Ruth in my life.

"By noon peace and victory filled my soul; there was assurance He had taken 'Isaac' and now my face turned toward China. The pain of giving up my 'love' was sweet in the new relationship between my soul and the Saviour, for nothing was between, and He had received my sacrifice of love. The next day testimony to the joy and radiance on my face amazed me, for the pain within my heart was sharp. Hence He taught the lesson He had promised to teach the week before—the joy of the Holy Ghost—for there was joy bubbling out that did not originate from me."

As the days added into weeks, however, it was almost a repeat of the days right after my original calling to the Jew. It seemed from every direction and in various ways the Jew was brought to my attention. Further word was received by Mike:

"Quietly and restfully my soul waited while He drew up the blueprints of His will, adding a little daily. Abundant opportunities to serve Him here through the slides, and in other ways kept me in His constant joy, satisfied whatever He would do and whenever He chose to do it. With my face turned toward China, burden for those people became increased and temptation to revive my 'Isaac' decreased. However, at the same time, circumstances began to open things for work in various ways for the Jew. (Until now the Lord has not given me the liberty to send in the application to Bob Hammond.) Peace and rest in complete submission to His will saturated my life and kept me stable, not trying to decide one way or another, content to know in His time His perfect will."

202

Step by step the workings of the Lord became more clear to me. The ardent fervent frequent prayers from a Jewish soul that longed after the salvation of his own people were being answered to his joy as Mike later read:

"As time has separated between me and the day 'Isaac' was offered up, assurance has increased that September 11–13 was a trial, and one which will cause me to know now and always that this precious ministry to the Jew belongs to Him and is only a loaned talent to be multiplied by His grace and power. Never again will He permit me to think of it as 'my ministry.' There is confidence that my work for Him, for the present at least, is to raise up prayer for Israel and the Jew.

"The burden for 'our' people is at times overwhelming and the compulsion to raise up prayer for them so strong, there is no peace in turning from it. In His mercy and sweetness He gave to me explicitly for this ministry Numbers 11: 14, 17. With Moses I cried, 'I am not able to bear all this people alone, because it is too heavy for me.' And the Lord said, 'I will take of the spirit which is upon thee, and will put it upon them; and they shall bear the burden of the people with thee, that thou bear it not thyself alone.' "

CHAPTER XXXIV

THE LIFE OF FAITH

THE TELEPHONE RANG SHARPLY! Quickly I grabbed up my calendar and pen. My impression proved correct—it was another request to present the pictures of Israel, this time to a ladies' missionary society.

It was gratifying to see the response to Israel's need for prayer and the hearing of the Gospel from various groups who opened their doors to my presentation. An awareness of the Christian's responsibility to reach Jewish neighbors, friends, and co-workers was being awakened or stimulated in one here and one there by the faithful working of the Holy Spirit. The burden embedded deep within my soul was reaching out even as He had promised, to the prayer shoulders of other burden bearers.

Though I never solicited a meeting or an offering, for a time love offerings received for my labors balanced out pretty well against my meager needs. Still in possession of my brother Clifford's gas and oil credit card, I resorted to it whenever circumstances made it mandatory. In the early fall I began to realize I had found the credit card necessary all too often. It seemed I had come away empty handed from a number of my last meetings. I took the matter to the Lord in prayer, refusing to mention my needs to anyone. I couldn't understand why, but once again the Lord seemed to be withholding His monetary blessings from me. I was serving Him in His work and using my funds for only the barest necessities, even disregarding some personal needs, feeling the ministry was more important than comfortable living.

In recent months my soul had been much exercised in reading of the life of faith of *Rees Howells, Intercessor*, written by Norman Grubb. This man of God had refused to act even upon the revealed direction of God to build a Bible school until all needed funds had been brought in, without solicitation, by God alone. And thus the will of God was proved. It is much easier for the flesh to devise a way to obtain money and ask God's blessing upon it than quietly to wait upon God's way and time—the way of pure faith. And this was the way I had felt led to go.

In evaluating my circumstances, it seemed the Lord provided enough to keep me going from day to day but not enough to cover the indebtedness I was incurring to my brother for gas and oil. The burden of this indebtedness began to weigh heavily upon me as I realized he could not afford to cover the gas bills which I could not pay each month. The financial web was growing tighter and tighter around me, and I could not seem to break it.

About this time I found a trip south necessary to take care of some business. My calendar allowed for a week's absence which I took as an indication of the Lord's will and timing. One matter led me to San Bernardino where I was shown warm hospitality by Mrs. Blakely, Mike's first and very adept Bible teacher after he was saved. Her love for the Bible had created within her a deep love for the Jew and an earnest interest in Israel.

Upon learning that I had brought my slides with me, she gathered together a group of friends in her home to view them. Thrilled with their message she asked if I would come to San Bernardino after the Christmas holidays to present them in various churches if she would arrange a number of meetings for me. Gladly I gave assent, silently pondering, "Could this be the beginning of an extended ministry of raising up prayer for the Jew and Israel perhaps even throughout the United States?"

An errand took me into downtown Los Angeles where parking space is often hard to find. Locating an empty street near the place of my business, I pulled over to the curb. It seemed strange mine was the only car parked along the entire block, but I could not see any prohibitive signs. Seeing no outward reason why I should not park there, I shrugged off an intuitive feeling of uneasiness and hurried to take care of my business. When I returned a short time later, much to my chagrin, there was a piece of paper stuck under my windshield wiper. Apprehensively I retrieved the paper which verified my fears—a parking ticket! A second check of all nearby signs still uncovered no indication of its being unlawful to park there. Under the circumstances I felt treated quite unfairly; nonetheless I still possessed the ticket that must be paid.

My consolation came from the Word of God, "All things work together for good to them that love God, to them who are the called according to his purpose . . . to be conformed to the image of his Son. . ." (Rom. 8:28, 29). I could only commit it to the Lord to bring good out of it. Perhaps the incident would not have magnified itself under ordinary circumstances, but it proved to be the pressure point that would revolutionize my way of living and extricate me from that financial web once for all!

Upon investigation I learned the violation required a five dollar fine. That was the sum total of all I had left for the four hundred miles home to Sacramento, apart from Clifford's reliable credit card! The expenses incurred during my trip had been a little more than I had anticipated, and I didn't feel I would dare get out on the highway without any cash in the event of an emergency. Weighing all things I decided to mail the fine from Sacramento as soon as possible after my return.

As the long miles toward home stretched out before me, there was considerable time to reflect upon my uncomfortable circumstances. It was obvious the Lord had not been blessing me financially as my income was never sufficient to bring me out of the red—to clear up my debts, and now another unpaid debt—an unnecessary five dollar ticket!

It certainly could not be the Lord's will for me not to pay my debts when Paul's letters were so explicit concerning the mind of the Lord for us—the members of the Body of Christ. Romans 13:8 plagued my thinking, "Owe no man anything, but to love one another . . . " I owed my brother what was fast becoming an enormous gas bill which I could not pay. There was no reason to doubt my being in the center of the Lord's will for me at this time since there had been leading here and none out from here. The ministry of the slides had seen His anointing and blessing, but not my financial status!

I felt no liberty to, nor could I ethically look for a secular job as I felt I might be led away from Sacramento at any time. If the Lord did not open a Jewish ministry to me here, then it had to be elsewhere. The Lord had not retracted my calling to the Jew! Therefore why hadn't the Lord seen to it that I could pay my bills?

Then it was that the still small voice spoke clearly—"Who made your bills?" The implication was unavoidable. The Lord had certainly not made my bills, I had! Even though I had done it for the ministry into which He had called me, still I had done it! My spiritual eyes were being opened. How typical of the workings of the flesh to dive in head first and then cry for help to be pulled out! Would it not have been far better to believe that He would supply for whatever He had called me to do if I waited upon Him for it, rather than devising means and methods, and perhaps jumping ahead of the Lord?

George Mueller and Rees Howells, two spiritual giants, had proved the Lord over and over. Their policy was never to tell a need to man or woman—only the Lord—and then to wait (not run or devise) until that need was supplied His way and in His time. And the Lord had met their needs of literally many thousands of dollars over many years' time!

Early in Mike's Christian experience he had been taught this marvelous life of faith by the enlightenment of the Holy Spirit. The Lord's instrument had been a Christian speaker to a Christian Business Men's meeting who had verbally attacked what he called cross-eyed faith—that is telling God and asking the people; or as he also put it "having one eye on God and the other on the Christian's pocket-book." Then and there Mike determined never to present his needs to anyone but the Lord, and on the basis of Romans 13:8, never to incur debt.

I recalled Mike's having said that if the Lord did not supply food, then starvation would be the way the Lord would want to take him home. In thinking back over the length of our friendship, I had never known Mike to have financial problems like mine. He was even blessed financially, never seeming to lack, and often being able to help others!

As for me I was always having to borrow from here or there to get by. In going to Israel I had refinanced my car. In Israel

I had had to borrow from Mike when my money did not come for school. To come home I had to withdraw from my investment with my uncle. To start my slide ministry I borrowed from Dad; to drive my car—my brother's credit card. Something was very wrong!

All things considered I, too, now determined in my heart and mind that no matter what happened from here on in, I would go forward only as the Lord supplied. If there was not enough money to put gas in the tank to get me to a meeting, I would have to believe that the meeting was not of the Lord, and trust the Lord to make things right or understood. The Lord heard my new step of faith that day and was soon to test me that I might prove my commitment, thereby exercising my new faith unto growth.

Ruth, the Moabitess, had received instruction for preparing herself before she was to reveal her heart to Boaz. The thought pleased me. Could this be the Lord's way of preparing me to live this life of faith, even as Mike already did, before His bringing of us together? The pieces of the puzzle seemed to be working together into a beautiful picture—but one I must see through the eyes of the Lord. And if this were so, what of Mike's choice to serve the Lord alone? Many things were at the same time clear and yet vague in my thinking that day.

Upon my arrival in Sacramento I returned the credit card to Clifford against his many objections. "Keep it just to have in case of an emergency at least," he pleaded. "What if you break down on the highway without money and get stranded?"

I appreciated his brotherly concern, but I knew what I must do. "Cliff, from now on I must trust the Lord entirely for my finances. If I get stranded on the highway, then He will rescue me in some way. From here on in I'm trusting the Lord to provide for what He directs me to do, and I intend to abstain from whatever He withholds."

The first testing came immediately. I had arrived back in Sacramento from my trip with only a five dollar bill and a penny or two. In my mind the five dollars belonged to the Department of Motor Vehicles for the ticket I had received in Los Angeles. However, I did not have the means of the money order or the postage stamp to mail in the fine, and would not ask for help or even tell my circumstance lest it appear as a hint. Living with Mother I was not lacking for the daily necessities. Prayerfully I waited upon the Lord for several weeks determined not to ask for the few cents needed should I even be called into court for negligence to pay my fine.

During this waiting period a situation arose in which I badly needed my typewriter, but since my return from Israel the typewriter which had been shipped back in my trunk was not working properly. I decided I must get it repaired and trust the Lord to supply by the time it was fixed. Carefully praying for clear guidance as to the repair shop which the Lord would have me patronize resulted in a strong pull toward one in particular.

To park near the repair shop it was necessary to drop my last penny in change in the parking meter in front. With the prayer that the repair would not be too costly, I entered the shop, expecting to receive an estimate and return for the machine later. A kind gentleman took the machine and I waited as he checked it.

Within minutes he approached me with the words, "A part of this machine has been bent out of shape. Did you drop it?"

"Why no!" The surprise expressed in my answer gave way to doubtful questioning, "But then maybe it was dropped at that. I just returned from Israel and it was shipped back in my trunk. Perhaps the trunk had been dropped. I wouldn't know."

The serviceman was immediately interested, "Oh? Why were you in Israel?" His question led to a testimony and witness which he received eagerly. Then he revealed that he also was a Christian, but living far from the Lord. Suddenly he asked me to wait a few minutes while he would see what he could do with the typewriter.

By now I realized my time on the parking meter outside was spent, and I could not afford another ticket (especially not having paid for the other one as yet!). My only alternative was to drive the car several blocks away where there were no meters and walk back. Walking back to the shop I pondered what to do about the typewriter if he had fixed it already. I could use the five dollars I was holding for that ticket and supposed I would have to do so. But what if the cost was more than five dollars? An earnest prayer of pleading went up, "Lord, please don't let it cost more than five dollars. You know I haven't more, and I don't even feel this money really belongs to me as I owe it to someone else. Yet I don't know what else to do, since I do need the typewriter right away. If this is of Thee, please, undertake in some way." If it was more than five dollars I knew I would just have to leave the typewriter there until I was able to reclaim it.

Just minutes after my return the typewriter was slid across the counter to me with, "I was able to straighten it pretty well, and it should work all right now!"

Upon expressing my appreciation I asked somewhat fearfully what the cost was for the repair. With a warm smile and a wave of his hand toward the door he replied, "Nothing. Just pick up the machine and walk through that door with it."

Surprise subsided into gratitude, and with a heart overflowing with thanksgiving I fairly sailed out of the shop. I joyfully concluded that this wayward son of the living God was evidencing a first step toward getting back into right relationship with the Lord by helping one of His servants. Whatever the reason, the Lord had definitely led and undertaken all the way. He had honored my determination and desire never again to borrow to work out my problems or needs. Shortly thereafter it was with no little relief to my conscience that I was able to pay my parking fine. However, money was still coming in rather slowly, and though I was not aware of it the ultimate test was yet at hand. I was learning that it is the little places of trials and testings that prepare us for the big ones.

Mother's cousin in Hanford (some two hundred miles from Sacramento) had made request for me to come there to present my slides to her church. I was glad for the further outreach. Subsequently, she made three engagements for me with the promise of a love offering to cover expenses when I came.

As the set time approached I knew I did not have sufficient funds for gas to get to Hanford. Only one more meeting was scheduled before I would have to leave to fulfill my appointment—a missionary meeting in a church across the street from Mother's house. I wouldn't need gas money for that meeting at least! And as far as I knew it was my last hope. For days I continually beseeched the Lord, reminding Him of my need, fully aware that if He did not supply apart from my asking or borrowing, I would have to cancel the Hanford meetings. As embarrassing as that might be I would have to conclude, though, in such event, that they were not of Him.

The evening of the missionary meeting, with hopeful heart I went forth, carrying my equipment with me across the street.

It was encouraging to know that Mother, remaining at home, had taken up the banner of prayer in behalf of my need. Whether or not she was in perfect accord with my new determination to live by faith alone, at least she stood behind me in my conviction.

As the group was assembling I proceeded to set up my screen and projector. And then this night of all nights everything seemed to go wrong! In plugging in my extension cord the frayed end (which had just recently been fixed) shorted out. One of the men scouted up another one in the church to substitute for mine. But when I saw it was a heavy duty cord I voiced my fear of using it, for previously when doing so the cord had blown out the bulb in my projector. Upon being assured that such really should not happen—the size of the cord shouldn't make any difference—I hesitantly gave consent. Everything appeared all right at first when suddenly, out flickered the bulb! Fortunately we were able to obtain another projector from the pastor's house several doors away. After only a short delay I was able to present our tour of the Holy Land, emphasizing my burden of prayer for Israel.

My presentation completed, the group proceeded to take up an offering—for their own missionaries! My heart sank. Recently I had poured out my heart to a number of missionary groups such as this one, watched them take up an offering for their own missionaries and send me away with a thank you and a hand shake. As bravely as I could I committed it to the Lord, "All right, Lord. Thy will be done." No gas money, no bulb, no extension cord—all added up to no meeting either!

Then just as the meeting was closing, one gentleman rose to his feet and began, "Mrs. Carter was very gracious to give her time to come and show us her very inspiring slides this evening. Unfortunately both her cord and projector bulb burned out. I feel we should take up an offering to buy her a new bulb at least! I could hardly believe my ears! What had appeared on the surface as ill fortune had been the Lord's way of moving this man's heart to meet my unrevealed needs. Gratefully I accepted this token of their desire to help my misfortune and returned home shouting a song in my heart. Upon counting the handful of change received I was doubly blessed to find it just enough for a new bulb plus a tank of gas to get to Hanford the next morning!

My financial status began to improve at that point and never again did I get involved in a web of debt—nor did I ever lack for anything I really needed. Over and over again He would prove the veracity of His word in my daily living, and Psalm 84:11, "No good thing will he withhold from them that walk uprightly," became a moment by moment reality. As I would later be able to testify—the life of complete faith (full dependence upon the Lord for everything) is the most stressless way of living in this world, for He never fails and delights to give His children good gifts.

As the Christmas season neared, the Lord provided about six weeks' employment with the downtown Bible Book Store. This not only augmented my income, providing for some car repairs and extras which helped at the time, but also gave precious opportunities to serve Him.

Meanwhile, continued contact through the mails enabled me to keep a consistent witness before Miriam in London. Her letters of loneliness, insecurity, and betrayal by her own family gave rise to sympathetic intercession for her. Jesus Christ as the only true and lasting answer was presented over and over. I was thankful to learn other Hebrew Christians there in London were befriending her as well. Surely God's Word would soon reap a harvest in this fertile heart.

CHAPTER XXXV

TO THE ENDS OF THE EARTH?

WORK IN THE Blue Ridge Mountains, although in many ways trying, had been full and rewarding. There had been numerous speaking and preaching opportunities among under-privileged children in numerous public schools presenting, as well as the Gospel message, the grand history, grievous present, and glorious future of the Jew in God's program.

It was amusing to Mike to find that most of these children had never knowingly seen a Jew and would stare at him as though he had horns or had recently ventured here from Mars. Taking everything literally as is the inherent nature of children to do, they were sure the Children of Israel were juveniles even as they themselves.

In spite of a busy schedule which included more than seventy-five speaking engagements within a two-month period, as well as God's blessing upon the work, Mike's heart could not be content with laboring solely among the Gentiles. There was decided disappointment that the expected contacts with a Jew here and there had not been realized.

Meanwhile my soul had not been able to rest peacefully in Mike's departure from Jewish missionary work. Striving often in fervent prayer that the Lord would lead him back to his own people who so desperately need his testimony was my bur-dened soul's only release. Thus upon picking up a letter from Mike early in November the words I read stirred anew the chords of praise:

"The other day there was such a heavy longing in my heart for Israel. . . .

213

"This work in Samaria has left me with a deeper burden for her! It has enabled me to see how few breathe a prayer for the Jew! As a result my heart burns even more intensely that the Lord Jesus will lead me back to working among His own!

"December 9 continues to remain the deadline insofar as ministering in this area is concerned. A call has come from a Hebrew Christian worker in Washington, D.C., to join hands in the ministry among the Jews there. Thus far it seems that the Lord would have me go there to look into things. However, it seems to me that He is leading back to California (that the Washington call will be turned down). If so, it would be shortly before Christmas Day before I'd reach California."

Upon learning of Mike's possible return to California just before Christmas, I felt strongly compelled to invite him to spend the holiday with my family and me and our mutual Christian friends in Sacramento. His acceptance was contingent, of course, upon the Lord's leading in Washington, D.C.

In Washington Mike investigated the offer from the mission to share in Jewish evangelism there. He was confronted with the need and saw the possibilities of the work, but after careful, prayerful consideration, the witness to his own heart was, "No, not here."

In searching out the mind of God and pondering the Holy Spirit's use of Acts 1:8 in his life, having traversed Samaria, he halfway anticipated the word of a ship at hand to take him to the ends of the earth. But with no evidence of a ship or an apparent leading on out, and with the pressure of an expected decision, he persevered in prayer for a definite sense of direction. "Lord Jesus, be pleased to show me Your will for me. Perhaps even by a letter today You would direct me!"

A little later in the morning Mike received his mail—one letter—and misaddressed! As he thoughtfully handled that envelope he marvelled that it should have reached him, improperly addressed to a stranger in Washington, D.C. His heart and hope ascended heavenward, "Lord, please let your direction be in this letter in some way!" Then with a sense of expectancy he tore open the envelope to find it was from Claude, his spiritual father, in San Bernardino. He was altogether amazed but overjoyed as his eyes caught the words, "Dear Son, come home!"

214

So it was that less than a week before Christmas I found a card in the mailbox, postmarked Ohio. "The Lord has made it clear to me that it is His will for me to return to California, praise His Name! Thus, it will be possible for me to be with you for Christmas. Am now en route and, Lord willing, will inform you of the exact day of arrival."

Wednesday morning, the twenty-second, just before I left for work a strong impression came upon me, "Put out fresh towels for Mike in the bathroom." Unable to ignore such a strong compulsion, I obeyed and also put a note on the front door as to where Mike could find me to get a key to the house.

Mid-afternoon the telephone in the Bible Book Store rang. It was for me. The familiar voice on the other end brought a flush of excitement and verified the divine origin of the compulsion to put out the towels in the morning! Hurrying home after work I could not cease giving thanks for the joy of anticipated fellowship once again with Mike, after thinking our paths might never cross again.

While Mother and I were preparing dinner in the kitchen that evening, the doorbell rang. Mike offered to answer it for us and came back in a few moments with a puzzled expression on his face. "Special Delivery," he announced, "from me! I thought when I found your note on the door you had received this, telling of my arrival today! Just how did you know?"

We were all quite amused that Mike had arrived in time to receive his own special delivery letter at the door. "The Lord told me," I answered and related my experience of the morning. And none of us could doubt the Lord's hand in all this, that it was assuredly His will for Mike to be with us.

The week passed all too quickly, filled as it was with visiting, services, dinner invitations, and preaching opportunities for Mike. Unknown to me he was looking for some sign that he had not been mistaken in believing the Lord had revealed my love to him. The fact that the Lord was directing him back home from Samaria, rather than to the ends of the earth as he had expected, caused Mike to wonder if the giving up of his love could have also been a temporary thing. And if so, he pondered, did Ruth really care for him enough to be his wife?

At the same time I was hoping for some sign from him

that the Lord was moving his heart in my direction and that he no longer felt the Lord had called him to a life of celibacy. Not a word or sign passed between us, but there was no mistaking at times the magnetic bond of love transmitted between us. However, we both regarded this love as of spiritual origin only—a beautiful fellowship in the Lord!

When Mike's departure to San Bernardino came, I was glad to be able to look forward to seeing him in about five weeks when I was due to show my slides there. Mike, on the other hand, did not then voice the doubts he entertained. For some reason he did not expect the meetings to develop. Although I was confident of the Lord's leading to San Bernardino, I had no idea of the impact it would have on both our lives.

Ruth, the Moabitess, had received her preparation for her presentation to Boaz in the house of her mother-in-law. Then she was sent out alone to the place of Boaz's abiding.

CHAPTER XXXVI

INTREAT ME NOT . . .

Now IT WAS MY TURN to think I was going to the ends of the earth! Sacramento had proved one thing to me all over again! I could not effectively alone, especially as a woman, begin to reach the Jewish community. The Lord had not opened a work to me here any more than He had in Israel. Nevertheless, during the same period He had used me through the slides to give understanding and to burden many to pray for the lost Jew and Israel. Time and again I had witnessed the Lord's anointing upon the slides. Now the door had opened to present their message in San Bernardino. Would another door open after San Bernardino and another and another?

The thought of raising up prayer groups even across America for these precious, spiritually exiled souls thrilled me. And the grand climax perhaps by then could be an open door back to Israel, this time to remain and labor. There had been a continuous strong sense that I had not yet found the place where I belonged, where I could rest in His vineyard. If I could not effectively serve alone any better in America than I could in Israel, I might as well be where my heart dwelt anyway!

A warm welcome was awaiting my arrival in San Bernardino on February 5. Mrs. Blakely had arranged a full schedule of meetings for me covering more than a month. Extensive previous prayer had prepared the way for an enthusiastic reception of the slides and their message everywhere. There were many evidences that the Lord was doing a work in Israel's behalf, through them bringing assurance of His direction in all of this and confidence concerning the future.

There were other definite signs of the Lord's hand upon my life and labors. A blessed, though puzzling, event occurred at a ladies' missionary meeting one afternoon in Fontana, near San Bernardino. Just prior to the showing of my slides the women had been working on a very unique quilt. It was being made up of large squares of vari-patterned material (sewed together) upon which were appliqued plain hearts which in turn had been embroidered with scripture references. From where I was sitting only one reference was plainly visible, and I wondered if the Lord was speaking encouragement to my heart when I saw the reference, Ruth 1:16, 17. Could this be a token from Him, as I wanted to believe, that Ruth would indeed be fulfilled—completed in my life?

Mike often came to Mrs. Blakely's home for a time of fellowship and Bible study in the morning, and so it was an added blessing to be with him in this way again. It did grieve me, however, to find he was not enjoying the fullness of the Lord. The radiant beauty of the Spirit of Christ which had attracted me to him early in our acquaintance was not shining from his countenance. I was aware of an unfortunate misunderstanding in recent months that had left Mike feeling let down by Christian friends who were very dear to him. This heartache on top of his family's rejection (his mother had not answered his letters for eight months now), plus the discouragement of not having seen the ministry unto the Israel of San Bernardino open as he had hoped, had brought on a spirit of depression and robbed him of the fullness of joy in the Lord.

Now the heaviness that was weighing upon his spirit became my own burden of concern for him. I beseeched the Lord for the privilege of being able in some way to encourage and help lift the spirit of darkness. I wanted him to know there was someone besides the Lord who truly cared.

February 11 was at hand. This would be Mike's fourth spiritual birthday. Aware of how much his spiritual birthdays meant to him, how precious he regarded each anniversary of the day of his spiritual liberation from the darkness that had constantly enshrouded and plagued his life, I prayed for some way to be used to bless perhaps this last one that I would be able to share in this small way with him.

As Mike felt his place was definitely in San Bernardino, and

218

I expected to move on within a few weeks, with Israel hopefully once again my ultimate goal, it seemed doubtful the Lord was going to bring us together, especially since He had not done so by now. A strong desire came upon me while praying, to write him a good-bye birthday note, with the assurance of my loyal and God-given love in the Gospel always.

Knowing that Mike had made plans to be in Los Angeles for his anniversary, when he came to Mrs. Blakely's for Bible study the morning of the 10th, the birthday note which had been written was given to him with the explicit instructions not to be opened until the 11th!

In Los Angeles on the morning of the 11th, Mike was looking to the Lord for a special blessing such as the Lord had usually given him on each of his previous spiritual birthdays. Suddenly he remembered the note. With a feeling of expectation he retrieved it from a jacket pocket. Prayerfully he opened it and began to read:

"May our precious Lord and sweet Saviour make this the most blessed day of your life heretofore. May He give to you all of His fullness, and sweep you into His gracious love, showering you with peace and joy.

"This may be the last spiritual birthday of yours in my life, for it seems the Lord is leading our lives apart as I face toward Israel and you settle down in your work here. Mike, always know my prayers will be with you as long as He gives me breath to breathe and thoughts in my head and heart to pray. If ever you feel alone and unloved, remember there are two who will love you always, our precious Lord and I—even that you might be edified to know that besides the Lord there is one here on earth standing behind you in her heart.

"Mike, my only desire is that your life may be full of joy and that your ministry might be what He has shown me it can be. My God-given love seeks satisfaction only in seeing you the man of God He has purposed since before the world that you should be. And so my prayer for you is that you may receive all of God's very, very best both now and always. May each day be full of grace and may the sunshine of His smile rest upon you.

"Happy spiritual birthday from one who will always remember you because God has engraved you upon my heart. Ruth."

As the reality of what he was reading settled upon him, joy and conflict began to flood him. Here was more than the sign he had sought in Sacramento—even proof that he had understood aright the Lord's revelation to him months before. He knew now, beyond doubt, that this love was more than that of Christian friendship. Assurance had filled him of Ruth's personal love for him—the same assurance Boaz must have felt when his Ruth presented herself for his protection on the threshingfloor.

But now what should he do? He had given Ruth up to the Lord for the calling to the fields beyond. And yet the Lord had brought him back home from the fields instead of thrusting him on out as he had anticipated. Did this mean he was now at liberty to ask Ruth to be his wife? Or should he because of the shortness of time, the wickedness of the day, and the great need of the lost remain unhampered by any earthly ties such as a family?

And so the conflict in thought continued: Perhaps because of the evil of the day a married man could have more freedom in his ministry—less cause to be misunderstood! Then too, he had seen in Israel the balance of the woman's part in the ministry complementing the man's, even as God had purposed from the beginning when He gave Adam a helpmeet! Only the clear mind of the Lord could resolve such conflict!

And another parallel was being fulfilled, for it was even as Naomi had predicted, ". . .the man will not be in rest, until he have finished the thing this day" (Ruth 3:18).

Having returned to San Bernardino the night of the 12th, still unsettled as to the Lord's will, Mike sat in his bachelor apartment alone. He knew he would see Ruth on the morrow, for the Spragues (the family who had led him to Christ) had invited her to dinner in order to meet her. They had heard much of Ruth and felt she might well be the answer to their prayers for a Christian wife for Mike. They had done all they could through the months to encourage Mike that now what he needed most was the Lord's helpmeet for him.

As Mike sat there pondering, a tremendous wave of loneliness suddenly swept over him. Looking around he thought, "Is this all I have to look forward to in the future should the Lord tarry?" A sense of being alone as he had rarely experienced in the past revealed to him the emptiness and sorrow of coming to the close of one's life alone. Down on his knees before the Lord earnestly, determinedly seeking His will for him, Mike received his answer and knew what he must do.

I awoke Sunday morning with a feeling of nervous excitement. Already the soft February sun had begun to melt away the early morning dew and the clear sky promised one of those lovely warm winter days that draw so many to southern California. The realization that Mike now knew the cherished secret of my heart sent a nervous tingling down my spine. What would be his reaction? Would he be fearful of continuing our close friendship and seek cessation of our fellowship? Or would he be his warm and friendly self, having accepted my note in the spirit of encouragement in which it was given?

Even though I had in essence said good-bye, there was always the slight hope underneath that if we did not lose contact with each other, that yet someday the Lord would bring us together in the ministry I had envisioned. Just why He had withheld at this time I was not to question, but rather to receive His withholding as well as His giving with praise and thanksgiving.

My stomach fluttered a little when the telephone jangled. Answering, Mrs. Blakely spoke a few words and then came to my room. "Mike would like to speak to you, Ruth dear."

If only I could stop shaking inside! Calling upon all the self control I could muster and whispering a prayer for inner calmness, I tried not to appear emotional. I was thankful he couldn't know the claminess of my hands as I picked up the receiver. "Good morning, Mike."

The sound of his same friendly voice at the other end of the line brought a measure of relief. "The Spragues have asked me to bring you to their house for dinner after church, and since they live next door to the church, if it is all right with you, I'll pick you up in time for Sunday school." Arrangements were made, and not altogether successfully, I tried to hide my nervous anticipation! At least he wasn't cutting off our fellowship immediately, I reassured myself.

When Mike came for me I rejoiced to see that the Lord had restored to some degree the joy of his salvation to him. The heaviness that weighted him down when I had last seen him four days earlier had been lifted. Too, I was greatly relieved to note that our bond of fellowship was as cordial as before the note. On the way to Sunday school Mike remarked, "We have some things to talk about later, so as soon as we can after dinner we'll get away from the Spragues!" I nodded agreement, wondering what he meant, not daring to allow impatience or eagerness to have a voice.

The Spragues were lovely to me and it was a special blessing to finally meet the family who had been used so greatly in Mike's life. As soon after dinner as could be considered polite, Mike excused us as he had planned. Pulling away from the Spragues' house, he debated as to where we could talk without interruption, finally recalling that he had seen a park where we could enjoy the warm sunshine as we discussed some matters. Receiving my approval, we were off for the park and were soon settled at a picnic table with our Bibles open before us. The voices and laughter of children at play and of those enjoying the loveliness of the park soon was lost to our awareness as Mike unfolded his story.

"In order to relate all I have to say I must go back and start at the beginning."

Breathlessly and fearfully I waited as he quietly and deliberately chose his words.

"When I first met you, Ruth, at Biola, I was impressed by your love for the Lord and your zeal for Him. I appreciated your fellowship and rejoiced in your love for my people. But my feeling for you was only in the spiritual realm. When we were brought together in Israel, first at the airport and then at length in the language Ulpan, frankly I wondered why it should be! At times I was glad, and at times—well you know how we both felt at times!

"It became apparent it was for mutual benefit spiritually and otherwise too, but now I know the Lord had longer ranged purposes. You have known all along that I have felt the Lord would have me serve Him alone, that in view of the shortness of time and the tremendous needs of work to be done I should give my all to Him." At that moment it truly seemed this was good-bye and I was thankful my heart was sweetly—though painfully—yielded to His will.

Mike went on, "At the same time I wanted the Lord's best for my life. And so I prayed, 'Lord, if You want me married, if this is best for me and my ministry, then please bring the girl of your choice into my life!' Through the years I had wanted a wife and home and family, but was always afraid to marry for fear of committing suicide, leaving an innocent wife and children behind to suffer. After my conversion this block had been removed, but to all appearances it seemed I could serve the Lord better alone.

"Then through our fellowship in Israel the Lord began to work in my heart, at first unrecognized by me. After leaving Israel I began to realize how much you were in my heart and that the Lord had given me a love for you—that of a man for a woman, one that he would want for his wife."

It was unbelievable! Was this reality or just another of those beautiful waking dreams I had cherished for so long? These were the words that I had so longed to hear. The Lord had indeed spoken to my heart of his love—but also of his sacrifice. I dared not raise my hopes too high. Was this still ultimately good-bye?

Conscious of the impact of his words Mike went on, "Now however, I had to ascertain the Lord's will in the matter! Was marriage for me? On my way back to San Bernardino last summer from New York, I picked up a hitch-hiker. Here was someone who could be impartial, so I wanted to get his viewpoint. After telling him somewhat about us, our backgrounds, spiritual desires and aspirations, I was really startled to hear him say he thought you were certainly the one for me and I ought to marry you.

"In Michigan I had also told my mother a little about you and she encouraged me to marry, too. So when I learned I must go through Sacramento on my way back to Southern California, I wondered if the Lord was in reality directing my way to you. During my brief stay in Sacramento, I was hoping for a sign from you that you cared for me. I saw nothing but Christian love. Nevertheless, soon after returning to San Bernardino, the Lord clearly revealed to me that you did love me, and then asked me to put you on the altar as He had a work for me to do alone."

As he recounted his leading to West Virginia, on to Washington, D.C., only to be turned around and headed home again, my heart thrilled at the marvelous working of the Spirit of God.

It was my turn now to reveal to him the precious outworking of "Ruth" in my life. With the book open before him he saw the parallel immediately: Ruth, a little Gentile widow, had forsaken her land and people to become one with the Jews. Then by an act of God she was brought into the life of Boaz, an eligible Jewish bachelor, while out in the fields of Israel.

"The Lord revealed to me your love also, Mike, and even that you had given me up for Him. I could not rebel or fight or even plead against such devotion to Christ for I, too, was asked to place you upon the altar of sacrifice—not once but twice!" I recounted my experiences in Israel and later the fullness of the test of willingness to go to China.

Mike continued, "When the Lord brought me back to Sacramento at Christmas time, I wondered then if it was to show me that the sacrifice was only temporary and He would bring us together. However, there was no sign or indication from the Lord or you!"

As he talked, over and over my heart would soar with hope, flutter with fear, and then crash with pain! After all of this, was it still to be good-bye?

"Somehow I didn't really expect you to come to San Bernardino with your pictures, and when you did I wondered, 'Why, Lord? What is this all about?' When I received your note for my spiritual birthday, I expected a blessing from it, as I always receive a blessing from your letters. I waited until I was alone to read it."

My heart sank once again as he told of the conflict into which it cast him and his determination not to quit the Lord's presence until he had the Lord's mind and knew His will in the matter once and for all. The only thing that gave me inner strength and outward composure was the assurance that His grace is sufficient no matter what, and my heart was upon His altar of sacrifice awaiting His good pleasure.

Mike was concluding, "Even so, the Lord did show me that a dedicated man can be married in this evil generation and be in the perfect center of His will. However, at this time I feel led of the Lord to try to work among the Jewish people here in San Bernardino and you feel the Lord is possibly leading you back to Israel. You, of course, even as I, must know the mind of the Lord for yourself."

He paused and in the quietness of that moment my mind grasped for a straw to cling to as I prepared myself for his apparent forthcoming words of departure with a possibility of marriage in the future should the Lord at some time be pleased to direct us together.

His words broke the momentary silence. "And so I guess there is nothing left for me to say, except to ask you to be my wife!"

So sure that he was going to say, "There is nothing left for me to say—but good-bye," I was stunned into silence. Almost frantically I searched for the mind of the Lord. Though I had wanted this for so long, I was so prepared to accept a good-bye from him that I couldn't say yes, and certainly not no! It seemed my faculties of utterance had departed leaving me speechless, while the thoughts flashed through my mind: "Should I say, 'Let me think about it, or give me time to pray about it'?"

The moments of silence became a fearful agony to Mike. Inwardly he pled, "Don't let her say 'no' or even 'wait,' Lord."

Suddenly my eyes fell upon the Bible before us that lay open to the Book of Ruth. It was as though Someone else took hold of my tongue and I found the words tumbling out of my mouth, "My answer to you is Ruth 1:16, 17."

Half fearfully, half hopefully, not knowing what Ruth 1:16, 17 contained, Mike began to read, "And Ruth said, Intreat me not to leave thee, or to return from following after thee: for whither thou goest, I will go; and where thou lodgest, I will lodge: thy people shall be my people, and thy God my God: where thou diest, will I die, and there will I be buried: the Lord do so to me, and more also, if ought but death part thee and me."

Trying to grasp the significance of what had just transpired, we fell silent before the Lord. It had come upon us so fast there was now a struggle to comprehend that the Lord had actually consummated our long awaited heart's desire. Then finding his voice, Mike sweetly declared, "I think this calls for a kiss, don't you?" and reaching over kissed me for the first time. Then two hearts, knit together in love, bowed in humble thanksgiving and praise before the wonderful One who had planned it all and brought us to this day.

Part IV   IN THE HEART AND HOME OF BOAZ

CHAPTER IV of RUTH of the HOLY BIBLE

CHAPTER XXXVII

FULFILLMENT

THE FOLLOWING DAY BROUGHT VIA THE MAIL a thrilling token of the Lord's seal of blessing upon our prospective united ministry. Picking up a letter with a British postmark, Mike noted it was from Miriam. In turning the letter over to break the seal, Mike's eyes caught the neatly penned words across the back of the envelope. His heart leaped within as his mind comprehended the message his eyes were recording! "As of this writing I believe I have been born-again. Pray for me!"

As time would prove, this one for whom we both, together and apart, had travailed in word and prayer had indeed found solace and peace—a new life—in birth from above. Miriam, the first known fruit of our combined efforts, we felt certain to be the Lord's indication of a fruitful future together.

Four days later I awakened to the realization that though we had shared a great deal of Christian fellowship, Mike had never courted me—had never asked me for a date as such! Faced with the fact, he promptly rectified the situation by asking me out. Needless to say I was only too glad to accept, and so we enjoyed our first actual date four days after our engagement!

At first we enjoyed the anticipation of surprising our friends with the announcement of our betrothal. But right from the beginning the surprise was destined to be ours, for we found scores of people had been praying to that end. Those who knew Mike had prayed the Lord would give him a helpmeet; others seeing my need had prayed for a husband for me. Still others who knew both of us felt we would complement each other's ministry and had prayed accordingly.

We could hardly wait to surprise, so we thought, our very dear mutual friend of Biola days, Dr. Feinberg. We went to see him at our first opportunity and glowingly shared our joyful news, only to be taken aback when he nonchalantly responded with, "What took you so long?"

Prayerfully looking to the Lord to consummate our wedding plans, we sought His leading in every detail. A first and important decision was the setting of the date. Considering all things we felt that the first Sunday in April would be a suitable time, allowing for the fulfillment of present commitments as well as the working out of details for the wedding. While seeking the Lord's mind, Mike took from his wallet a pocket calendar to see upon which date the first Sunday fell. We looked at each other in amazement! It was almost as though the Lord himself had spoken—which indeed He actually had! The Scripture text printed at the bottom of the card stood out in bold type. "This is the day which the Lord hath made; we will rejoice and be glad in it" (Ps. 118:24). We were satisfied that April 3 was the Lord's choice!

It proved to be a beautiful warm Palm Sunday. In the afternoon more than four hundred guests gathered at the little church behind which four years earlier a desperate Mike Perl had sought privacy and stood alone calling to the Lord with all of his heart. This modest but lovely little church, which rang with his first radiant testimony to newness of life through union with Christ, would significantly witness this next most joyous union about to be wrought in his life.

Since "Ruth" had become my story woven into the tapestry of my life, it was only fitting that her love story should be the setting of our wedding ceremony. Diane came from Sacramento to read excerpts from the Book of Ruth to the waiting audience, revealing the story of the Gentile widow who forsook all to become one with the Jews and reaped a rich harvest in the heart and home of Boaz.

The beautiful words and music of "The Holy City" followed, adding Jewish color and projecting us back to our beloved Israel, where our precious Messiah had set into motion the chain of events that had culminated in this day. A wedding could not be complete without words of love pledged one to another. Our wedding song beautifully portrayed not only this love for one another given by Him, but also our two hearts, knit together as one in love, turned in dedication to adore and serve Him. The words would long linger upon our ears and in our hearts, "We pledge our life to Christ our Lord, to do His will, obey His Word. . . ."

Then as hearts bowed in quiet meditation before Him, chords of the immortal words of Ruth's dedication and devotion to the people and God of Israel completed the preparation for our appearances.

Pastor Bill Reed, a friend of Mike's since shortly after his new birth, and a true friend of Israel for many years, fittingly officiated for us. His words were carefully chosen. "Mike, and according to your Hebrew name, Meir, wilt thou have this woman to be thy lawfully wedded wife, to live together after God's ordinance in the holy state of matrimony?"

"I will."

"Wilt thou love her, comfort her, honor her, and keep her in sickness and in health and forsaking all others keep thyself solely for her so long as you both shall live?"

Mike's voice was deep with emotion as he turned to face me, "And now . . . fear not; I will do to thee all that thou requirest: for all the city of my people doth know that thou art a virtuous woman. And now it is true that I am thy near kinsman; howbeit there is a kinsman nearer than I . . . the Lord God of Israel under whose wings thou art come to trust" (Ruth 3:11, 12; 2:12b).

Pastor Reed continued, "June, and according to your Hebrew name, Ruth, wilt thou have this man to be thy lawfully wedded husband to live together after God's ordinance in the holy state of matrimony?"

"I will."

"Wilt thou love, honor, serve, obey, and keep him in sickness and in health and forsaking all others keep thyself solely for him so long as you both shall live?"

With the same deep meaning as the Ruth who first voiced the words, I repeated my pledge to my Boaz, his God and his people. "Intreat me not to leave thee, or to return from following after thee: for whither thou goest, I will go; and where thou lodgest, I will lodge: thy people shall be my people, and thy God my God: where thou diest, will I die, and there will I be buried: the Lord do so to me, and more also, if ought but death part thee and me" (Ruth 1:16, 17).

"What tokens of this love covenant do you bestow upon each other?"

Mike answered, "A pair of rings."

We had designed our matching wedding rings ourselves as a tribute and testimony to our faith and calling. Alternately engraved upon the broad white gold bands were the star of David portraying Israel and the Old Covenant, and the cross representing the New Covenant, the fulfillment of the Old.

Addressing the congregation of witnesses Pastor Reed continued. "The wedding ring, which is a complete circle, is a fitting emblem of eternity. Being composed of a circle it is a constant reminder to us not only of the undying love now pledged between these two, but also of the untarnishable and eternal love of God who is now uniting this home together. . . .

"And now since these two lives before us are both of Jewish descent, it is very fitting that we bring a great spiritual truth into this ceremony from the Hebrew Scriptures themselves concerning the God whom they love and worship and seek to honor. In Deut. 6:4 are these wonderful and significant words, 'Hear, O Israel: the Lord our God is one Lord.' In the Hebrew the word Echod, which means one, contains a great message, for it signifies not the idea of a single one but the thought of a union—a united one.

"In the Scriptures God uses this same Hebrew word for one to designate the holy union which is to exist between a man and his wife: they two shall be one flesh (Gen. 2:24). This is a great mystery and God has also used it in the New Testament for the beautiful symbol of the bond and the love that exists between Christ and His Church. In Ephesians 5 of the New Testament we read, 'So ought men to love their wives as their own bodies. He that loveth his wife loveth himself. For no man ever yet hated his own flesh; but nourisheth and cherisheth it, even as the Lord the church. . . . As the church is subject unto Christ, so let the wives be to their own husbands in everything' (Eph. 5:28, 29, 24).

"Therefore, Meir and Ruth, as you receive and give these rings, may the God of heaven look upon you and add His manifold blessing upon you, your lives, your home, your love, and your service for Him; and may He keep these vows inviolate until in His will death do you part."

Our voices in turn repeated after Pastor Reed's, "With this ring, Ruth (Meir), I thee wed in the name of the Lord Jesus Christ." ("That in all things He might have the preeminence.")

Pastor Reed continued, "As a final symbol of this holy union, will you two now join your right hands?" And addressing the audience, "For as much as Meir and Ruth have consented together in holy wedlock and have witnessed the same before God and this company and thereto have pledged their faith each to the other by giving and receiving a ring and by joining their right hands, I now pronounce them man and wife together in the name of the Lord Jesus Christ. What God hath joined together let no man put asunder. 'And so Boaz [Meir] took Ruth and she was his wife. . .' (Ruth 4:13a). Let us pray:

"Our Father and our God as these two lives are kneeling before us now we cannot help but think back to the chain of events that has brought them together. We know that it is entirely of Your doing, for to us it seems as though it was a golden chain of events that has been welded together to bring these two lives to this moment. And, our Father, we feel that the chain is not yet complete, but that You have a service for them together in holy union, and to that end we pray that You will bless them.

"As the name of Meir means 'light bringer,' we pray their lives may truly bring light to those whom they meet, to those they contact both of their own people and of those of the Gentiles. And we pray as the name of Ruth means 'friendship' that many, O God, might be brought into the friendship that they long in their hearts that their home shall manifest, a place, a haven, where many shall learn the name of Jesus and the love that comes down from heaven. To that end we pray that You will bless and seal this union in the name of our Saviour, the Lord Jesus Christ."

In that sacred moment the strains of song committing our future life's journey together with Christ to the keeping and enabling power of our Saviour who had brought us together sealed our wedding prayer. Rising from our knees and sealing our vows to each other with a kiss, we turned to face the world as Mr. and Mrs. Mike Perl.

CHAPTER XXXVIII

THY PEOPLE—MY PEOPLE

IT IS REASONABLE TO ASSUME from the biblical account that Ruth remained and settled in the city and home of her husband Boaz, and there fulfilled the will of the Lord for her.

Mike's vision of the spiritual need of the more than five thousand Jews of the San Bernardino valley who were without a messianic witness had drawn and redrawn him to this area for several years. The circumstances in Israel that had closed the door to us nearly a year before had not changed and until they did or the Lord clearly moved us out in that direction again, it was not reasonable to return.

And so weighing together the vision of the need, the burden, and the opportunity, it seemed apparent we should wait upon the Lord for an opening of the doors to a ministry here. Perhaps a token of the Lord's leading could be surmised from the fact that there had been five unsaved Jews in attendance at our wedding, among whom were the jeweler and his wife through whom we had designed and obtained our wedding bands.

Upon returning from our honeymoon, we rented a modest little furnished two-bedroom house, one bedroom of which Mike used as his office and study. Such were the humble beginnings of what is now the Hebrew Christian Witness, an independent non-denominational, non-profit faith mission to our people in San Bernardino and the surrounding areas.

From the beginning I was to realize fully the wisdom and perfect workings of the Lord through my financial difficulties, which had resulted in my receiving of the gift of faith for subsistence in this material world. From the time two years earlier when Mike had severed his only source of income, the G.I. Bill, by leaving Biola College in order to go to Israel, he had subsisted by total reliance upon the Lord's provision. It had been a joyous experience for him to see the Lord supply his every need; however, when he was contemplating marriage the question arose in his mind, "Do I dare, or ethically should I, ask Ruth to marry me without a regular income?" Peace and assurance came with the witness to his heart—if this is of the Lord He will provide for Ruth, too!

My preparation by the Lord made it easy for me to join Mike in his ministry of faith—to wait together upon the Lord alone for the supply of each and every need. Our policy from the beginning was and is never to voice a financial need personally or for the ministry on the horizontal level, bringing our requests to Him alone in private. Consistency meant to us never appealing or hinting for funds in any way, including never passing a collection plate at meetings. And right from the beginning He has proved himself faithful, the Giver of every good and perfect gift.

Early in our ministry we saw a need arising which we estimated would require several hundred dollars to meet. Friends concerned about helping us reach the needy Jews in our area had been used of the Lord through their gifts to us to provide our daily necessities, but from whence would such an amount as several hundred dollars come? We went to the only One who had the answer and could meet the need.

One day we picked up a letter from a dear couple in a nearby city, and were amazed to find a check enclosed for $500. The need, as it turned out, required a sum of $492.

It wasn't until sometime later, when meeting with the couple, that we related the incident of the Lord's provision through them. They rejoiced to know beyond a doubt that they definitely had been led of the Lord to send us such a large amount. They recalled their reasoning as to whether or not the two of us living in a rental and without a church building or program for which to supply could possibly need such an amount. The prompting of the Lord had been so strong they let it overrule their reasoning and obediently sent the check, much to their ultimate joy and thanksgiving as well as ours.

236

Pioneering is always a slow uphill climb, and as we sought, often painstakingly, for Jewish contacts, we became convinced of the tremendous value of getting the Word into the Jewish home by means of radio. While Mike was discussing the possibilities and voicing his intention of looking into the costs of a thirty-minute broadcast at one of the local radio stations, one of his listeners, a businessman, spoke up, "Let me know what you learn." When the requested information was given him a little later he offered, "Contract for a quarter year to be paid in advance and send me the bill!"

Thus began the only weekly evangelistic message of its kind in the area, geared to reaching unsaved Jews by identifying the Jewish Messiah through Old Testament prophecies. It was destined to continue for many years and to be the channel to salvation for Jew and Gentile alike. For twelve full years the prorgam has continued—without one solicitation or hint for financial help—paid for currently, if not in advance. We are convinced that when the funds are not brought in by the direct touch of the Lord upon hearts, it will be His time to discontinue the broadcasts.

As time passed it became evident that in order to broaden our ministry and reach out in a larger sphere to help more people by means of classes and meetings, and also in view of our prospective family, we would need larger and more adequate quarters. Rents for what we needed were exorbitant, and we felt we could not buy without a regular income. What to do? Again the matter was placed before the Lord. In direct answer to prayer the Lord led through circumstances to a three-bedroom home with a building on the rear of the lot which converted very nicely into a study and office for Mike. We were able to assume a mortgage already against the house without the usually required regular income for security, and our needs were met at monthly payments much less than rent would have been.

From the beginning, however, Mike felt concerned about the mortgage, which he came to consider an indebtedness as well as an investment. Again we took the matter privately to the Lord in prayer. Without our solicitation He moved upon hearts over a period of time, and several large gifts came to us specified to be applied against the mortgage of the home. Seven years exactly to the very time of our purchase the mortgage was paid in full, and our only indebtedness was cleared!

It was a blessing and a joy to see the Lord adequately furnish our home, providing each necessary item in a variety of ways, each in answer to prayer. So when our car began showing signs of terminal old age, it was with a spirit of anticipation we waited upon the Lord to see how He would meet this need.

One morning after Mike had fulfilled a commitment out of town, he paid a call on a business friend whose fervent concern in life was to help get the Gospel out to Jew and Gentile alike. After a few words of greeting he bluntly inquired of Mike, "Do you need any money?"

Not wanting to place himself in the position of asking of anyone other than the Lord for our needs Mike answered, "There are a couple of things we are praying about."

Our friend refused to be put off. "Well, what are they?"

Knowing that behind the prodding there was definite purpose, Mike truthfully revealed, "One is for better transportation. We have a little money on hand, but whether it is for a car or not the Lord hasn't shown us clearly as yet."

Whereupon Mike saw him turn to his wife with the words, "Let's buy them a new Cadillac."

Knowing this was not mere jest Mike quickly intervened, "No!"

"Why not? You need good transportation."

The ministry had already taught Mike, "My people would surely say then that I was in the ministry for the money. They are always seeking a motive, not willing to accept my true reason for being a missionary."

"Well, how about a used Cadillac then?"

"No. The Lord has not impressed me that way."

"How has He impressed you?"

"That in the work we need a good used station wagon, and in the low-end price bracket."

The Lord had touched a heart again and the end result of that conversation saw an excellent two-year-old station wagon added to the work. He has never failed to grant in precious ways one single need, small or large, to our family life or ministry—all in answer to prayer alone. But even more significant, the spiritual dividends to a life and labor of faith will always far outweigh the material.

Personal contacts at first in the main were slow in coming

and somewhat difficult to obtain. In time prayer would open many doors to Jewish businessmen in their shops and places of business, and Jewish families in their homes. Jewish fruit is said to be 'hand-picked'—meaning one here and one there that has been lovingly labored over often for a long period of time. Mike's twelve years of running from the Lord and Claude has taught us patience. The obstacles of prejudice and persecution are not torn down over night. We would face the question time and again, "If there is a God, where was He when Hitler killed the six million?"

The majority do not realize that the door of escape was offered to the Jews of Germany before the inferno was upon them, but most refused to heed the danger signs because of the difficulty of picking up and starting all over again elsewhere. And how can you convince them that Gentiles—not true Christians—murdered their families and loved ones? Only the display of genuine, divine love, backed by fervent prayer over a long period of time, can melt the bitterness and opposition to messianic truth.

"Is God a man that He should have a wife?" is often the Jewish argument encountered against the Trinity. "Say you believe Jesus to be the Messiah, but don't say that He is God, the Son." Over and over we would declare that God's Son is mentioned in the Old Testament Scriptures. Proverbs 30:4 asks in speaking of God, "And what is his Son's name if thou canst tell?" And in Psalm 2:7, God states to the Messiah, "Thou art my Son." We have found it to be today as the Apostle Paul declared almost two thousand years ago, "But their minds were blinded... in the reading of the old testament; which veil is done away in Christ. But even unto this day, when Moses is read, the veil is upon their heart" (II Cor. 3:14, 15).

Thankfully, every now and then, we would find one who, like ripened fruit, was ready to be picked. Momele, early in our ministry, was just such a one. After hearing only a few times the claims of Jesus as Messiah from Old Testament passages, she believed in her mind that He must be the One Israel had long awaited.

As Mike and I together called on her in her home, we quickly ascertained her readiness to receive Him as her Kaporah, her sin-bearer. Asked if she wanted to receive Him into her heart, here and now, she unhesitatingly responded in the affirmative. At eighty years of age, with the faith of a little child, kneeling between Mike and me, she received the greatest of all gifts, salvation in and through her own Messiah. Her spiritual hunger and eagerness for the Word greatly rewarded our efforts until the Lord called her home several years later.

One day we received word from a Christian brother in a nearby town that he had sent Gospel tracts to an inmate of our city jail. By return mail he had received a word of thanks for his concern with the message, "I read the literature but I can't believe it. I am a Jew." With only this information at his disposal Mike paid him a call in the jail. Seeking to understand his need so as to be better able to help him, Mike inquired as to the reason for his imprisonment, and was astonished to hear, "Double murder."

Lawrence, who had strayed far from his moral Jewish upbringing, was deeply concerned about his sins and his need to be ready to meet God. Could such as he be forgiven, and how? Mike quickly assured him of the all-sufficient sacrifice of the Jewish Messiah made available to all—even such as he!

After a few weeks of counselling during the time before the trial, Mike found him one day with a completely transformed countenance. Suspecting the answer Mike eagerly asked, "Lawrence, has something happened to you?"

With a joy that was inconsistent with his circumstances, he radiantly testified of assurance of his sins forgiven through the blood atonement of the Messiah who had died for him. Although in time society found him guilty and demanded the full payment for his sins, it only served (according to his own anticipation) to usher him into the presence of that One whom he loved much because he had been forgiven much.

Florence who came from an orthodox Jewish background was willing to seek help for the problems involving her Gentile husband. Through a mutual Christian friend we were called into the home. As we tried to help both husband and wife, she told us she was appreciative of our trying to help her husband, but we were not to waste our efforts on her as she had no spiritual interest whatsoever.

Refusing to be discouraged from helping her see her spiritual need, we eventually rejoiced to see her open her heart to the Messiah. She came to testify that the problems which once overwhelmed her and threatened to engulf her have become stepping-stones to eternal rewards. Though conditions have not bettered, she possesses an inner strength and peace, a hope and joy evident to those who know her.

She rejoices not only in her own salvation but also that of her fully Jewish daughter (by a previous marriage) who with her two small sons was deserted by her Gentile husband. When Joan found the world held no solution to her personal needs or that of her fatherless sons, she was drawn to the Saviour.

Joan had been in our home many times and as she later confessed had felt the peacefulness of the presence of the Lord, while beholding the love and oneness a husband and wife can have in Christ. She was a direct answer to Pastor Reed's prayer, for in our home she had seen and tasted of the haven and the love that comes down from heaven, thus becoming convinced that Jesus was the answer for herself and her boys too!

Lynn, facing the breakup of her marriage, sought help. Puzzled by a neighbor's continuously happy disposition in the midst of a troubled home, Lynn inquired of her, "What makes you so happy all the time, Linda?"

Looking at Lynn thoughtfully she asked, "Do you really want to know?"

Although stating she did, she was totally unprepared for the answer, "Jesus is in my heart."

Rather than accept her answer, Lynn thought she could discredit this explanation with her age-old question, "Listen, how can a virgin have a baby?" Then scoffingly, "That is impossible!"

This time Lynn's defenses were completely torn down. "Lynn, God can do anything."

Suddenly she realized that if God can take the dust of the earth and create a man, He would have no problem whatever of causing a virgin to conceive if He so willed.

Realizing her inadequacy in dealing with a Jewess whose background was so entirely different, Linda subsequently brought her to us for counselling. She frequently attended our Hebrew Christian Witness Fellowship meetings, and upon hearing what the Lord had done for other Jews who had become followers of Christ, she saw in Him her only hope.

One evening she began reading the true account of a Jewish family who had recognized in Jesus the fulfillment of all the

Old Testament messianic prophecies. Unable to put the book down, in the wee hours of the morning, as she read of the acceptance of Jesus by the mother in the book, Lynn also dropped to her knees and bowed before her Lord and her God.

All through her life Lynn had tried to cover up the fact of her Jewish origin because of the prejudice against her people. She soon was amazed to see how the Gentile Christians love the Jews and learned it was a precious privilege to have been born one of God's chosen seed. Today she is quick to tell that she is proud to be a Jew, a completed Jew, one who did not stop short in accepting all the plan of God revealed in her own Messiah.

Irving was always gracious, but underneath he sometimes disliked seeing us come through the door of his florist shop. He just wasn't interested in spiritual things and had no time for them, being much too busy building his business. But when business reverses came, he found he had no foundation to stand upon, nothing to see him through. He began to look for purpose and meaning to life. Then our witness of the Word of many months, plus faithful friendship during his crisis time, bore fruit early one morning on the Los Angeles freeway!

While driving home from the flower market, his weighty problems racing through his mind seemed about to crush him. In utter despair he cried out, "All right, God. I give up. Do whatever You want with me!" Into the darkness of that moment light suddenly flooded through. In his mind it seemed as though he saw written across the sky, "Jesus *is* the Messiah, my Messiah!" And Irving knew he had experienced life from above. Time was soon to see the conversion of his wife and two sons as well.

The daughter of a deceased rabbi from Algiers and only in this country a few years, Yvette was told of our meetings by a woman who had heard our radio broadcast. Seeking peace of heart and mind she willingly came to investigate. She was impressed. Here were people who radiated and spoke convincingly of the peace she was seeking. As she listened to the Word she recognized that what we taught of Jesus was what her father years ago had told her of the Messiah. In a short time by the hearing of the Word, faith was born into her heart and filled her with the peace and joy she had so desired.

Although Phil had been ordained as a rabbi, he never took

a congregation. Choosing rather to continue his studies in law school, he eventually went before the bar and was licensed to practice even before the United States Supreme Court. He soon found that success and recognition could not satisfy his deep inner needs and longings, and he unsuccessfully sought peace and rest in other places. Eventually emotional disturbance necessitated hospitalization near San Bernardino.

It was at this point that a fine Christian from the hospital told him of Mike and his testimony. After a time he expressed a desire to meet Mike and a meeting was arranged. On the first call he inquired of Mike, "How long have you believed this? And how long have you been making it known publicly?"

Ten years seemed to satisfy Phil that this was real and lasting. Realizing that in essence the claims of Christ were on trial in that man's mind that day, Mike gave an "eye-witness" account of his personal testimony of what Christ had done for him, following it up with many messianic scriptures. In concluding his case, Mike pointed Phil to the God of Israel for faith to believe, and exhorted him to pray to the God in whom he as an ordained rabbi had believed for the truth.

Upon making his second call Mike was overjoyed to hear, "I hope you don't think that I've acted hastily, or that you have borne undue pressure upon me, but I believe I've been reborn." Soon Phil's changed life and joyous testimony bore witness to his claim.

The Lord had indeed led us to that needy field of hungry hearts to which we had so longed to minister, and we have found rest and satisfaction serving Mike's people who are now my own. And yet the blessing of being allowed to help harvest over thirty dividends of fruit among "our people" thus far, has not come without real spiritual battles. But together we rejoice that the battle is not ours but the Lord's, who "always causeth us to triumph in Christ" (II Cor. 2:14).

CHAPTER XXXIX

FRUITFULNESS

"Lo, CHILDREN ARE an heritage of the Lord: and the fruit of the womb is his reward" (Ps. 127:3). ". . .and she bare a son" (Ruth 4:13).

As much as we longed for children, Mike and I both would have preferred to be childless rather than to bring into the world one who would not accept the Lord's gift of salvation from eternal punishment—ultimately one to dishonor the Lord and aid Satan's forces. Thus as we earnestly petitioned for a son, we asked our desire be granted only if he would be one who would be saved, who would bring honor and glory to the Lord.

And so when we knew that David was on the way, it was with confidence that we began to pray for his salvation to come at the very earliest age possible for him! To a lesser degree I prayed it might please the Lord to grant him red hair like his father had!

Just two years after our marriage little red-haired David made his debut into this world. Right from the beginning while rocking and cuddling him, before he could even begin to understand a word, we spoke to him of the loving Saviour. We felt certain that the Holy Spirit could influence even this tiny soul in an atmosphere permeated with the Word of Christ bathed in prayer.

As he grew, in daily contact with the ministry, he learned early to pray the thoughts of his heart, and as is natural for a child had no problems with unbelief. From his earliest understanding he was taught that no one goes to heaven unless he has Jesus in his heart, and that there is a dreadful hell to shun as well as a heaven to gain.

One day when David was just past three years of age, Daddy was asked to call upon a Gentile man who desired to be saved. After a time Mike called home to report the joyous news of the man's having received Christ. I told David the good news to which he questioned, "And now he can go to heaven?"

To my affirmative reply he further questioned, "Mama, are you saved?"

"Yes." I waited knowing something was going on in this little mind.

"Is Daddy saved?"

"Yes." There was a brief silence. Then rather than lose a good opportunity I asked, "David, are you saved?"

Matter-of-factly he answered, "No. Not yet."

"When are you going to be saved?" I further inquired.

Without hesitation he informed me, "When I get to be a big man."

Whereupon I explained that he needn't wait that long. "Whenever you are sure you want Jesus to come into your heart and wash your sins away, you can just ask Him."

A few months passed. While David and I were having a friendly chat over our lunch one day, he made mention of the time he would be going to heaven. "I want to take my toy doggie with me when we go to the Lord Jesus' house. If He has one up there already, I can throw it back down again."

Containing my inner chuckle, seeking not to miss any natural opportunity to guide him along spiritual lines, I reminded him that only Christians can go to heaven when Jesus comes for us—inferring that he was speaking of something that he could not count on as yet. I was taken by surprise when he almost indignantly let me know, "But I am going to heaven! I am a Christian!"

This was so contrary to his past responses I questioned, "Why do you say that? What makes you think so?"

Then as though it were the most natural happening in the world, he answered, "Because I asked Jesus to come into my heart."

My mother-heart was overwhelmed. "When? Where?"

Then he explained in his childish way, "The other day by the door in the hall. I kneeled down and asked Jesus to come into my heart."

Later wanting to satisfy my own mind as to whether or not this little one just past three and a half years of age had really understood what he had done, I further questioned, "Why did you ask Jesus into your heart, David?"

His words were very revealing, "Because I don't want to go to hell."

As he continued to grow in stature as well as increase in knowledge, his spiritual understanding bore witness to the reality of his experience. By the time he was four and a half when Daddy secretly decided to test his understanding, he surprised us with his answers. Daddy had asked, "David, who is the Redeemer?"

The answer came forthrightly, "The Lord Jesus."

"What did he redeem us from?"

"Our sins."

"How did He redeem us?"

"He died on the cross."

Thinking to catch him now, "Then He is still dead?"

"No. He arose three days later."

By the time he was five and a half and attending kindergarten in a Christian Day School, his teacher remarked that she wished all of her children had the spiritual understanding that David revealed. Such understanding comes only by the enlightenment of the Holy Spirit within the soul. The Lord had indeed graciously answered "the earliest age possible for him."

We found the prayer life of a small child in his unfettered faith not only a challenge but very amusing at times. At the age of five David was very original in his prayers to the simple prayer that none of the door knobs would fall off the doors (we had had trouble with one in particular), to the far reaching concern that the Lord would help him get lots and lots of money so he could build thousands and thousands of homes for the orphans.

One night I was sure my ears had deceived me when hearing his prayer until afterwards upon my questioning he removed any doubts. "And Lord Jesus, when the devil is fishing sometime, let him catch a whale that will come up out of the water and hit him on the head, and then splash back in again! Amen."

When David was born we had more or less but mistakenly expected him to have curly hair because of his father's very curly hair. So when we knew Ruth Anna was to adorn our string of Perls, we began praying not only for red hair but curly hair, too, especially if it was to be a girl and if, of course, it would be pleasing to the Lord.

These we knew were only minor details, but the Lord had said, "Ye have not because ye ask not" (James 4:2), and we had already learned through multiplied experiences that He delights in giving His children the desires of their hearts. Perhaps my desire stemmed from the fact of my own disappointment through the years that I had not inherited my mother's beautiful naturally curly hair. How blessed we were with the arrival of our golden-red curly haired, blue-eyed Ruthie!

From our first knowledge of her coming we had prayed once again that the Lord's hand might be upon her from the beginning and she would receive Him at the very earliest age possible for her. Before the age of four she indicated clear understanding of Jesus' having died for her sins. (It doesn't take long for a child to show forth the fruits of the inherent sin nature they are born with or to recognize their feeling of guilt after lying or disobeying or taking something not theirs!)

She had loved Jesus from her first knowledge of Him and amazed people with her very mature prayers, but the day came when she was not sure He was in her heart. So at the age of four, in order to be certain, she knelt between Mommy and Daddy and asked Jesus into her heart. From that day she has not doubted her salvation. In fact she becomes indignant if anyone even suggests she might not be a Christian. Her love of spiritual things and intercessory prayers in behalf of others would erase anyone else's doubts too!

Rachél (pronounced Ra-shell) Joy with her auburn curls was our Christmas baby. We were anticipating a "Daniel" and so had only a first name "Rachél" picked out when she made her appearance. (I was glad that I had prayed, "Lord, if it could possibly be a girl, may she have curly hair, too!")

David was just past three and a half years of age when she was due, and the morning we announced we thought it was time for Mommy to go to the hospital, in the midst of all the scurrying around him, he knelt right down where he was on the floor in the hall and prayed, "Lord Jesus, please help Daniel to hurry up and get here, 'cause I'm tired of waiting."

When Daniel turned out to be "Rachél" (on December 23), we sought the Lord for a middle name. The carol "Joy to the World" had been going through Mike's mind, and when he told me, suggesting Joy, spontaneously I responded, "Our Christmas Joy!" So it was that our Rachél Joy arrived home from the hospital on her first Christmas day in a big red stocking with a tinkling bell attached to it. Her bubbling-over, joyous personality ever since has revealed the Lord's wisdom in naming her!

Our prayers for her salvation had also been "at the earliest age possible for her." One Sunday evening when she wasn't feeling well, just after I had tucked her into bed (she was barely three and a half at the time), she suddenly said to me, "Mommy, I want to pray."

"What do you want to pray about?" The usual bedtime prayers had been said.

"I want to ask Jesus into my heart."

Neither wanting to encourage a premature decision, nor to hinder the genuine working of the Holy Spirit, I proceeded cautiously. "Why do you want to, Rachel?" As we hadn't been talking of salvation I wondered what had prompted her decision.

"So He will wash my sins away so I can go to heaven someday."

Recognizing understanding, but still not wanting to push in any way, I replied, "If you really want Jesus to come into your heart, just bow your head and tell Him about it."

By now she was sitting up in bed. Tiny little hands folded, and a serious little curly head bowed in prayer. "Lord Jesus, please come into my heart and wash my sins away so I can go to heaven someday. Amen." The simple faith of a little child, as always, was acceptable to the Lord. Her first testimony was to Daddy when he came home, "Daddy, I'm a Christian now, too, 'cuz I asked Jesus to come into my heart."

The simplicity of the wondrous Gospel can be early understood and yet its depths will not be fully comprehended until we sit at the foot of His throne in the Glory. Nor will the endless ages of eternity ever exhaust the marvels of that grace already received into our hearts but barely tasted down here.

Now together as a family we continue to sow and to glean in the fields of the barren souls of Israel's sons and daughters— our people—awaiting that day when the Shofar will sound, announcing the end of the harvest and calling us home from the day's labor. Our momentary anticipation rings out clearly, echoing and re-echoing in the words of our little ones whenever Daddy leaves the house to go somewhere. "Shalom. The Lord bless you, and I'll see you later, Daddy dear, either when you come home or in the air, if Jesus comes first."

EPILOGUE

Now nearly thirty-eight years later we have found God always to have been faithful in meeting our needs as a ministry and as a family. As in the beginning, we have never passed a collection plate, hinted at our needs, solicited meetings, materials, equipment, etc. The Lord Himself is our only paymaster (Philippians 4:19). He has used many and varied sources. A good example is the gift to cover this reprinting of our book by a beloved Christian brother whom we have yet to meet! We have never lacked a need, and have often been able to share with and help others.

The Lord has broadened our ministry to include the Low Desert as far as Indio, the High Desert as far as Victorville and environs, South as far as Sun City, and West almost to Los Angeles. This would include more than 20,000 Jewish people. We are now on four different radio stations covering this territory and all the way to the Mexican border.

One Saturday evening a Jewish woman whom we had not as yet met fell asleep listening to the San Bernardino station on which our program is carried. Joannne had grown up in Long Beach during World War II. Her parents, fearing that persecution might come also to the Jews in America told her not to let anyone know that she was Jewish. They even sent her to a Catholic school. She fell in love with the Jesus she learned about, but her parents told her He was only for the Gentiles, and she could not believe in Him. After a life of many troubles and heartaches she ended up in San Bernardino. Having fallen asleep with the radio on, she awakened to hear Mike speaking in Hebrew as well as English. It brought back memories of her early Jewish childhood. The message from the Old Testament Prophecies proving Jesus is Messiah were a revelation to her. When Mike said that Jesus was for everyone, Jews and Gentiles alike, she thought, ''Then I can have Him too!'' A few days later she walked for two hours to get to our fellowship meeting in order to tell us that she had received her Messiah when Mike had given a prayer of invitation at the close of the broadcast.

A part of our hearts has always been in Israel. We have had the privilege of leading four tours back to that beloved land, and are now planning our fifth. During our last tour the Lord gave us the privilege of leading a proprietor of one of the souvenir shops to his Messiah. In sharing with him he told of a dream he had had in which he was standing with Jesus on one side of him and an angel on the other. Then they took him by the hands and together they went up. He didn't know what the dream meant. We told him that we believed the Lord sent us to tell him, and explained about the rapture. We told him that Messiah Jesus came first to be a sacrifice for our sins, went back to Heaven and would return to bring peace and righteousness to this world through the nation of Israel. But before He did there would be seven years of tribulation culminating in the War of Armageddon. However, before the tribulation, He would take His people, those who had invited Him into their lives as Messiah and Savior, out of this world. When we asked him if he had ever invited Jesus into his life, he replied, "No." When asked if he wanted to, he answered, "Why not?" We then lead him in a prayer of acceptance. Miraculously, no one came into his shop all this time. Later, when we returned, the shop was full of customers! Subsequent contacts with him have assured us that his salvation is real.

In 1982, Mike felt he wanted to improve his Hebrew. He learned of a Rabbi who had given up his congregation, and was now teaching Hebrew. Maurice was originally from Morocco, and migrated to Israel as a young man. There he was ordained as a Rabbi, and fought in three of Israel's wars, including her War of Independence. Later he came to America, and after leading a congregation in Corona, California, ended up in Riverside, near us. Mike asked him if he would be willing to teach him Hebrew, letting him know he was a Hebrew Christian. He answered, "Why not? I teach other Christians." During their study each week, Mike would ask Maurice to help him translate various Messianic prophecies. When studying Isaiah 53, Maurice said, "I can see why the Christians believe this speaks of Jesus." Mike in return asked, "Of whom do you say it speaks?" to which he replied, "I don't know." A short time later Maurice informed Mike that he could no longer refute the Scriptures. He was ready to accept Jesus as his Messiah and Savior. Several months later he accompanied us on a tour to Israel, where he took his first communion at the Garden Tomb in Jerusalem. As we visited many of the holy sites he was amazed, telling us that the many years he had lived there he never knew these places existed. For the past nine years he has been an integral part of our mission, helping to win his own people to the Lord.

Also, it has been our joy to have our daughter, Rachél, working with us full time in our ministry. Saved at the age of three and a half, she was called of the Lord to Jewish Missions at the age of nine. After high school, she attended Biola College, and returned home to become an indispensable part of the Hebrew Christian Witness.

We have had the joy of seeing over 200 Jewish people come to accept their Messiah, as well as over 300 Gentiles come to the Lord, since our ministry began. We long for the day when the Deliverer will come out of Zion, and turn away ungodliness from Jacob (Romans 11:26); when they will look upon Him whom they have pierced (Zechariah 12:10), and realize that ''neither is there salvation in any other; for there is no other name under Heaven given among men whereby we must be saved'' (Acts 4:12). We stand convinced that the day of Israel's redemption is near at hand.

EPILOGUE II

We have now completed our thirty-ninth year of marriage and ministry, and also our fifth tour to Israel. It was a beautiful blessing to spend an evening in Tel Aviv in the home of the proprietor who we led to the Lord seven years previously. He asked me, "Do you remember the dream I told you about? "Oh, Yes," I replied. "Well I never had one like it before, nor have I had since! I don't understand it!" Joyfully I explained, "The Lord just used that to bring you to Himself." And he agreed! His wife informed us she believes in God, but not Jesus. Our hearts long to see them united in their Messiah.

We were excited to see banners displayed particularly in the orthodox sections stating in Hebrew, "Prepare yourself to greet the Messiah." They, of course, do not mean Jesus. They are expecting the Messiah for the first time. We also saw displayed at The Temple Institute in Jerusalem various articles that have been constructed for use in the Temple as soon as it is rebuilt. They say that they are 100% authentic and ready for use. They include, among other things, a silver decanter for the drink offerings, the High Priest's lottery box, a harp for the Levites to use in singing, the High Priest's robe, and the silver crown that says 'Holiness to the Lord' on it. The very fact that these Israeli's are preparing for the rebuilding of the Temple we believe is a sure sign of the soon coming of the Lord.

The only thing hindering the rebuilding is the fact that the Temple Mount area is in the control of the Arabs presently, given to them by Israel, because of the two mosques standing on it. In the Lord's timing that will change and the Temple will be built!

Early this year, 1994, it was our blessing to meet for the first time the very gracious gentleman who paid for the last two printings of our book. He just celebrated his eighty-sixth birthday and is truly a very special servant of the Lord.

We are now grandparents for the fourth time. It warms our hearts to hear Ruthie's three and one half year old, Lyndsay say, "Pray for me," and "The Lord bless you." And what a joy to know David's Jordan, also three and one half years old, prays for "Gramma" and "Papa" every night! Our prayer is that they may open their hearts to our Lord at the earliest age possible for them, even as their parents did.

We continue to rejoice in our Lord Messiah's great faithfulness, looking for that day when our "Blessed Hope" (Titus 2:13) will be realized and we will be Home forever with Him. "Through Heaven's door we will soar, if Jesus comes in '94, to be with Him forevermore!"